I0802017

Sex in the archives

Manchester University Press

Sex in the archives

Writing American sexual histories

Barry Reay

Manchester University Press

Published by Manchester University Press
Altrincham Street, Manchester M1 7JA
www.manchesteruniversitypress.co.uk

British Library Cataloguing-in-Publication Data
A catalogue record for this book is available from the British Library

ISBN 978 1 5261 2453 1 hardback

ISBN 978 1 5261 2454 8 paperback

First published 2019

Typeset in Garamond by
Servis Filmsetting Ltd, Stockport, Cheshire
Printed and bound in Great Britain by TJ International Ltd, Padstow, Cornwall

For Amos Badertscher, Baltimore's sexual archivist

Contents

Figures

Acknowledgements

Although there is only a little swinging and no Fatwa sex in this book, I am still reminded of the brilliant Larry David as I write these acknowledgements. Do the thank-yous demonstrate the appropriate level of gratitude? Is the praise fulsome enough? Will any expressed regret be sufficient? Should I curb or indulge my enthusiasm?

As the reader will discover, I have spent considerable time in the archives, so perhaps I should start there. I remain impressed with the friendliness and efficiency of the libraries and archives that I have consulted for material on various aspects of the history of American sex. The Library of the Kinsey Institute at Indiana University has been absolutely crucial to my research. Liana Zhou, Director, Library and Special Collections, and Shawn Wilson, Associate Director of Collections, have been welcoming and helpful for more years than any of us would care to recall. I am also deeply appreciative of the assistance of the staff at the University of Chicago Library Special Collections Research Center; Archives of American Art, Smithsonian Institution; Grainger Museum Collection, University of Melbourne; Houghton Library, Harvard University; Yale University's Beinecke Rare Book and Manuscript Library; Gay, Lesbian, Bisexual, Transgender Historical Society, San Francisco; San Francisco History Center, San Francisco Public Library; the Leslie–Lohman Museum of Gay and Lesbian Art, New York; The Forbes Collection, New York; and the personal archive of ANONYMOUS.

One of my favourite destinations, however, is the New York Public Library, a true national treasure. Here I am especially indebted to Tal Nadan, Reference Archivist in the Manuscripts and Archives Division, for her help and encouragement with material that has been used in several chapters. I think that she has been somewhat bemused by the fact that among the first to view new archival holdings in a New York repository has been a researcher all the way from New Zealand.

I would like to express my thanks to the following for their permission to use illustrative material reproduced in this book: Grainger Museum, Photographic Collection, University of Melbourne; Richard Taddei; Faulkner–Morgan Pagan Babies Archive; The Bancroft Library, University of California, Berkeley; The Kinsey Institute; Archives of American Art, Smithsonian Institution; The Forbes Collection, New York; Getty Images; Estate of Samuel Steward (Michael Williams); Whitney Museum of American Art; Viscopy Limited, Australia; Schlesinger Library, Radcliffe Institute, Harvard University; Estate of Bettye Lane (Gary O'Neil); The Dittrick Medical History Center, Case Western Reserve University; Google Inc.; MasturbateForPeace.com; Annie Sprinkle; Steven Morowitz (VIDEO-X-PIX); and Amos Badertscher. Fuller citation will be made in the appropriate captions. Every effort has been made to trace the copyright owners of the images used in this book and anyone claiming copyright should contact this author.

Earlier versions of chapters 2 and 6 appeared in *History Workshop Journal*, 73:1 (Oxford University Press, 2012) and *Radical History Review*, 122 (Duke University Press, 2015). Chapter 7 was originally published in *Porn Studies*, 3:3 (Routledge, 2016), copyright Taylor & Francis, available online: www.tandfonline.com doi:10.1080/23268743.2016.1141704. Chapter 4 draws on an article from *Journal of Historical Sociology*, 27:1 (John Wiley & Sons, 2014). I am grateful to the publishers for permission to use these materials.

Apart from those mentioned elsewhere in the acknowledgements, a miscellany of friends, colleagues, and editors, archivists, and interested parties have played varied roles of reassurance, enthusiasm, criticism, amusement, and distraction (they will know which): Henry Abelove, Laura Accinelli, Nicholas Accinelli, Chrysoula Artemis, Feona Attwood, William Badertscher, Leonard Bell, Chris Brickell, Iain Buchanan, Malcolm Campbell, Jonathan Coleman, Luis Corteguera, Jennifer Curtin, Samuel Delany, Patricia Delara, Sam Dresser, Christopher Forbes, Heather Gaunt, Jeff Gomez, Claire Gooder, Laura Gowing, Lauren Gunn, the students of History 102 (*Sexual Histories*) and 206/306 (*Making Sex*), Catherine Johnson-Roehr, Bonnie Kirchstein, Daniel Marshall, Kiah Mccarthy, Gregory Minissale, John Morrow, Kevin Murphy, Kim Phillips, Jonathan Scott, Clarissa Smith, Justin Spring, Annie Sprinkle, Craig Symes, Annette Timm, Zeb Tortorici, Marta Vicente, Michael Williams, Tim Wilson, Philippa Wyatt, and Joe Zizek. I know I may have forgotten someone. If so, I am (Larry!) distraught, devastated.

Then there is family, who have little choice in their contributions. Athina

Tsoulis, Alexa Tsoulis-Reay, Kristina Tsoulis-Reay, and Mark Rodda are all creative people with their own curiosities and careers, but they have been amazingly tolerant of my preoccupations, which, in any case, are rather tame compared to facets of Alexa's ('What it's like to date a horse?') journalistic portfolio.

Finally, there are those without whom there would have been no book. Emma Brennan, my commissioning editor at Manchester University Press, is always such a pleasure to work with, and was there from the moment the book started to take shape, indeed negotiated its formation. Apart from the joy experienced in working with them, my co-authors Erin Griffey (Chapter 2), Nina Attwood (Chapter 7), and Branka Bogdan (Chapter 9) have generously agreed to let me use their work for those respective chapters. Nina has also acted as a research and editorial assistant, so her contribution is singular.

I thank the University of Auckland on a daily basis for awarding me the Keith Sinclair Chair in History, which has provided support for my work in sexual history. Whether the late Keith Sinclair would have approved of all my research topics is another matter entirely.

Above all, in my special acknowledgements, I am indebted to the remarkable photographer Amos Badertscher, who so enjoyed my earlier book *New York Hustlers* that he urged me to write another one. I have come to know Amos during the last few years; he is both the subject of Chapter 9 and the creator of the photograph used on the cover. I do hope that the book's dedication is some recognition of his importance – and not just to what follows.

Prologue

If Jacques Derrida was permitted a Note, Exergue, Preamble, and Foreword in his *Archive Fever* (1996), I might at least be allowed a Prologue. I promise not to move to a Postscript immediately after my Theses.[1]

It is not mentioned in Jennifer Tyburczy's *Sex Museums* (2016), presumably because it is not a museum totally devoted to sexual matters, yet Melbourne University's Grainger Museum contains an intriguing archive within an archive, or rather an archive within a museum – and, even more absorbingly, one devoted to queer *heterosexuality*.[2] The US-based, Australian composer and pianist Percy Grainger, best known for his composition *Country Gardens* (1918–19), was responsible for what he termed the 'Lust Branch Collection', which he considered an important component of his legacy. Hence the Grainger Museum's vast musicological and ethnographic collection also contains its founder's sex archive of whips, photographs (*Self beaten, Kansas City* [1933] is my favourite), sexological works, explicit personal descriptions of the receiving and inflicting of sexual pain, and paeans to the advantages of 'self-help' (masturbation) and the joys of oral sex (see Figures 1–3).[3] 'I want *every inch* of your body baptised by the fires of my pain-wooing', he wrote to his wife Ella Ström from New York in 1930, in a letter in his archive,

> I want every inch of my body baptised by the fires of your pain-wooing. I want to be scorched, flayed, plucked, sucked, pricked, tweeted, ripped, bitten by you all over my body, just as I want to do those things to you, before we close for the crowning act of sex-pierce-ment . . . I want 1000s of years of civilisation torn away. I want a lifetime of modern training uprooted. I want terrible anguish . . . I want to know *at your hands* what I otherwise have not yet known.[4]

Grainger, as he explained in the contents of his envelope 'Do Not open Until 10 Years after My Death' (1956), was convinced that his sex archive

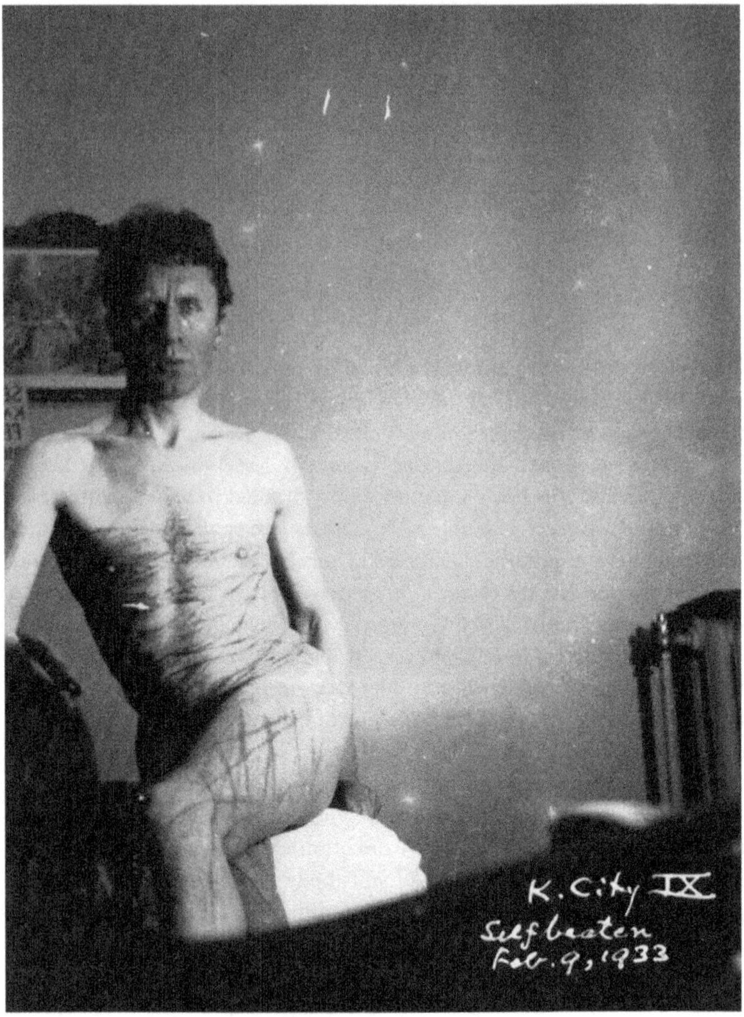

1 Percy Grainger, Kansas City IX Self beaten, Feb. 9, 1933. From Grainger Museum, Photographic Collection, University of Melbourne.

contained what would become important social documents and mementos when society became more enlightened in sexual matters.[5] 'If only one could get the whole world to unite in making the earth a temple of sexual intensity', he had written in 1908, 'Men & women both eager for the fleshy bliss of it all . . . how both sexes could go to hell in joy & oblivion.'[6] He

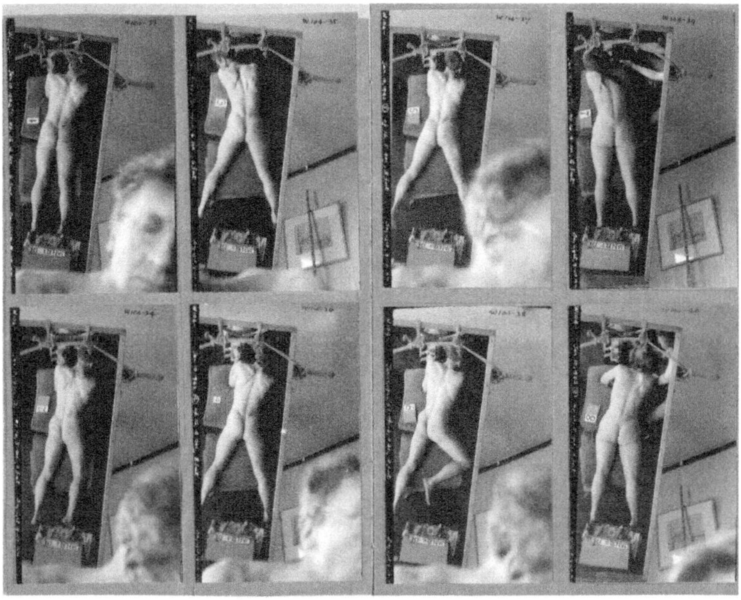

2 Percy Grainger, Photo-Skills Guide, 1942. From Grainger Museum, Photographic Collection, University of Melbourne.

believed too that his sexual passions and musical talents were closely linked. In 1910 he reported a week of travelling concert performances, late nights, erotic reading, self-flagellation, and frequent masturbation ('naughtiness'): 'and all the days almost shaking with such lewdness and sexual fantasies. But I feel quite well and fresh, although Tschaikowsky [*sic*] 3 days in a row is tiring.'[7] Sex was important to him. 'Of course I am glad to have my works done, to have bookings come so long in the season', he wrote to his wife from his hotel in Chicago in 1930; 'Yet none of that reaches my soul or stills the wild hunger that is in me. Only in sex do I really awake.'[8] In the same year he confided to a fellow composer, Roger Quilter, that he lived for his lusts, '& I do not care if they kill me or others . . . That is how I live: Following my lusts, & composing now & then on the side.'[9]

Grainger was, in Michael Piggott's apt description, an 'autoarchivist', constantly aware of preserving for posterity.[10] 'So the little sweetie thinks she can take all my extremely interesting letters to the grave with her, if she dies', he chided his lover Karen Holten in 1908; 'My letters will be admired by a yet-unborn generation; can't you see that I always write with an eye to a possible public? . . . I always hope that my letters will be handed over

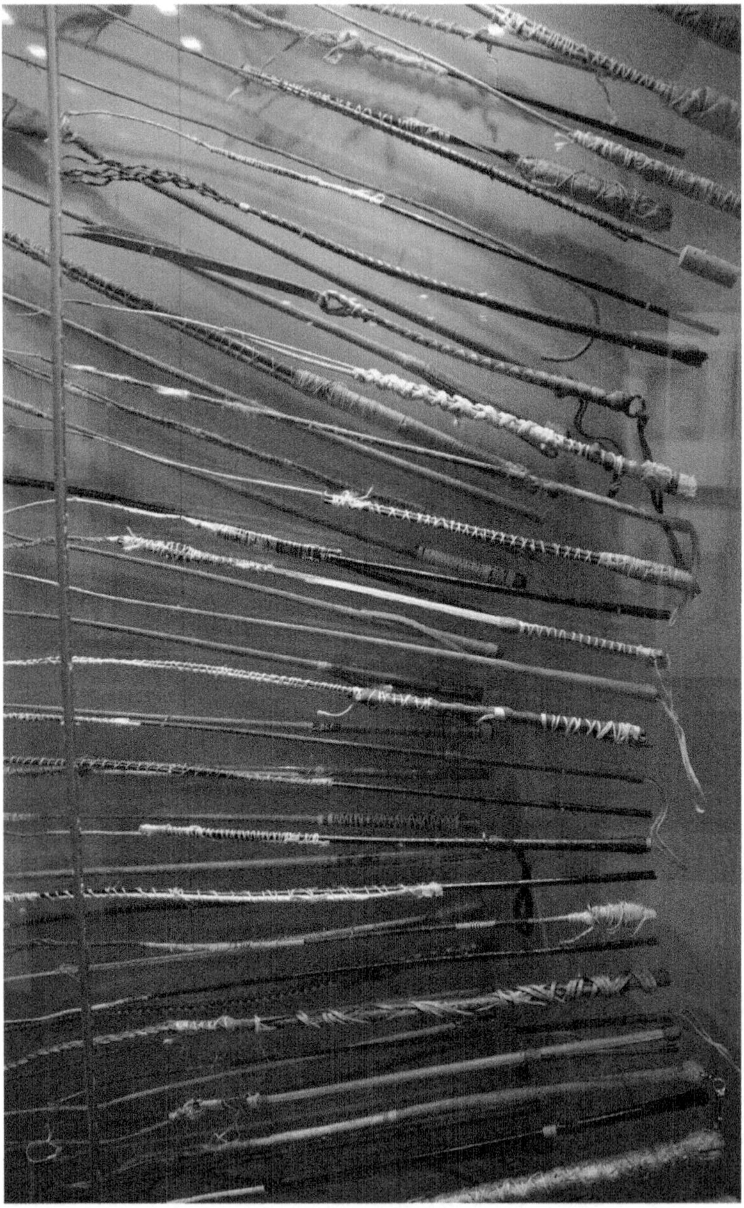

3 Exhibition of a selection of Percy Grainger's whips. Photograph of display in Grainger Museum, University of Melbourne, 2017.

to immortality one day.'[11] He initiated, shaped, and ensured the physical foundations of his archive and memorial to himself and his mother Rose, achieving, almost on his own, as Piggott points out, 'what was to become a core function of librarians and archivists'.[12]

Grainger was unusual in his autoarchivism, his single-minded pursuit of a sexual legacy and the conviction that it would benefit society. He was rare too in his early recognition of an archival intent, unique in his ability to form an actual archive of brick and mortar: no metaphorical or virtual archives for him. Grainger explicitly urged the openers of 'Do Not open Until 10 Years after My Death' not to destroy its contents – 'I fervently hope that whoever opens the package will regard my wishes *that none of the contents of the package be destroyed*, but lodged with some medical or historic or scientific society or library that may wish to investigate the nature & habits of creative Australians' – and the openers observed his wishes and placed its contents in the archive of their originator, the creative Australian himself.[13] He was fortunate in this as well.

Those whom you will encounter in this book may also have been aware of a future audience. One knew that he was keeping a gay diary during a special period of gay history; however, his primary motivation was personal gratification rather than instructing future generations. The diary is there because it served a sexual function. Others were methodical in their charting of their sexual interactions, but would not have accumulated so much detail had they not been encouraged, in the name of sex research, by the remarkable Alfred Kinsey. The sex in the archives in the pages that follow is much less systematic than Grainger's autoarchivism. It is the result of surveillance. Or it exists because someone got into trouble. Or it was driven by economic need. Or we have it because it was not thrown out with the trash. Or it is an archive of accident in numerous other ways. As the founder of a vast photographic collection once told me, while it might appear purposeful, everything in his life, including the formation of his archive, had been accidental.

Notes

1 J. Derrida, *Archive Fever: A Freudian Impression* (Chicago, 1996).

2 J. Tyburczy, *Sex Museums: The Politics and Performance of Display* (Chicago, 2016). For the formation of the museum, see B. Nemec, '"I am hungry for fame-after-death": Percy Grainger's quest for immortality through his museum', *reCollections: Journal of the National Museum of Australia*, 2:2 (2007), 180–200; B. Allison, A. B. Krautschneider, and K. Dreyfus, 'The Grainger Museum: then,

now, and in the future', in P. Thwaites (ed.), *The New Percy Grainger Companion* (Woodbridge, Suffolk, 2010), ch. 13.

3 The best published selections from Grainger's archive, including sexual matters, are K. Dreyfus (ed.), *The Farthest North of Humanness: Letters of Percy Grainger, 1901–14* (London, 1985), and M. Gillies, D. Pear, and M. Carroll (eds), *Self-Portrait of Percy Grainger* (Melbourne, 2006), esp. pp. 93–100, 113–24, 160–2, 166–8, and pp. 97, 114, 161 for self-help. For a useful short essay on Grainger and sex, see D. Pear, 'The passions of Percy', *Meanjin*, 62:2 (2003), 59–66.

4 Grainger Museum Collection, University of Melbourne (hereafter, GM), Ella Ström Grainger Collection, Letter from Percy Grainger to Ella Ström Grainger, 12 January 1930. Emphasis in original.

5 Gillies, Pear, and Carroll (eds), *Self-Portrait of Percy Grainger*, p. 160. He established the museum between 1935 and 1955.

6 Dreyfus (ed.), *Letters of Percy Grainger*, p. 180.

7 Ibid., p. 366.

8 GM, Ella Ström Grainger Collection, Letter from Percy Grainger to Ella Ström Grainger, 25 January 1930.

9 GM, 2016/18, Unit 1, Folder 02.0139, Letter from Percy Grainger to Roger Quilter, 20 July 1930.

10 M. Piggott, 'Grainger the autoarchivist', in D. Pear (ed.), *Facing Percy Grainger* (Canberra, 2006), pp. 39–45.

11 Dreyfus (ed.), *Letters of Percy Grainger*, pp. 187–8.

12 Piggott, 'Grainger the autoarchivist', p. 45.

13 Gillies, Pear, and Carroll (eds), *Self-Portrait of Percy Grainger*, p. 160. Emphasis in the original.

Introduction

Antoinette Burton has noted that many of us have archive stories.[1] Significantly, this author's initial real archival meeting involved dust, both figuratively in the sense that it was in the old Public Record Office in Chancery Lane, an archetypal traditional archive, described by one commentator as church-like, an 'archival temple', and literally in that I became covered in dirt from the old (and rather large) bundles of tithe files that I was grappling with, somewhat innovatively it turned out, for my work on the seventeenth-century radical religious sect, the Quakers.[2] Consequently I had frequently to resort to the bathroom to wash the dirt of centuries off my hands and arms. Fortunately, this was before Carolyn Steedman's *Dust* (2001), with its invocation of the spectre of anthrax.[3]

So the physicality of inquiry is significant, especially, one might predict, in research dealing with sex. My book *Watching Hannah* (2002) drew on photographs, sketches, diaries, and journals in Trinity College, Cambridge, the collection of Arthur Munby, a Victorian lawyer, civil servant, and poet who married a servant called Hannah Cullwick and who was obsessed with working women and female bodily deformity (the two were connected in his mind).[4] One of his preoccupations was with women's hands, and although common archival practice for handling photographic material, it seemed bizarre to be made to wear white gloves to examine the photographs in the collection: an almost fetishistic confirmation of Munby's fetish. Carol Mavor, who consulted the same repository and donned similar gloves, described her archival research as an erotic encounter: 'the photographs (and the diaries), for me, are overflowing with sexuality, flesh, desire'. 'I am drawn to this missing picture: it represents Hannah's invisible flesh. I want to touch it. I caress the place of her absence with gloved fingers.'[5] She began and ended her essay with reference to the white gloves. In retrospect, it was a significant moment, for critics have described the historian's relationship to the archive and the primary source document as fetishistic or fantastical in their obsession with actually touching the past.[6]

What I have been calling the archives vary in nature, and I have visited many of them – not all represented in this book – in the twenty years since my research and writing took a sexual turn. They range, in my own more recent experience, from the grandeur of the New York Public Library, Beaux-Arts landmark building on Fifth Avenue and 42nd Street, to the modern architectural beauty of the Beinecke Library, or the more understated Main Library of the San Francisco Public Library, temporary daytime home to so many of that city's homeless who share its space with researchers. The archive can consist of a mural in a hotel, or drawings and paintings in the collection of a wealthy patron. When researching Chapter 2 on the artist Edward Melcarth, Erin Griffey and I travelled to the Forbes Gallery's warehouse, The Fortress, in Queens in New York, which indeed looked like and was as secure as a citadel, where our hosts set out a whole room of Melcarth's work (see Figure 4). (Malcolm Forbes, the billionaire owner of *Forbes* magazine, had patronised both hustlers – male sex workers – and the always-struggling Melcarth.) The following day, we went to the newly refurbished and rather exclusive Pierre Hotel in Manhattan, where in the

4 At the Fortress (with Erin Griffey). Photographed by author, 2010.

1960s Melcarth had painted a mural using hustlers as models and to carry out the actual labour. (There are photographs in Chapter 2.)

Or the archive can be in a room in an apartment, the product of one person's private obsession. In 2007, while working on *New York Hustlers* (2010), I contacted an artist called Richard Taddei, who had known the aforementioned Melcarth. It transpired that Taddei also painted and photographed hustlers, but those of another generation – Melcarth in the 1950s and 1960s, and Taddei in the 1980s and 1990s (see Figure 5).[7] His apartment was then on West 47th Street, deliberately located to be near male prostitution, and he had stacks of photographic albums, a scanner, and digital copies of both his and Melcarth's photographs. I spent the morning there with him, took him to lunch, and then in the afternoon and evening we selected what I wanted while he scanned them and copied the files on to disk for me, emailing others later. It was a remarkable archive of Melcarth's photography, much of which Taddei has moved to the Archives of American Art, Smithsonian Institution, in Washington DC, where many of the images now reside.[8]

The title of this book is not entirely original, although I did not think about this when I wrote Chapter 6. Bonnie Smith used the phrase 'sex in the archives' to describe a type of nineteenth-century male fetishism of archival research where a collection was like a 'virgin' ('I long for the moment I have access to her . . . whether she is pretty or not') and a rare book was caressed because it was 'enveloped in skin, like a woman'.[9] But the sex in the archives here is of an entirely different order to that possessive, masculine, empirical quest for a history of politics, diplomacy, and . . . well, anything other than the history of sex. The subject topics covered in this book are wide ranging: rethinking the art history of homoeroticism; casual sex before casual sex; early trans history; New York queer sex; masturbation; pornography; Baltimore's sexual cultures. The duality indicated by the book's title reflects its two principal themes: it deals with archival form and archival content, the archives of the histories of sex and the sexual histories contained in those archives. It is an experiment in writing an American sexual history that refuses the confines of identity sexuality studies, spanning the spectrum of queer, trans, and the allegedly 'normal'; and it includes masturbation, perhaps the queerest sex of all. What unites this project is a fascination with sex at the margins, sex that refuses the classificatory frameworks of heterosexuality and homosexuality, and that demonstrates gender and sexual indecision and flexibility. It is sex that also conceptually challenges the supposed demarcations of pre and post gay liberation, for the pre-Stonewall

5 Richard Taddei, photograph of New York hustler, 1980s. Collection of Richard Taddei.

years as they are usually called, the time before the gay identity politics of the late 1960s and early 1970s, were ones of immense sexual richness and variability, as we will see in Chapters 2 and 3.

But the book, as will be discussed in Chapter 1, is also an exploration of the role of the archive in such histories. The sex discussed is located both in the margins of the archives, what has been termed the counterarchive, but also, importantly, in the pockets of recorded desire located in the most traditional and respectable repositories. Hence we will encounter the erotic art of the Kinsey Institute (Chapter 2); Thomas Painter's hustler dossiers and Samuel Steward's very personal and extensive visual and written record of casual sex (Chapter 3); the University of Chicago Library's holdings of the work of 1920s sociologists, mapping the sexual opportunities to be found in the anonymity and freedom of the furnished rooms' district of Chicago (Chapter 4); the New York Public Library's collection of the investigators' reports for the moral reformers of New York's Committee of Fourteen that chart sex in dance halls, massage parlours, hotels, and restaurants in the early twentieth century (Chapter 4); the San Francisco History Center's life course diaries of Lou Sullivan, transitioning from heterosexual woman to gay man (Chapter 5); gay masturbatory journals in the New York Public Library that are of such a sexually explicit nature, and name so many people, that they were embargoed for seventy-five years until I gained special permission to read them (Chapter 6); the private archive of the amateur pornographer known as ANONYMOUS who, with a team of straight women, wrote gay male erotic fiction for publication in the 1990s (Chapter 7); the scattered archive of masturbation, not located in any specific institution or private holding but generated through evidentiary remains from recent US history (Chapter 8); and Amos Badertscher's intensely intimate, lifetime photographic dossier on Baltimore's sexual cultures, ranging from the 1960s to the 2000s (Chapter 9). The sexual histories in this book are those where pornography and sexual research are indistinguishable; where art and pornography intersect; and where today's personal obsession becomes tomorrow's archive.

Notes

1 A. Burton, 'Introduction: archive fever, archive stories', in A. Burton (ed.), *Archive Stories: Facts, Fictions, and the Writing of History* (Durham, NC, 2005), pp. 1–24.

2 For the Public Record Office as archival temple, see E. Ketelaar, 'The panoptical archive', in F. X. Blouin and W. G. Rosenburg (eds), *Archives, Documentation,*

and Institutions of Social Memory (Ann Arbor, MI, 2006), pp. 144–50, at pp. 146–7; and for the Quakers and tithes, B. Reay, 'Quaker opposition to tithes, 1652–1660', *Past and Present*, 86 (1980), 98–120.

3 C. Steedman, *Dust* (Manchester, 2001), pp. 23–5, 28–9.

4 B. Reay, *Watching Hannah: Sexuality, Horror, and Bodily De-Formation in Victorian England* (London, 2002).

5 C. Mavor, *Pleasures Taken: Performances of Sexuality and Loss in Victorian Photographs* (Durham, NC, 1995), pp. 78, 84.

6 See J. Tollebeek, '"Turned to dust and tears": revisiting the archive', *History and Theory*, 43:2 (2004), 237–48; A. Buchanan, 'Strangely unfamiliar: ideas of the archive from outside the discipline', in J. Hill (ed.), *The Future of Archives and Recordkeeping: A Reader* (London, 2011), ch. 3.

7 B. Reay, *New York Hustlers: Masculinity and Sex in Modern America* (Manchester, 2010).

8 See www.aaa.si.edu/collections/edward-melcarth-papers-7865 (last accessed 26 April 2018).

9 B. G. Smith, *The Gender of History: Men, Women, and Historical Practice* (Cambridge, MA, 2000), pp. 119, 124.

1

The lure of the archive

From long-forgotten first encounters to more memorable recent incidents, archives are central to the experiences of many – though now not all – historians. Carolyn Steedman's famous book *Dust* (2001), which originated as a study of the archive but turned out to be about the writing of history, begins both with an observation on the paradigmatic role of the archive in the craft of the historian and the recognition that many historians never experience archival dust.[1] Ironically, I am writing about the lure of the archive, in this material sense, after the so-called archival turn has long since turned, the meaning of the word archive has become overstretched, and we have reached the point when it is conceivable 'to construct an archive of archive studies'.[2] The role of digitisation and the Internet means that archival material can be accessed from a computer almost anywhere, and the Internet itself can become an archive, or rather innumerable archives, including YouTube, 'the world's default media archive' of 1.2 billion videos.[3] Thus, by 2011, 'The Archive' was already one of Sherry Turkle's 'evocative objects'; and Susan Yee could write hauntingly about the loss of the physical in the face of the digital as the drawings in Paris's Le Corbusier archive were copied on to an online database.[4]

For those with an archival past (in the older sense), however, the traces persist, like the layers of suppressed memory in psychotherapy. Arlette Farge has written not just about what historians do with the archives and the excitement of discovery, but also of the hard slog that goes into archival work, and the more mundane, but no less interesting, aspects of archival work, the jostling for a prime seat, the petty bureaucracies, the disappointments, the physicality of inquiry, what Natalie Zemon Davis has termed the experience of research, the smells, the feeling, the dust.[5]

There are elegiac accounts of 'the beauty of archival work . . . the tactile experience of engagement – to touch, literally to commune, with the dead', and of how inferior the 'digital surrogate' is in comparison.[6] Lisa Jardine refers to the 'particular thrill' of linking to the past through an archival document, of (with tongue in cheek) 'more emotional investment . . . than is proper for a professional historian'.[7] Joan Wallach Scott prefers the metaphors of *jouissance* and *la petite mort* (the little death: orgasm) for the intellectual excitement that can be generated by the contents of an archive (while simultaneously recognising the possibility of misrepresentation by 'dullards').[8] Brent Hayes Edwards has an elegant essay on the 'taste of the archive', the sensation of uncovering an incongruous photograph of an unknown young man emerging from a 1930s' Parisian urinal, found in the archives of the Jamaican writer Claude McKay in Yale University's Beinecke Rare Book and Manuscript Library; he invokes Michel Foucault's description, 'vibration', as way of capturing the feelings of exhilaration involved in encountering the past through such material remnants.[9] Despite his familiarity with the work and world of Robert Mapplethorpe, Jonathan Weinberg was nonetheless excited by seeing in Mapplethorpe's archive a membership card for the New York S/M club The Mineshaft (more of which in Chapter 6) and feeling the pleasure of being in the presence of something handled by the dead artist.[10] Whether or not those who feel that they are directly touching the past are in fact, as Emily Robinson says, being 'simultaneously made aware of its unreachability' is perhaps another issue.[11]

What is the archive? Steedman provides a useful starting point: 'that prosaic place where the written and fragmentary traces of the past are put in boxes and folders, bound up, stored, catalogued'.[12] We all know that modern archives began as custodians of national memory; that they 'create' as well as 'store'.[13] Achille Mbembe has described the traditional archive as a cross between a 'temple and a cemetery'.[14] But the term can be used in a wider sense too. To stay with Steedman, the archive can simply be 'a name for the many places in which the past (which does not now exist, but which once did really happen; which cannot be retrieved, but which may be represented) has deposited some traces and fragments'.[15] For Charles Merewether, it is 'a repository or ordered system of documents or records, both verbal and visual, that is the foundation from which history is written'.[16] The archive can be the police records of the Archives Nationales, used to such compelling effect by Arlette Farge, or the Public Record Office, the site of Steedman's archival fever.[17] It can be devotional in the form of the medieval French Books of Hours (archives of prayer) or the votive boards in Italian churches (an archive of miracles, stretching from the Renaissance to the present day).[18]

It is possible to distinguish between the classical or privileged archive (on the one hand) and the popular archive (on the other).[19] Indeed, the archive has become inflated in its usage, both in terms of the definition of the repository (what qualifies as an archive) and with regard to the record itself, becoming 'a kind of loose signifier for a disparate set of concepts'.[20] Markus Miessen and his collaborators set up a project to explore the archive beyond the traditional archive, counterarchives of a dizzying range and variety, in a book entitled *The Archive as a Productive Space of Conflict* (2016) that itself became the archive of that journeying.[21] The archive can be understood as metaphor, 'a rhetorical trope'.[22] Anjali Arondekar refers to its 'figurative flexibility'.[23] It can stand in for history itself.[24] Or it can represent, especially in science, far more, a fantasy of 'past, present, and future', what the ever perspicacious Lorraine Daston has termed an archive phantasmagoria.[25]

So the word archive has now to encompass a huge expansion of source material in a digital age.[26] It can range, quite literally, from O. J. Simpson to the Simpsons: that is, comprising the commentary and coverage generated by a high-profile trial such as that of the celebrity sportsman;[27] or entailing most things relating to the long-running animated series, catalogued in the Web-based *Simpsons Archive*.[28] One could think of an 'ex-static archive . . . not assembled behind stone walls, but suspended in a liquid element behind a luminous screen . . . a virtual repository of knowledge without visible limits, an archive in which the material becomes immaterial'.[29] When we log into our computer desktops we are simultaneously entering our own personal archives as well as potentially accessing innumerable online archives.[30] We are all 'miniarchivists'.[31] The earlier-referred-to phantasmagoria is evident in the fascinating, personal, archive-of-the-self projects discussed by Rebecca Lemov: the renowned futurist Buckminster Fuller's Chronofile, documenting his life every fifteen minutes for over sixty years, which now appears rather primitive in terms of the undigitised material that it generated, though of course visionary in terms of its scope; Gordon Bell's MyLifeBits archive, chronicling his personal everything; and Chris Dancy's recording of his life every thirty seconds. Lemov does not specify whether these archives of the self are also sexual archives, though if they include 'everything', presumably they are.[32]

Digital technology has facilitated the rise of what is termed the rogue archive and the rogue archivist, with everyone their own collector and assessor, providing both quantity and democratisation, though not necessarily permanency, to archival practice.[33] One example is the fan archive, particularly slash fan fiction (fan fiction's earliest iteration in print form as fanzine in the 1960s and 1970s is discussed later as the backdrop to the female-authored gay male pornography featured in Chapter 7). The genre of erotic and gender variant fandom expanded exponentially from the 1990s, with the Internet generating new archives such as Fanfiction.net and Archive of Our Own that both incorporate and expand the possibilities of earlier fan fiction while remaining steadfastly experimental in terms of sexuality and gender.[34] To paraphrase aficionados, fan stories are bisexually erotic, and fan archives function as queer female spaces.[35] These texts are also 'archontic', archive-like, in nature, always growing, never complete.[36] And it is worth stressing the sheer numbers involved in this archival proliferation. Fanfiction.net has 1.2 million unique authors and nearly 140 million story reviews.[37] Archive of Our Own has over a million users and nearly 3 million works in its archive.[38]

The archival turn has been especially evident in the visual arts. 'I quickly found myself at a loss when I sat down to introduce these proceedings', wrote the editor of a book aptly called *Lost in the Archives*, 'overcome not only by the intense profusion of the offerings, but by the excessive quality of the thing itself: every heap by now an archive, each archive already one too many . . . What isn't an archive these days?'[39] Although there is a much longer history, with a claimed archival turn for the 1920s, it is difficult to escape the multiplicity of examples of archivally themed art from the 1990s and 2000s.[40] Perhaps it was a pivotal moment when the studio-archive of the Brazilian artist Paulo Bruscky, bristling with all sorts of paper and celluloid matter, including thousands of works of Mail Art, itself became an exhibit at the São Paulo Biennial in 2004.[41] However, the archival impulse in modern art can be seen everywhere.[42] The installation artist Christian Boltanski's haunting imagery of the lost property of the inhabitants of Munich or the workers of Halifax, and his *Les Archives de C. B. 1965–1988* (1989), which Kate Albers argues is not an archive, are but the best known of many interpretations of the visual archive.[43] Thomas Demand's *Archive* (1995) is a photographic print of a constructed archive of identical, undated, unclassified – possibly empty – boxes: 'Not the past, only phantoms of empty boxes.'[44]

The archival turn in modern art includes the annals of sex. Marina Abramović's archive of performance involves masturbation and self-harm.[45] The photographer Nan Goldin's slide show of more than 700 images, 'The Ballad of Sexual Dependency', catalogues her intimate relationships in the late 1970s and 1980s.[46] Goldin once said that taking a picture of someone was tactile. 'It's a caress. My pictures often come from erotic desire. It's like having safe sex.'[47] Or we could consider the German artist/film-maker Michael Brynntrup's *Loverfilm* (1996), a personal archive of casual sex, twenty-one minutes of lovers named and (possibly) pictured, though the facticity of the representation is never established: 'The imagery for this film is purely coincidental and derived from a different context. The imagery originates from my personal archive. The images were shot by myself or taken from public media sources. Some images were given to me as a personal memoir by those photographed.'[48] Some art archives linger between categories; Arthur C. Danto said that Mapplethorpe 'played with the edge that separates art and mere pornography' and that this element was central to his whole artistic schema.[49] Jonathan D. Katz has termed it the twinning of formal perfection and sexual provocation.[50]

For the artists Gilbert & George, on the other hand, the archive lies behind rather than in their art: an archive of images used in their pictures, boxes of all the designs for their work, all the articles written about them ('There's a very good title here from 1992 . . . it just says "Fifty dead fucking Jesuses"'), thousands of social photographs, installation archives, transparencies of their pictures, incidental files of images (that 'might turn out to be very important'), letters, and their 'Male Sex' Library. George claimed that it was possible to trace their thematic trajectory merely through the titles in their press files.[51]

There are many other archives. We have the archives of terror, 'paper cadavers' in Kirsten Weld's chilling description.[52] We have the colonial archive, the postcolonial archive, the decolonial archive, and the 'imperial but not colonial' archive.[53] We have the domestic or living room or personal archives.[54] There are community archives, part of an older history-from-the-bottom-up or local history initiative, but given fresh impetus by the Internet.[55] The migrant archive provides traces of the past outside the 'official spaces of archivization'.[56] The archive of labour recovers the literary world of nineteenth-century, working-class, US women.[57]

The archive is also a site for the exercise of imagination, a 'place that is to do with longing and appropriation'.[58] Harriet Bradley writes of the 'pleasures, seductions and illusions of archival work'.[59] There are articles referring to the erotics of 'accessing the archival body', of how 'touching, smelling and stroking what remains of distinct material lives might elucidate arousal and certain other affective and haptic responses within the visitor to the archives'.[60] Joan Nestle, the founder of the Lesbian Herstory Archives, told Madhu Narayan that she saw archival research as an 'erotic exchange'.[61] (It has to be said that this is not an encounter that this, more detached, writer has personally experienced.)

Perhaps unsurprisingly, then, the archive has assumed a new significance in the history of sex. In such discussion it is not so much the archive of tradition, the repository of national record, that features, though it still plays a role as I will argue shortly, but more what have been termed (as we will return to in Chapter 9) archives of affect or the counterarchive, which privilege intimacy and personal longing, favour the non-normative, revel in the perverse, and confront easy assumptions of sexual identity (no nation-state guardianship and dry-as-dust chronicling here).[62] The queer archive, existing often as ephemera or in mere traces, is such a counterarchive.[63] 'Can our radical queer histories really provide the necessary ground from which to make our most fabulous queer dreams and desires a reality?' asked Ryan Conrad of his curated exhibition of photographs of queer activism in 1990s Maine; 'Hot dates, hot politics, hot pictures' was one participant's memory of the period.[64] Alana Kumbier has displayed the commitment involved in generating queer archives, but also, more poignantly, the difficulties, even resistance, she faced when trying to document the fluid, transient history of the drag king performers, a movement that she was part of in Columbus, Ohio, and in New Orleans in the late 1990s and the 2000s. In a sense, it was a noble failure: 'Concluding this chapter is difficult', she writes in a dispiriting ending, 'because both the projects I'm writing about – like all of the projects in this section of archiving from the ground up – have not been shut down or formally discontinued. There is still a page with information . . .'[65]

But there are happier stories. Robert Morgan and Jonathan Coleman's Faulkner–Morgan Pagan Babies Archive, located in Coleman's home in Lexington in Kentucky and dedicated to the LGBTQ history of that region, holds more than 12,000 items and is still growing; 'we are in a collecting phase', Coleman explained to me recently.[66] Partly named for the flamboyant artist Henry Faulkner, friend in New York in the 1940s and 1950s to Edward Melcarth and Thomas Painter (of this book), the archive includes oral histories and material exhibits as well as letters and photographs.[67]

The Internet has affected archival possibilities, as we will see when we discuss transgender. Jonathan Alexander and Jacqueline Rhodes have demonstrated the queer-world-making potentials of the World Wide Web, while simultaneously crafting their own lively queer archive from online artefacts and examples of subversions of heteronormativity.[68] Meanwhile, Kumbier dreams of digital archives of her drag king histories.[69] We might treat the museum too as counterarchival, if we are thinking of sexual artefacts: the Leather Archives & Museum in Chicago, the World Erotic Art Museum in Miami, or the Museum of Sex in New York.[70]

What have been termed porn archives also fall within the category of the counterarchive; and it is likely that there are many, yet to be 'discovered' personal collections of such material.[71] Surviving gay erotic films from the 1970s (retrospectively classified as pornography) are an important archive of male–male sexual fantasy and desire during that decade, when 'the search for sex' was central to gay male culture, but with many of its witnesses (its living archive) removed by the AIDS epidemic of the 1980s.[72] Similarly, Whitney Strub has demonstrated how a Cornell University archival collection of gay male pornographic VHS tapes from the 1980s and early 1990s, annotated and indexed by its compiler, can shed light on the erotic sensibilities of that period.[73] In other words, gay pornography can be used as 'an archive for the history of American sexuality'.[74] A recent book by Tim Dean, Steven Ruszczycky, and David Squires that outlines the diversity of archival pornography, including a bibliography of nearly forty relevant research centres, is itself a serious archive of pornography: from foreskin fetishism to amputee sex.[75] We should also include vernacular pornography, ranging from homemade or amateur art and writing to handmade objects such as wood or bone carvings – the Kinsey Institute has a large collection of such objects – material evidence for the embeddedness of sex in everyday American life.[76]

Yet it would be a mistake to limit the role of the archive in the history of sex to oppositional archivism and queering the archives. It is all too easy to dismiss the 'traditional archive'.[77] Sara Edenheim has warned against setting up the so-called scholar's archive as a 'phantasmatic projection that radicalizes the queer archive of feelings'.[78] Nor should we strictly separate the archive from the counterarchive; I have long been amused by the fact that Bryant Park, a historical haunt of hustlers and their clients, is right next to the walls of the august New York Public Library – as captured in one of Melcarth's photographs of rough trade leaning on the memorial to William Cullen Bryant (see Figure 6). Weinberg writes of the spotless white environment of the (exquisite) Getty Research Institute Library housing the archive of the artist/photographer Mapplethorpe, with sexual imagery, fisting, self-fucking, and leather bondage that still has the power to startle, either in the form of contact sheets and unpublished Polaroids or in the 'masterful perfection' of his more formal work.[79]

As well as the silences and the need to generate an absent historical trace, to counter ephemerality, I want to advocate for the richness of the sexual histories, the pockets of recorded desire, located in the most respectable repositories. After all, the New York Public Library has an extensive (though dispersed) erotica collection, and reportedly sent librarians to shop for adult material in Times Square in the 1970s to augment its holdings.[80]

6 Edward Melcarth, photograph of Bryant Park hustler, 1950s/1960s. Collection of Richard Taddei.

The library also has the Royal S. Marks AIDS Activist Video Collection, described as 'an affective archive of both AIDS activists' ingenuity and the technology used to document it'.[81] It is the repository for the Sixt Kapff files in the C. A. Tripp Papers, recording Kapff's sex with nearly 28,000 different men (Chapter 3), and the explicit, 1970s and 1980s sex diaries of David Louis Bowie (Chapter 6). Yale University's Beinecke Library contains the Samuel Steward archives, including his notorious Stud File and a box of whips and other BDSM paraphernalia (Chapter 3). Significantly, the list of pornography research collections in the *Porn Archives* anthology includes those most established of institutions, the British Library and the Bibliothèque Nationale, alongside the Museum of Sex and the Leather Archives.[82] The special issue of the *Art Journal* dealing with queer archives similarly lists the Beinecke and the Fales Library of New York University along with Brooklyn's Lesbian Herstory Archives and San Francisco's GLBT Historical Society.[83] Indeed, as sexual history becomes more mainstream, the divide between the archive and the counterarchive will lessen.[84] There is a sense, as has been said of museums, in which all archives are sex archives.[85]

The archival turn means that the archive's users have had to become more conscious of archival formation, of looking *at* archives as well as *through* them.[86] Archives have a partial and curated relationship with the past that they are said to represent, their contents culled by accident and the whims of a variety of intermediaries. Sometimes their actual presence is accidental – thus we have, somewhat predictably for a chance occurrence, the 'accidental archive', the most intriguing example of which is a seventeenth-century postmaster's trunk of unopened letters found in a museum in The Hague.[87] Archives are always indeterminate, consisting of the absent as well as the present. I love it that the personal archive of the curator Hans Ulrich Obrist, who has probably thought more about archives than any living person, has an archive of the 'unrealized projects' of artists and architects, eight hundred of them, too big, small, or unrealistic to be realised, or else censored or self-censored.[88] 'A necessary correlate to the textual profusion of the archive', writes Penelope Papailias, 'is the mystique of its gaps; the overwhelming textual clutter and its semblance of fullness is offset by the recognition of just how much is not there, of what had been lost, destroyed, confiscated, made off-limits, or never written down in the first place.'[89] The archives of the cultural critic Walter Benjamin, both extensive and idiosyncratic, are as noteworthy for their losses as for their dispersed survivals: the missing briefcase that possibly contained a manuscript on the concept of history; his lost library.[90]

Perhaps the deficit is more likely in the sexual archives. The archive of the sexologist Magnus Hirschfeld was dispersed after its partial, Nazi-initiated destruction in 1933. There are fragments in archives in London and Berlin and in the Kinsey Institute Library. There should also be boxes of his papers at the University of Minnesota, but the suitcase of documents located in Vancouver and saved from the garbage, purchased, and then destined for Minnesota, arrived empty![91] Ann Laura Stoler remembered visiting the French colonial archives in the late 1980s and ordering dossiers with promising subject matter ('clandestine prostitution in Cochin') only to discover that they no longer existed; 'they were delivered empty again and again'.[92] Richard Burton's missing secret report on male brothels in nineteenth-century Karáchi is another example, where, as Arondekar observes, 'an archival object comes into existence . . . only through its loss – a paradoxical archival emergence'.[93] Parts of the writer Franz Kafka's sexual history and self-torment, including both homoerotic desires and attraction to female sex workers, were ironed out of his published journals and correspondence – ironically, given that the same editor and friend, Max Brod, had gone against the writer's explicit wishes by saving his archives in the first place.[94] Nan Goldin's private diaries, which are yet to be released to the research community, unlike her public photographic record, have been partly destroyed by a jealous and violent lover, the result of the very sexual dependency that her archive represents.[95] And archival patrons will always perversely focus on the lacunae. The World Erotic Art Museum neglects the historical context of its exhibits. The Leather Archives and Museum representationally favours gay white men. The Museum of Sex is a 'museum for straight people'.[96]

In his history of sex and the post-war New York art scene, Gavin Butt consciously operates by what he calls 'whispering in the archive', focusing on gossip and innuendo rather than, as he sees it, 'conventional attention to the archival record'. Hence there is much mention of reimagining, unwritten suggestions, suspicions, unarticulated thought, what might have been, and 'speculative form[s] of analysis'.[97] While I have not found it necessary to whisper in a similar way – most of my archives speak rather loudly – it is true that histories are often patched together from the dispersed fragments of memory and archival traces. The hustler, Beat, and Kinsey contact Herbert Huncke has a shadowy historical presence; his drug addiction, rootless lifestyle, and petty criminal activity were not conducive to the accumulation of documentary evidence (the frequent, demanding letters from prison excepted). Yet there was enough in the archives of Columbia University, Stanford University, and elsewhere – journals and miscellaneous manuscripts, letters, literary references in the work of famous contemporaries such as Jack Kerouac and William Burroughs, remnants of Huncke's existence in the papers of his better-known friends, Allen Ginsberg and Irving Rosenthal – for him to become almost a leitmotif in my *New York Hustlers* book and for Hilary Holladay to write a biography.[98] Huncke is still there in cyberspace; you can watch him on YouTube, holding court at the Chelsea Hotel in the 1990s.[99]

The artist Henry Faulkner's sexual archive is similarly scattered. The Kinsey Institute has an archive of two hundred of Faulkner's photographs, left with Painter for safekeeping, and ending up in Bloomington (they were among those Painter described as masturbatory material, as we will see in Chapters 2 and 3). However the Faulkner–Morgan archive has four hundred more of these images from the 1940s and 1950s, and 2,000 in total from Faulkner's collection. When Faulkner died in Lexington in 1981, his companion Robert Morgan inherited his photographic albums as well as his (or someone else's) 'sailor top', stuffed cat, and doll heads. It is fascinating that among the numerous mementos of a prolific sexual history this personal archive includes pictures of hustlers individually recognisable from the Melcarth and Painter collections (see Figure 7).

Archiving transgender or trans* is almost a case study in the themes of the archival turn. Archives include what K. J. Rawson labels 'grassroots archives' such as the Sexual Minorities Archives, located in the archivist's home in Northampton, Massachusetts; community repositories such as the GLBT Historical Society in San Francisco; and the established, often university-based, institutional archive, comprising some of the repositories discussed in this chapter as well as, say, the University of Toronto's Sexual Representation Collection, the University of Michigan's National Transgender Library and Archive, or the Robert J. Stoller Papers in the Charles E. Young Research Library at the University of California, Los Angeles.[100] The archive can take the form of performance. Sean Dorsey embarks on archival research and oral history before translating those collected stories into dance. One of the lives choreographed is that of Lou Sullivan; and Dorsey read his diaries, just as I did for Chapter 5 of this book.[101] The archive can involve the visual arts.[102] Katie Herzog's *Transtextuality (Senate Bill 48)* (2013), now in the Los Angeles County Museum of Art, depicts 48 portraits of transgender writers.[103] Mariette Pathy Allen has been generating a transgender photographic archive since the 1970s, including famous names (Lou Sullivan is one) and moments in trans history.[104] More recently, Mark Seliger and Janet Mock's portfolio 'Christopher Street' has captured the variety of trans lives in New York in 2016.[105] And Zanele Muholi has been picturing what she calls 'gender within gender' in her arresting South African images.[106] However, the trans archive has its gaps too. Allen's oeuvre seems rather white and teleological.[107] Herzog's *Transtextuality (Senate Bill 48)* has been criticised for its blinkered representation of race and class.[108]

7 Henry Faulkner, scrapbooks of photographs from New York, 1940s/1950s. The photographs are of Faulkner, surrounded by images of a hustler whose photograph reappears in the next chapter (see Figure 20). Faulkner–Morgan Pagan Babies Archive.

Transgender artefacts range widely. They can take the form of photographs of trans before trans, as in the police before-and-after photographs of 'A bunch of female impersonators arrested in a house in Los Angeles' in 1927, wigged and then un-wigged, found in the personal scrapbook of

8 'Female Impersonators' arrested in a raid on a house in Los Angeles by the Los Angeles Police, 1927. In Jesse Brown Cook scrapbooks documenting San Francisco history and law enforcement [graphic], BANC PIC 1996.003:Volume 25:71a--fALB. Courtesy of The Bancroft Library, University of California, Berkeley.

a San Francisco police chief (see Figures 8–9). Or, in the same archive of negation – in Rebekah Edwards's exemplary reading – there is another such image from 1917: 'This is not a girl', a picture of Geraldine Portica.[109] The trans artefact can consist of an oral history: those living archives of desire, of those who are already dead, such as Teresita la Campesina, recalled so compellingly by Horacio N. Roque Ramirez – 'I'm an old lady now, but looking whory, you know. I refuse to lay down and look like an antique. I like to varnish myself'; or Susan Stryker's riveting collection of 1990s San Francisco interviews in the GLBT Historical Society Oral History Collection; or the more recently targeted oral histories of trans people of colour, missing from so many of the archives and histories of transgender.[110]

Like the archival queer, transgender has embraced the digital. Cyberspace provides the scope for 'transgender history to be provoked, recorded, disseminated, accessed, and preserved in ways untethered from traditional, offline, and analog practices of history'; and the curated Digital Transgender Archive is a most impressive demonstration of that very potential.[111] The trans* archive includes the 'living archive' of YouTube, with its cleverly

9 'Female Impersonators' arrested in a raid on a house in Los Angeles by the Los Angeles Police, 1927: 'The same bunch with their wigs off'. Jesse Brown Cook scrapbooks documenting San Francisco history and law enforcement [graphic], BANC PIC 1996.003:Volume 25:71b--fALB. Courtesy of The Bancroft Library, University of California, Berkeley.

crafted – if highly idealised – visual records of trans self-fashioning, the respective effects of testosterone and oestrogen on trans man masculinity and trans woman femininity.[112]

Finally, one could argue that the indeterminacy of trans is reflected in its archive. Is the history of what was then designated transsexuality really flattened in the gay histories of drag performers (Pittsburgh's House of Tilden), or by what was then called transvestism (at Casa Susanna, or in *Transvestia*)?[113] Or is the sexual and gender indecipherability at the transsexual moment of the 1960s and 1970s the very essence of that period's transness?[114]

The queer archive, as the editors of special issues of *Radical History Review* have claimed, 'might be described . . . as a space where one cobbles together historical understandings of sexuality and gender through an appraisal of presences and absences'.[115] Hopefully the readers of what follows will not confront 'negation in abundance', holes and absences amid excess.[116] But there are instances of archival absences. For example, the missing photographs and journals from David Louis Bowie's obsessive collecting, burgled from his home and discussed in Chapter 6, may eventually surface – or they may be lost forever. Much of Steward's archive (Chapter 3) could easily have disappeared. Apart from copies made for Kinsey, his papers mouldered, scattered throughout his house, and then, after his death, in a friend's attic, until his biographer Justin Spring arranged their acquisition by the Beinecke Library, where they now reside, with a kind of supplementary, shadow, archival presence at the Kinsey Institute.[117]

Whatever the intent of the originator of the archive, its content can be censored when it reaches the archivist. There is the example of the South African Anglican priest whose letters were embargoed and certain items in his collection destroyed to protect the reputation of a man who may well have wanted the reality of his life to be revealed.[118] Matthew Reisz has similarly written of his grandmother Winifred de Kok's intimate correspondence with the sex reformer Havelock Ellis, discussing masturbation and undinism or urolagnia (urine play), which, without the knowledge of the family, was held back from researchers in the Ellis archive at the British Library in an effort to spare the perceived blushes of her descendants. Reisz, not one to blush readily, only discovered its existence in 2003.[119]

Or the archive is there, or probably there, but frustratingly inaccessible. Steven Maynard, an innovative historian of homosexuality, has outlined the decades-long irritations of trying to access the records of the Morality Department of the Toronto Police Force, housed in the Toronto Police Museum.[120] Vintage pornography, for example, may exist in the archive, but because backlogged acquisitions or donations build up without ever being catalogued, it is therefore effectively lost in the archive, possibly forever.[121] Even the Kinsey Institute demonstrates the limits of the archive in generating sexual history. While it stands alone as an archive entirely devoted to sexual matters, protected over the years by the determination of its founders, its independent incorporation (until 2016), and location in Indiana University, this most sexually tolerant of institutions has boundaries.[122] Not all of the Kinsey's holdings are accessible to the researcher: the secret films of human sexual activity, including Steward's, remain secret; sections of Steward's Kinsey collaboration, with an incomplete copy of his famous Stud File of thousands of sexual contacts, have been unavailable for viewing.[123]

Certainly archives are never static. The Transgender Archives at the University of Victoria, in Canada, is a relatively new archive (2011), formed out of the collection of Rikki Swan and the papers of Reed Erickson.[124] The Lesbian Herstory Archives, which has been described as an 'always-in-process archive', began in Joan Nestle's pantry in 1976 and spilled out throughout her apartment before moving to its current location in Brooklyn.[125] The Mapplethorpe archive started as a couple of portfolios under the artist's bed in Brooklyn in the 1960s and ended up, enormously expanded ('Robert saved everything'), in the Getty Research Institute with selected exhibitions in the Los Angeles County Museum of Art.[126] Nan Goldin's slide show has been constantly re-edited and reshown, with music, as live performance, video, film, and in printed form, moving from clubs in the 1980s to the Whitney, and, most recently, to a major exhibition at New York's Museum of Modern Art (2016–17).[127] Its meaning has shifted from an insider's chronicle of gendered violence and sexual obsession to a memorial of loss to drug addiction and AIDS, and, for the artist herself, from a record of her world as it really was (in 1986), 'without glorification', to (in 1996) a visual encapsulation of the out-dated 'notion of self-destruction as glamorous'.[128] So there is the kind of fluidity that Stuart Hall thought desirable in the composition of an archive.[129] The New York Public Library's Schomburg Center for Research in Black Culture has just acquired the letters of James Baldwin, previously held by the Baldwin estate, though some of the correspondence, presumably of a sexual nature, has been embargoed for another twenty years.[130] And, as I write this, the Archives of Lesbian Oral Testimony have announced their 'Bridging the Gap' research initiative, which will allow users to upload their own oral history interviews.[131]

Some of the sexual annals discussed later in this book demonstrate similar archival flux. Richard Taddei's archive of hustler photographs (aside from those now in the Smithsonian Institute) has moved from his West 47th Street Manhattan apartment to a house in Montgomery, New York. The Forbes Gallery is no more, so the Melcarth archive remains partly in Forbes family ownership and partly in the galleries and private collections to which it has been dispersed. ANONYMOUS's archive of the changes made to rewritten gay classics (see Chapter 7) may vanish when he does, though vestiges will be left in digital copies of the files and the chapter in this book which describes his endeavours. Badertscher's vast photographic archive (see Chapter 9), including ongoing digital enlargements of previous negatives to 18" x 24" prints, is destined for the Leslie–Lohman Museum of Gay and Lesbian Art in New York. But it also includes the stories that he continues to write and rewrite, and which he has been sending to this author for his own digital collection of Badertscher's works:

> John, always known as JJ, lived in Dundalk, east of Baltimore City and all of it a formidably mixed bag of humanity – a working class neighborhood

> where most of the people weren't working. His mother had died of cancer and he lived in one of the units of subsidized housing alone with his father, a man on various disabilities. When he would call in the early morning when I would be recovering from a hangover, he would begin to describe in excruciating detail the color and shape of every item he was wearing, the type and color of shoes, his exact location on Dundalk Avenue, the names of the streets he would be passing, some drab significant landmarks and in which direction he was headed and the precise time he would be doing this. All of this for my ravenous pain ravaged curiosity so I just couldn't miss him. As if this was humanly possible. When I met him he would invariably begin telling me one of his labyrinthine, either slightly harmless or unsettling stories about himself or his father or a particularly dysfunctional neighbor and sometimes the details would change each time he told it. Really, his life was in another dimension. If John was on a particular mission in life, either now or in the not too distant future, I'm pretty sure he didn't know what it was.[132]

Perhaps this observation of a photographic subject will be included in the margins of an enlarged print. Possibly it will remain a discrete story. And so the Badertscher archive still grows.

Notes

1 C. Steedman, *Dust* (Manchester, 2001), p. x.

2 B. Hutchinson and S. Weller, 'Archive time', *Comparative Critical Studies*, 8:2–3 (2011), 133–53, quote at 133. Though the literature on the archives and history is now extensive, and will be drawn on in what follows, a good starting point is F. X. Blouin and W. G. Rosenberg, *Processing the Past: Contesting Authority in History and the Archives* (New York, 2011).

3 R. Prelinger, 'The appearance of archives', in P. Snickars and P. Vonderau (eds), *The YouTube Reader* (Stockholm, 2009), pp. 268–74; the video statistic comes from http://tubularinsights.com/youtube-changes-33-percent-a-year/ (last accessed 26 April 2018). The numbers in the *YouTube Reader* were out of date before it was even published.

4 S. Yee, 'The archive', in S. Tuttle (ed.), *Evocative Objects: Things We Think With* (Cambridge, MA, 2011), pp. 31–6.

5 N. Z. Davis, 'Foreword', in A. Farge, *The Allure of the Archives*, trans. T. Scott-Railton (New Haven, CT, 2013), pp. ix–xvi.

6 L. Bernard, 'Unpacking the archive', *The Yale Review*, 99:4 (2011), 93–107, quote at 97–8.

7 L. Jardine, *Temptation in the Archives: Essays in Golden Age Dutch Culture* (London, 2015), p. viii.

8 J. W. Scott, *The Fantasy of Feminist History* (Durham, NC, 2011), p. 148.

9 B. H. Edwards, 'The taste of the archive', *Callaloo*, 35:4 (2012), 944–72, quotes at 944, 945. He starts the article with the photograph and reveals the identity of its subject later. However, the mystery was somewhat undermined for this reader because I recognised the young man immediately as Charles Henri Ford.

10 J. Weinberg, 'The promiscuity of the archive', in F. Terpak and M. Brunnick (eds), *Robert Mapplethorpe: The Archive* (Los Angeles, 2016), pp. 185–99, at p. 187.

11 E. Robinson, 'Touching the void: affective history and the impossible', *Rethinking History*, 14:4 (2010), 503–20, quote at 517.

12 C. Steedman, 'The space of memory: in an archive', *History of the Human Sciences*, 11:4 (1998), 65–83, quote at 67.

13 See R. H. Brown and B. Davis-Brown, 'The making of memory: the politics of archives, libraries and museums in the construction of national consciousness', *History of the Human Sciences*, 11:4 (1998), 17–32, quotes at 20.

14 A. Mbembe, 'The power of the archive and its limits', in C. Hamilton et al. (eds), *Refiguring the Archive* (Dordrecht, 2002), pp. 19–26, quote at p. 19.

15 Steedman, 'Space of memory', 67.

16 C. Merewether, 'Introduction//art and the archive', in C. Merewether (ed.), *The Archive: Documents of Contemporary Art* (London, 2006), pp. 10–17, quote at p. 10.

17 Farge, *Allure of the Archives*; Steedman, *Dust*.

18 V. Reinburg, *French Books of Hours: Making an Archive of Prayer, c. 1400–1600* (Cambridge, 2012); M. Laven, 'Recording miracles in Renaissance Italy', in L. Corens, K. Peters, and A. Walsham (eds), *The Social History of the Archive: Record-Keeping in Early Modern Europe* (Oxford, 2016), pp. 191–212.

19 M. Lynch, 'Archives in formation: privileged spaces, popular archives and paper trails', *History of the Human Sciences*, 12:2 (1999), 65–87.

20 M. Manoff, 'Theories of the archive: from across the disciplines', *Portal: Libraries and the Academy*, 4:1 (2004), 9–25, quote at 10.

21 M. Miessen et al. (eds), *The Archive as a Productive Space of Conflict* (Berlin, 2016). A point made by two of the editors on p. 27.

22 M. O'Driscoll and E. Bishop, 'Archiving "archiving"', *English Studies in Canada*, 30:1 (2004), 1–16, quote at 4.

23 A. Arondekar, *For the Record: On Sexuality and the Colonial Archive in India* (Durham, NC, 2009), p. 2.

24 E. Yate, 'The history of archives: the state of the discipline', *Book History*, 18 (2015), 332–59.

25 L. Daston, 'Introduction: third nature', in L. Daston (ed.), *Science in the Archives: Pasts, Presents, Futures* (Chicago, 2017), pp. 1–14, quote at p. 12.

26 See Blouin and Rosenberg, *Processing the Past*, ch. 10: 'Archives and the cyberinfrastructure'.

27 Lynch, 'Archives in formation', 75–9.

28 R. Wolf, 'The scholar and the fan', in M. A. Holly and M. Smith (eds), *What is Research in the Visual Arts? Obsession, Archive, Encounter* (Williamstown, MA, 2008), pp. 158–67.

29 P. J. Voss and M. J. Werner, 'Towards a poetics of the archive: introduction', *Studies in the Literary Imagination*, 32:1 (1999), i–viii, quote at ii.

30 K. Eichhorn, 'Archival genres: gathering texts and reading spaces', *Invisible Culture: An Electronic Journal for Visual Culture*, 12 (2008), 1–9.

31 J. Parikka, 'Archival media theory', in W. Ernst, *Digital Memory and the Archive*, ed. J. Parikka (Minneapolis, MN, 2013), pp. 1–22, quote at p. 2.

32 R. Lemov, 'Archives-of-self: the vicissitudes of time and self in a technologically determinist future', in Daston (ed.), *Science in the Archives*, ch. 10.

33 A. De Kosnick, *Rogue Archives: Digital Cultural Memory and Media Fandom* (Cambridge, MA, 2016).

34 For the upsurge of erotic Internet fandom literature, see K. Hellekson and K. Busse (eds), *Fan Fiction and Fan Communities in the Age of the Internet: New Essays* (Jefferson, NC, 2006); S. Cumberland, 'Private uses of cyberspace: women, desire, and fan culture', in M. C. Kearney (ed.), *The Gender and Media Reader* (New York, 2012), ch. 48; A. Lothian, 'Archival anarchies: online fandom, subcultural conservation, and the transformative work of digital ephemera', *International Journal of Cultural Studies*, 16:6 (2012), 541–56; A. Jameson (ed.), *Fic: Why Fanfiction is Taking Over the World* (Dallas, 2013); De Kosnick, *Rogue Archives*, ch. 3.

35 E. Lackner, B. L. Lucas, and R. A. Reid, 'Cunning linguists: the bisexual erotics of *Words/Silence/Flesh*', in Hellekson and Busse (eds), *Fan Fiction and Fan Communities*, ch. 8; K. Busse, 'My life is a WIP on my LJ: slashing the slasher and the reality of celebrity and Internet performance', in ibid., ch. 9; A. Lothian, K. Busse, and R. A. Reid, '"Yearning void and infinite potential": online slash fandom as queer female space', *English Language Notes*, 45:2 (2007), 103–11.

36 A. Derecho, 'Archontic literature: a definition, a history, and several theories of fan fiction', in Hellekson and Busse (eds), *Fan Fiction and Fan Communities*, ch. 1.

37 De Kosnick, *Rogue Archives*, p. 342.

38 In March 2017: https://archiveofourown.org/ (last accessed 26 April 2018).

39 R. Comay, 'Introduction', in R. Comay (ed.), *Lost in the Archives* (Toronto, 2002), pp. 12–15, quote at p. 12.

40 S. Spieker, *The Big Archive: Art from Bureaucracy* (Cambridge, MA, 2008).

41 S. Osthoff, *Performing the Archive: The Transformation of the Archive in Contemporary Art from Repository of Documents to Art Medium* (New York, 2009), pp. 23–4, 139–50.

42 H. Foster, 'An archival impulse', *October*, 110 (2004), 3–22. For other examples, see B. von Bismarck et al., *Interarchive: Archivarische Praktiken und Handlungsräume im zeitgenössischen Kunstfeld / Archival Practices and

Sites in the Contemporary Art Field (Cologne, 2002); Comay (ed.), *Lost in the Archives*; O. Enwezor, *Archive Fever: Uses of the Document in Contemporary Art* (New York, 2008); E. van Elphen, 'Archival obsessions and obsessive archives', in Holly and Smith (eds), *What is Research in the Visual Arts*, pp. 65–84; G. Borggreen and R. Gade (eds), *Performing Archives/Archives of Performance* (Copenhagen, 2013); T. T. Latimer et al., 'Forum: conversations on queer affect and queer archives', *Art Journal*, 72:2 (2013); A. Downey (ed.), *Dissonant Archives: Contemporary Visual Culture and Contested Narratives in the Middle East* (New York, 2015); F. de Jong, 'At work in the archive: introduction to special issue', *World Art*, 6:1 (2016), 3–17; G. Palladini and M. Pustianaz (eds), *Lexicon for an Affective Archive* (Chicago, 2017).

43 R. Hobbs, 'Boltanski's visual archives', *History of the Human Sciences*, 11:4 (1998), 121–40; K. P. Albers, '"It's not an archive": Christian Boltanski's *Les Archives de C. B., 1965–1988*', *Visual Resources*, 27:3 (2011), 249–66.

44 Spieker, *The Big Archive*, pp. 192–3.

45 G. Minissale, 'Performing the curator, curating the performer: Abramović's *Seven Easy Pieces*', in C. Jeffery (ed.), *The Artist as Curator* (Bristol, 2015), ch. 7.

46 N. Goldin, *The Ballad of Sexual Dependency* (New York, 1996).

47 N. Goldin and T. Kawachi (eds), *Nan Goldin: Couples and Loneliness* (Tokyo, 1998), p. 58.

48 M. Brynntrup, 'Loverfilm', in Comay (ed.), *Lost in the Archives*, pp. 464–80, quote at p. 467; R. Curtis, 'From the diary to the webcam: Michael Brynntrup and the medial self', in R. Halle and R. Steingröver (eds), *After the Avant-Garde: Contemporary German and Austrian Experimental Film* (Rochester, NY, 2008), ch. 11.

49 A. C. Danto, *Playing With the Edge: The Photographic Achievement of Robert Mapplethorpe* (Berkeley and Los Angeles, 1998), quote at pp. 76–7. See also R. Meyer, 'Mapplethorped: art, photography, and the pornographic imagination', in P. Martineau and B. Salvesen (eds), *Robert Mapplethorpe: The Photographs* (Los Angeles, 2016), pp. 231–43.

50 J. D. Katz, 'Robert Mapplethorpe's queer classicism: the substance of style', in Martineau and Salvesen (eds), *Robert Mapplethorpe: The Photographs*, pp. 257–69.

51 H. U. Obrist, 'Interview with Gilbert & George', in von Bismarck et al., *Interarchive*, pp. 48–58, quote at p. 50.

52 K. Weld, *Paper Cadavers: The Archives of Dictatorship in Guatemala* (Durham, NC, 2014).

53 A. L. Stoler, 'Colonial archives and the arts of governance: on the content in the form', in Hamilton et al. (eds), *Refiguring the Archive*, pp. 83–102; A. L. Stoller, *Along the Archival Grain: Epistemic Anxieties and Colonial Common Sense* (Princeton, NJ, 2009); J. Allman, 'Phantoms of the archive: Kwame Nkrumah, a Nazi pilot named Hanna, and the contingencies of post-colonial history-writing', *American Historical Review*, 118:1 (2013), 104–29;

P. Basu and F. de Jong, 'Utopian archives, decolonial affordances: introduction to special issue', *Social Anthropology/Anthropologie Sociale*, 24:1 (2016), 5–19; C. McGranahan, 'Imperial but not colonial: archival truths. British India, and the case of the "naughty" Tibetans', *Comparative Studies in Society and History*, 59:1 (2017), 68–95.

54 A. B. Burton, *Dwelling in the Archive: Women Writing House, Home, and History in Late Colonial India* (New York, 2003); P. Papailias, *Genres of Recollection: Archival Poetics and Modern Greece* (New York, 2005), p. 2.

55 A. Finn, 'Community histories, community archives: some opportunities and challenges', *Journal of the Society of Archivists*, 28:2 (2007), 151–76.

56 R. Lazo, 'Migrant archives', in R. Castronovo and S. K. Gilman (eds), *States of Emergency: The Object of American Studies* (Chapel Hill, NC, 2009), pp. 36–54, quote at p. 37.

57 L. Merish, *Archives of Labor: Working-Class Women and Literary Culture in the Antebellum United States* (Durham, NC, 2017).

58 Steedman, 'Space of memory', 76.

59 H. Bradley, 'The seductions of the archive: voices lost and found', *History of the Human Sciences*, 12:2 (1999), 107–22, quote at 109.

60 J. A. Lee, 'Be/longing in the archival body: eros and the "endearing" value of material lives', *Archival Science*, 16:1 (2016), 33–51, quotes at 33. This archival sensuousness permeates at least two of the essays in A. L. Stone and J. Cantrell (eds), *Out of the Closet, Into the Archives: Researching Sexual Histories* (Albany, NY, 2015): see J. R. Enszer, 'Feverishly lesbian-feminist: archival objects and queer desires', ch. 6; and R. L. Fullan, 'Victory celebration for Essex Charles Hemphill; or, what Essex saved', ch. 8.

61 M. Narayan, 'At home with the Lesbian Herstory Archives', *Enculturation: A Journal of Rhetoric, Writing, and Culture*, 15 (2013): www.enculturation.net/lesbian-herstory-archives (last accessed 26 April 2018).

62 For a useful summary, see T. Dean, 'Introduction: pornography, technology, archive', in T. Dean, S. Ruszczycky, and D. Squires (eds), *Porn Archives* (Durham, NC, 2014), pp. 1–26.

63 See, for example, J. E. Muñoz, 'Ephemera as evidence: introductory notes to queer acts', *Women & Performance: A Journal of Feminist Theory*, 8:2 (1996), 5–16; P. Hegarty, 'Harry Stack Sullivan and his chums: archive fever in American psychiatry?', *History of the Human Sciences*, 18:3 (2005), 35–53; M. Danbolt, J. Rowley, and L. Wolthers (eds), *Lost and Found: Queerying the Archive* (Copenhagen, 2010); D. Marshall, K. P. Murphy, and Z. Tortorici (eds), 'Queering archives', *Radical History Review*, 120 (2014) and 122 (2015) [journal special issues]; K. J. Rawson and A. Devor (eds), 'Archives and archiving', *TSQ*, 2:4 (2015) [journal special issue]; Stone and Cantrell (eds), *Out of the Closet, Into the Archives*.

64 R. Conrad et al., *Future of the Past: Reviving the Queer Archive* (Portland ME, 2009), no pagination.

65 A. Kumbier, *Ephemeral Material: Queering the Archives* (Sacramento, CA, 2014), p. 151.
66 FaceTime conversation with Jonathan Coleman, March 2017.
67 See www.facebook.com/FaulknerMorganArchive/ (last accessed 26 April 2018). I have benefited greatly from email conversations with Coleman.
68 J. Alexander and J. Rhodes, 'Queer rhetoric and the pleasures of the archive', *Enculturation: A Journal of Rhetoric, Writing, and Culture*, 13 (2012): http://enculturation.net/queer-rhetoric-and-the-pleasures-of-the-archive (last accessed 26 April 2018).
69 Kumbier, *Ephemeral Material*, p. 151.
70 J. Tyburczy, *Sex Museums: The Politics and Performance of Display* (Chicago, 2016).
71 J. Mercer, 'The secret history: porn archives, "personal" collections and British universities', *Porn Studies*, 1:4 (2014), 411–14.
72 L. Hilderbrand, 'Historical fantasies: 1970s gay male pornography in the archives', in C. Bronstein and W. Strub (eds), *Porno Chic and the Sex Wars: American Sexual Representation in the 1970s* (Amherst and Boston, MA, 2016), ch. 13, quote at p. 345.
73 W. Strub, 'Indexing desire: the gay male pornographic video collection as affective archive', in Stone and Cantrell (eds), *Out of the Closet, Into the Archives*, ch. 5.
74 J. Escoffier, 'Sex in the seventies: gay porn cinema as an archive for the history of American sexuality', *Journal of the History of Sexuality*, 26:1 (2017), 88–113.
75 Dean, Ruszczycky, and Squires (eds), *Porn Archives*, esp. chs 19, 21, and appendix. See also, for another example, S. Nomine, 'Pornographic website as public history archive: a case study', in R. Wexelbaum (ed.), *Queers Online: LGBT Digital Practices in Libraries, Archives, and Museums* (Sacramento, CA, 2014), pp. 19–41.
76 L. Z. Sigel, 'Handmade and homemade: vernacular expressions of American sexual history', *Journal of the History of Sexuality*, 25:3 (2016), 437–62.
77 As in J. Rowley and L. Wolthers, 'Lost and found: querying the archive', in Danbolt, Rowley, and Wolthers (eds), *Lost and Found*, pp. 9–23, quote at p. 11.
78 S. Edenheim, 'Lost and never found: the queer archive of feelings and its historical propriety', *Differences*, 24:3 (2014), 36–62, quote at 41.
79 Weinberg, 'Promiscuity of the archive', in Terpak and Brunnick (eds), *Robert Mapplethorpe: The Archive*, pp. 185–99. For some of the 1,500 Polaroids, see also S. Wolf, *Polaroids: Mapplethorpe* (Munich, 2013). And for Katz's brilliant essay on Mapplethorpe's queer classicism, accompanied by examples of the more formal photographs, see his 'Robert Mapplethorpe's queer classicism', in Martineau and Salvesen (eds), *Robert Mapplethorpe: The Photographs*, pp. 257–69, quote at p. 257.

80 E. Sciolino, 'Lifting the veil on the New York Public Library's erotica collection', *The New York Times*, 1 January 2016: www.nytimes.com/2016/01/03/nyregion/lifting-the-veil-on-the-new-york-public-librarys-erotica-collection.html (last accessed 26 April 2018).
81 J. Hubbard, 'Fever in the archive', *GLQ*, 7:1 (2001), 183–92; L. Hilderbrand, 'Retroactivism', *GLQ*, 12:2 (2006), 303–17, quote at 308.
82 C. Shanley, 'Clandestine catalogs: a bibliography of porn research collections', in Dean, Ruszczycky, and Squires (eds), *Porn Archives*, appendix.
83 T. T. Latimer, 'Conversations on queer affect and queer archives', *Art Journal*, 72:2 (2013), 33–7.
84 J. Weeks, *What is Sexual History?* (Cambridge, 2016), p. 124.
85 I am alluding to Tyburczy, *Sex Museums*, 'Introduction: all museums are sex museums'.
86 K. Burns, *Into the Archive: Writing and Power in Colonial Peru* (Durham, NC, 2010), p. 125. My emphasis.
87 R. Ahrendt and D. Van der Linden, 'The postmaster's piggy bank: experiencing the accidental archive', *French Historical Studies*, 40:2 (2017), 189–213. Even more intriguing is the authors' decision not to seek that the remaining sealed letters be opened (some have been opened and some not) in order to preserve their material integrity. I am not sure that this historian could exercise such restraint.
88 M. Miessen and H. U. Obrist, 'Archiving in formation', in Miessen et al. (eds), *Archive as a Productive Space of Conflict*, pp. 539–54, at p. 542.
89 Papailias, *Genres of Recollection*, p. 20.
90 E. Wizisla, 'Preface', in U. Marx et al. (eds), *Walter Benjamin's Archive: Images, Texts, Signs* (London, 2007), pp. 1–6.
91 H. Bauer, *The Hirschfeld Archives: Violence, Death, and Modern Queer Culture* (Philadelphia, 2017), pp. 3–4.
92 A. L. Stoler, *Carnal Knowledge and Imperial Power: Race and the Intimate in Colonial Rule* (Berkeley and Los Angeles, 2010), pp. 15–16.
93 Arondekar, *For the Record*, p. 30.
94 M. A. Anderson, 'Kafka, homosexuality, and the aesthetics of "male culture"', in R. Robertson and E. Timms (eds), *Gender and Politics in Austrian Fiction* (Edinburgh, 1996), pp. 79–99; J. Zilcosky, 'Kafka's remains', in Comay (ed.), Lost in the Archives, pp. 630–44; S. Friedländer, *Franz Kafka: The Poet of Shame and Guilt* (New Haven, CT, 2013), ch. 3. Whether Kafka's explicitly expressed wishes reflected his unexpressed wishes is another matter.
95 Goldin, *Ballad of Sexual Dependency*, p. 8.
96 See J. Tyburczy, 'Perverting the museum: the politics and performance of sexual artefacts', in M. Kohlke and L. Orza (eds), *Negotiating Sexual Idioms: Image, Text, Performance* (Amsterdam, 2008), pp. 145–70, quote at p. 158.
97 G. Butt, *Between You and Me: Queer Disclosures in the New York Art World, 1948–1963* (Durham, NC, 2005), pp. 16–21.

98 B. Reay, *New York Hustlers: Masculinity and Sex in Modern America* (Manchester, 2010), pp. 1–2, 4, 23, 77, 82, 111, 112, 130–1, 225–6, 263–71; H. Holladay, *American Hipster: A Life of Herbert Huncke* (New York, 2013).

99 www.youtube.com/watch?v=SFc34SU8Cbk (last accessed 26 April 2018).

100 K. J. Rawson, 'Accessing transgender // desiring queer(er?) archival logics', *Archivaria*, 68 (2009), 123–40, quote at 126; G. Koskovich, 'Displaying the queer past: purposes, publics, and possibilities at the GLBT History Museum', *QED: A Journal in GLBTQ Worldmaking*, 1:2 (2014), 61–78; N. Matte, 'Without a minority/identity framework: highlighting trans archival materials at the University of Toronto's Sexual Representation Collection', *TSQ*, 2:4 (2015), 595–606; C. Joynt and K. Schilt, 'Anxiety at the archive', *TSQ*, 2:4 (2015), 635–44.

101 M. Crandall and S. W. Schwartz, 'Moving transgender histories: Sean Dorsey's trans archival practice', *TSQ*, 2:4 (2015), 565–77.

102 See J. Halberstam, *In a Queer Time and Place: Transgender Bodies, Subcultural Lives* (New York, 2005), ch. 5: 'Technotopias: representing transgender bodies in contemporary art'.

103 K. Besser, '*Transtextuality (Senate Bill 48)*: recovering and reimagining trans histories', *TSQ*, 2:4 (2015), 673–5; J. L. Mathiason, 'In Herzog's hands: *Transtextuality (Senate Bill 48)*', *TSQ*, 2:4 (2015), 679–82.

104 M. P. Allen, 'Momentum: a photo essay of the transgender community in the United States over 30 years, 1978–2007', *Sexuality Research & Social Policy*, 4:4 (2007), 92–105; M. P. Allen, 'Connecting body and mind: how transgendered people changed their self-image', *Women & Performance: A Journal of Feminist Theory*, 20:3 (2010), 267–83. Ironically, the caption for Sullivan's photograph was transposed with that of Steve Dain (another trans man, whom Sullivan knew): see Allen, 'Momentum', 95–6, Figures 9 and 10.

105 M. Seliger and J. Mock, 'Christopher Street: portraits of a transgender community', *The New Yorker*, 1 August 2016.

106 G. Baderoon, '"Gender within gender": Zanele Muholi's images of trans being and becoming', *Feminist Studies*, 37:2 (2011), 390–416.

107 My personal observation.

108 Z. Davy, 'Trans intelligentsia: a Western pictorial', *TSQ*, 2:4 (2015), 676–8.

109 R. Edwards, '"This is not a girl": a trans* archival reading', *TSQ*, 2:4 (2015), 650–65.

110 For Teresita la Campesina, see H. N. R. Ramirez, 'A living archive of desire: Teresita la Campesina and the embodiment of queer Latino community histories', in Burton (ed.), *Archival Stories*, pp. 111–35, quote at p. 112; H. N. R. Ramírez, 'Sharing queer authorities: collaborating for transgender Latina and gay Latino historical meanings', in N. A. Boyd and H. N. R. Ramírez (eds), *Bodies of Evidence: The Practice of Queer Oral History* (New York, 2012), ch. 10. For the Stryker interviews, see GLBT Historical

Society, San Francisco, Oral History Collection, GLBT-OH. And for the later oral history projects, E. P. Brown, 'Trans/feminist oral history', *TSQ*, 2:4 (2015), 666–72.

111 K. J. Rawson, 'Transgender worldmaking in cyberspace: historical activism on the Internet', *QED: A Journal in GLBTQ Worldmaking*, 1:2 (2014), 38–60, quote at 38; www.digitaltransgenderarchive.net/about/overview (last accessed 26 April 2018). See also K. J. Rawson, 'Rhetorical history 2.0: toward a digital transgender archive', *Enculturation: A Journal of Rhetoric, Writing, and Culture*, 15 (2013): www.enculturation.net/toward_digital_transgender_archive (last accessed 26 April 2018).

112 T. Raun, 'Archiving the wonders of testosterone via YouTube', *TSQ*, 2:4 (2015), 701–9, quote at 701; T. Raun, *Out Online: Trans Self-Representation and Community Building on YouTube* (London, 2016).

113 H. Apple, 'The $10,000 Woman: trans artifacts in the Pittsburgh Queer History Project archive', *TSQ*, 2:4 (2015), 553–64 (for drag); and B. Davis, 'Using archives to identify the trans* women of Casa Susanna', *TSQ*, 2:4 (2015), 621–34 (for Casa Susanna and *Transvestia*).

114 Something that I am currently working on for my forthcoming book *Trans America*.

115 D. Marshall, K. P. Murphy, and Z. Tortorci, 'Editors' introduction: queering archives: historical unravelings', *Radical History Review*, 120 (2014), 1–11, quote at 2.

116 For Green, see R. Green, 'Survival: ruminations on archival lacunae, 2002', in Merewether (ed.), *Archive*, pp. 49–55, quote at p. 49.

117 J. Spring, *Secret Historian: The Life and Times of Samuel Steward, Professor, Tattoo Artist, and Sexual Renegade* (New York, 2010), 'Afterword: The Steward Papers', pp. 407–14.

118 G. Reid, '"The history of the past is the trust of the present": preservation and excavation in the gay and lesbian archives of South Africa', in Hamilton et al. (eds), *Refiguring the Archive*, pp. 193–207, at pp. 193–4.

119 M. Reisz, 'When grandma was young', *Granta*, 90 (2005), 127–48.

120 S. Maynard, 'Police/archives', *Archivaria*, 68 (2009), 159–82.

121 D. Church, *Disposable Passions: Vintage Pornography and the Material Legacies of Adult Cinema* (New York, 2016), ch. 3. For the problem of access amid excess in film archives more generally, see J. Jones, *The Past is a Moving Picture: Preserving the Twentieth Century on Film* (Gainesville, FL, 2012), ch. 4.

122 For the Kinsey Institute and Library, see L. Zhou, 'Characteristics of material organization and classification in the Kinsey Institute Library', *Cataloging & Classification Quarterly*, 35:3–4 (2003), 335–53; J. B. Bright and R. Crowley, '"A quantity of offensive matter": private cases in public places', in Dean, Ruszczycky, and Squires (eds), *Porn Archives*, ch. 5. For the history of the institute and its recent loss of its independent incorporation (on the eve of its

seventy-year anniversary), see J. A. Allen et al., *The Kinsey Institute: The First Seventy Years* (Bloomington, IN, 2017). The institute is now under the full governance of the university (Allen et al., *Kinsey Institute*, p. 185).

123 Bright and Crowley, '"A quantity of offensive matter"', p. 115.

124 A. H. Devor, *The Transgender Archives: Foundations for the Future* (Vancouver, 2014); A. H. Devor and L. Wilson, 'Putting trans* history on the shelves: the Transgender Archives at the University of Victoria, Canada', in Stone and Cantrell (eds), *Out of the Closet, Into the Archives*, ch. 10.

125 J. J. Gieseking, 'Useful in/stability: the dialectical production of the social and spatial Lesbian Herstory Archives', *Radical History Review*, 122 (2015), 25–46, quote at 26. See also J. Nestle, 'The will to remember: the Lesbian Herstory Archives of New York', *Journal of Homosexuality*, 34:3–4 (1998), 225–35; P. J. Thistlethwaite, 'Building "a home of our own": the construction of the Lesbian History Archives', in J. V. Carmichael (ed.), *Daring to Find Our Names: The Search for Lesbigay Library History* (Westport, CT, 1998), ch. 12; K. Davy, 'Cultural memory and the lesbian archive', in G. E. Kirsch and L. Rohan (eds), *Beyond the Archives: Research as Lived Process* (Carbondale, IL, 2008), ch. 13; M. Narayan, 'At home with the Lesbian Herstory Archives', *Enculturation: A Journal of Rhetoric, Writing, and Culture*, 15 (2013): www.enculturation.net/lesbian-herstory-archives (last accessed 26 April 2018); S. D. Smith-Cruz, 'Tape-by-tape: digital practices and cataloguing rituals at the Lesbian Herstory Archives', in Wexelbaum (ed.), *Queers Online*, pp. 85–110; A. Beins, 'Making a place for lesbian life at the Lesbian Herstory Archive', in Stone and Cantrell (eds), *Out of the Closet, Into the Archives*, ch. 1; C. McKinney, 'Body, sex, interface: reckoning with images at the Lesbian History Archives', *Radical History Review*, 122 (2015), 115–28; and J. Nestle, 'Who were we to do such a thing? Grassroots necessities, grassroots dreaming: the LHA in its early years', *Radical History Review*, 122 (2015), 233–42.

126 See Terpak and Brunnick (eds), *Robert Mapplethorpe: The Archive*. The quote is from the essay by Patti Smith in the same volume, 'Picturing Robert', p. 7.

127 www.moma.org/calendar/exhibitions/1651 (last accessed 26 April 2018). See too the essay by Hilton Als, 'Dark rooms: revisiting Nan Goldin's "The Ballad of Sexual Dependency"', *The New Yorker*, 4 July 2016.

128 Compare Goldin, *Ballad of Sexual Dependency*, pp. 6–9 and 145–6.

129 S. Hall, 'Constituting an archive', *Third Text*, 15 (2001), 89–92.

130 J. Schuessler, 'James Baldwin's archive, long hidden, comes (mostly) into view', *New York Times*, 12 April 2017: www.nytimes.com/2017/04/12/arts/james-baldwins-archive-long-hidden-comes-mostly-into-view.html (last accessed 26 April 2018).

131 http://alotarchives.org/bridging-the-gap (last accessed 26 April 2018).

132 A. Badertscher, 'JJ, 2000', unpublished writing, 2016, Badertscher Collection, Baltimore.

2

Sexual portraits: Edward Melcarth and homoeroticism in modern American art

with Erin Griffey

The metaphor of the closet pervades historical interpretations of American art just as it pervades other cultural readings. In this peculiar way of seeing the past, the art historian's role is to reveal concealed meanings, to make the 'silenced gay self' speak, as Gavin Butt has expressed it.[1] 'Modes of disclosure: the construction of gay identity and the rise of Pop Art', the title of Kenneth Silver's early 1990s essay on American art in the late 1950s and early 1960s, captures the trope. Homosexuality was something hidden until spoken and named. 'Gay artists' helped to construct this emerging identity. If the author had been required to provide key words for a hypothetical synopsis of his essay then undoubtedly they would have included 'closet', 'concealment', and 'gay'.[2] There is no room for ambiguity in this labelling – labelling is what it is – for indistinctness is replaced by gay world-making. '[Jasper] Johns's early work is situated in a discourse, for those who could decipher it, of gay identity.' Johns, Charles Demuth, and Marsden Hartley were 'gay'.[3] Andy Warhol's sketch of a young sailor, *Boy with USN Tattoo* (1957), is presented as if its mere presence shores up the emergence of this hidden, homosexual identity.[4]

We see this anti-logic in another example of the closet in art historical interpretation, Jonathan Katz's essay on code in the work of Johns and Robert Rauschenberg:

> Johns and Rauschenberg are in the curious position of being understood as a pair, but not a couple. Yet they were a couple, and the rather obvious silences, ellipses, and omissions that penetrate the usual accounts of their history make no sense unless arrayed against an insistent and damaging homophobia that has led both artists actually to deny the substance of what they had together.[5]

They are gay artists who are a gay couple and whose sexual identity, even if they were not aware of it, was reflected, or rather can be decoded, in their art. There is no possibility that what Rauschenberg much later referred to as a 'tender and sensitive' relationship may have been just that, nor that his comment about the art world's awareness that 'the two most well-known, up and coming studs were affectionately involved' hinted at anything more complex, undefined, or sexually complicated than a gay couple.[6] As Katz writes: 'As a couple, they were able to reap the benefits of a shared subjectivity without having to identify or affiliate with a larger gay and lesbian community.'[7]

The closet – or implied closeting – is persistent. Jonathan Weinberg's discussion of the work of Demuth is positioned in terms of the hidden explicitness of his homoerotic watercolours.

> And so when we speak of the viewer in reference to these works, we are speaking of a peculiar construct, made up of the artist, intimate friends, and those who were meant to discover the work after Demuth's death. In this sense, the late pictures of sailors urinating [1930] have the quality of intimate confessions or of a memoir discovered long after its author has passed away. They could almost be illustrations for the kind of sexual tales told to the sexologist in strictest confidence . . .[8]

Demuth's *Turkish Bath Scene with Self-Portrait* (1918), allegedly, was literally kept in an owner's closet.[9]

This limiting use of sexual identity is not confined to early 1990s art criticism. A 2002 collection of scholarship on the art of Hartley contains reference to his 'determination to mask his identity as a gay man' and his encoding of the homoerotic.[10] For Randall Griffey, Hartley's homosexuality is hidden in his imagery of straight masculinity: 'as a national icon intended to be honored and glorified, the common man offered Hartley a useful trope in which he could encode his love and desire for beautiful men without necessarily revealing his homosexuality to the public'.[11] One of his paintings, *Down East Young Blades* (*c.* 1940), is described as '[a]t once a pictorial tribute to Maine's common men and a gay man's covert admission of same-sex desire'.[12] R. Tripp Evans's 2010 biography of Grant Evans, creator of the iconographic *American Gothic* (1930), likewise portrays him as a closeted homosexual – a reading that in this case leads to some rather bizarre over-interpretations of his art.[13]

Even Gavin Butt is not immune to the lure of the closet. True, his approach is different. He is interested in the web of meaning around a perceived opacity that may not have been opaque at all, for he has examined the role of gossip about the sexuality of artists in New York from the late 1940s to the early 1960s in informing perceptions of their work. Not just the interaction of verbal and visual discourse but suspicion too: 'those identifications and suspicions not spoken of, ones which might have remained as unarticulated thought but which nevertheless can be credited with animating the sexual meaning of art and artists in the period under review'.[14] Nonetheless, he still refers to the 'generally closeted treatment of homosexuality' in the art of the 1950s and early 1960s.[15] Consequently, Rauschenberg and Johns's alleged distance towards their fellow homosexual artist Warhol – 'You're too swish, and that upsets them . . . the *major painters* try to look straight' – is interpreted as evidence of their closeted homosexuality when it may merely have indicated their simple dislike of swish.[16]

Nor does the National Portrait Gallery's important new exhibition on same-sex desire in American portraiture quite manage to shake off such influences, despite the efforts of the authors of its companion volume. Thus the jacket-summary of the significantly named *Hide/Seek* (2010) refers to 'hidden impacts', 'code', and 'disguise'.[17]

Although recently reclaimed as a 'gay artist', indeed ironically undergoing a kind of retrospective closeting of his own, the subject of our study has not figured much in histories of the homoerotic in American art.[18] Thus he is hidden from art history in the sense of ignored rather than closeted, for we will see that he is the most unlikely candidate for the latter category. You will not find Edward Melcarth (1914–73) in the best recent histories of male homosexuality and American art: Weinberg's surveys and monographs and Richard Meyer's *Outlaw Representation* (2002).[19] There is no mention of Melcarth (born Edward Epstein), an American artist who worked in a wide variety of media and who was active from the 1930s to the early 1970s. He is not in the Smithsonian Institution's previously mentioned 2010–11 (controversial) exhibition on same-sex desire in American portraiture.[20]

Let us be clear that our subject was not always so spectral. In 1950 *Life* magazine named the 35-year-old as among the best young American artists and reproduced one of his paintings of Coney Island, in colour.[21] He exhibited as a painter, draughtsman, and sculptor and also practised as an illustrator, photographer, and designer. He taught art too: at the Parsons School of Design (Long Island), Columbia University, University of Washington (Seattle), University of Louisville, and the Arts Students League of New York, which still lists him among its 'instructors and lecturers – past and present'. The male nude preoccupied him throughout his career. Melcarth's output as a draughtsman covers everything from quotidian images of a mother and child to rape scenes, but it is dominated by the single male nude, positioned in a variety of angles, drawing attention to the tactility and availability of the subject (see Figure 10). He was spectacularly prolific. The biographies written to accompany his exhibitions during his lifetime celebrate his training: Chelsea School of Art followed by a four-year degree at Harvard and instruction under Karl Zerbe; his solo shows at dealer galleries in New York City as well as England, France, Belgium, Italy; and group shows at the Museum of Modern Art, Whitney Museum, Metropolitan Museum of Art, Carnegie Institute, Corcoran Gallery, and Chicago Art Institute among many others. But when Melcarth died in Venice in late 1973 (he had moved there in 1969), the bulk of his work remained unsold and in storage, until finally acquired by the Forbes Collection in 1980 and 1991.[22] His close friend Thomas Painter (more of whom shortly) speculated that the artist's lack of financial success had been influenced by his Jewish background, militant communism, and homosexuality.[23] Indeed the FBI surveillance files on Melcarth as a communist are an ironic source for the artist's career.[24]

In the face of the trends of abstraction and later pop art, Melcarth favoured figurative images in the tradition of Old Master 'history' paintings and representations of the nude. In his subject matter and breadth of media, Melcarth's work bears striking parallels with that of his celebrated contemporary, Paul Cadmus (1904–99). Melcarth's art includes impressive large-scale works, such as the painting *The Last Supper* (1962), bought by the billionaire Malcolm Forbes for his Manhattan townhouse, a ceiling mural for Broadway's Lunt-Fontanne theatre (1957), and the illusionistic wall paintings and sculpted busts for the rotunda of the Pierre Hotel in Manhattan (1968).

Melcarth's friend Painter, a fellow chronicler and photographer of New York hustlers, provided a link to the famous sex researcher Alfred Kinsey. This valued informant of Kinsey gifted three of Melcarth's drawings, all nudes executed in red chalk, to the Kinsey Institute in 1950, and the art archive contains a box of photographic reproductions of his drawings.[25] In fact Kinsey consulted Melcarth for his uncompleted project on the role of sex in art.[26] It is rarely that artists – homosexual or heterosexual – explain what it is that they consider erotic or sexual about their art. However, Melcarth collaborated with Kinsey on precisely this project. In a letter in 1947 the sex researcher thanked the artist for allowing him to photograph his art: 'I think that no one studying in our field has ever before had such an opportunity to look over an artist's production and get the sort of help

10 Edward Melcarth, photographic reproduction of drawing of two male figures, *c.* 1946. From the Collections of the Kinsey Institute, Indiana University. This is in the Art and Artifacts Collection, Box of photographic reproductions of Melcarth's drawings with Kinsey's notes: 'Er → M bcs strng bck + buttck NY. 46'. [That is: very erotic, masculine, biceps, strong back, buttocks, New York, 1946.]

which you gave us in interpreting the material that you drew.'[27] We use that material in this chapter.

Important collectors and patrons also purchased Melcarth's work. A list of pictures sold by Durlacher Brothers, among his dealers from 1941 till 1962, includes respected collectors such as Chick Austin, R. Kirk Askew (whose portrait he painted in 1941), and William T. Kempfer. The Museum of Fine Arts in Boston bought a self-portrait of Melcarth from Durlacher Brothers in 1942. Other familiar names appear as buyers: the playwright William Inge; the designer Van Day Truex, president of Parsons School of Design from 1942 till 1952, and director of design at Tiffany & Co. from 1955 till 1979; Edgar Kaufmann, Jr, architect, author, and head of the Industrial Design Department at the Museum of Modern Art; the artist James Whitney Fosburgh; and the architect Whitney Warren. The writer Gore Vidal bought a Coney Island scene, *Boardwalk* (1964). The composer Virgil Thomson owned a Melcarth sculpture, the heroic head of a hustler, which he kept in his Chelsea Hotel room; it was there when the *New York Times* did a piece on him in 1972.[28] Forbes purchased several others of Melcarth's 1960s paintings of working-class masculinity, including the suggestively named *Manhole* (1962), as well as *Trouble* (1962), *Movers* (1962), and *Rape of the Sabines* (1967). The Forbes Collection once had over 150 catalogued works by Melcarth, among them several sketchbooks and portfolios that themselves contain over 500 drawings and sketches. Ironically, Melcarth is best known for designing and manufacturing the Peggy Guggenheim surrealist sunglasses; he was a friend of Guggenheim's and painted a half-length nude portrait of her that is also in the Forbes Collection. That said, judging by the vast collection still in storage and unsold at his death, his work must have had a limited market, and indeed this is noted in the inventory of artworks made at his death. His hustler heads are still available, however, relatively inexpensively, on eBay.

So it is a peculiar stretch of logic that places Melcarth in the closet. Melcarth's enigma, for Jay Boda, is 'why a gay artist working in a style and with subject matter appealing to gay men is so unknown to them and will remain so for some time'. It is as if, for this art historian, the artist's oeuvre is closeted within the gallery (the Forbes), the museum (the Smithsonian), and, he might have added, the archive (the Kinsey Institute). But his point only holds if he means that this work is not now on constant public display.[29] Its generation and day-to-day circulation were by no means closeted. Nor, as we will learn, was its artist. Melcarth's many drawings of the male nude, photographs of hustlers, and paintings of masculine-looking men may well have suited homosexual viewers but they were also in keeping with an aesthetic of masculinity that appealed to a female audience. Moreover, his imagery extended beyond these subjects to embrace opposite-sex couples (both clothed and engaged in sex) and female nudes, as with the portrait of Peggy Guggenheim. Melcarth's sexual tastes were homosexual – though not limited to men[30] – but he moved in poly-perverse circles that we discuss later. Painter noted that Melcarth 'had many female admirers and, in lieu of himself, his trade [masculine companions] fucked them'.[31]

We will argue that whatever any aesthetic judgement about the quality of Melcarth's art, he is an important figure in the cultural history of male visual homoeroticism, an iconography of visual pleasure that focused on but was not confined to imagery of the male body. We will demonstrate that Melcarth's vision of the erotic was far broader than the traditional categories of sexuality that are perpetuated in histories of male homosexuality and American art – and that such a revisioning enables a reinterpretation of some of the better known images of homosexual art.

Melcarth, who would have been horrified to be described as gay rather than homosexual, once said that he needed daily sex for his creativity, cruising every night 'like a mad thing', sometimes all night, leaving little time for actual work![32] Like numerous homosexual men from the 1930s through to the late 1960s – including his friend the writer Gore Vidal and Vidal's friend the playwright Tennessee Williams – Melcarth was attracted to 'trade', the term for ostensibly straight, usually working-class men who might engage in homosexual sex. Painter, who shared an apartment with Melcarth, described the artist's sexual predilection for males who were 'young, tough and heavily muscular – and big, tall I mean'.[33] The closet seems quite the least appropriate metaphor for such longings. 'I think I have been to bed with five hundred boys', Vidal wrote in his diary in 1949, 'very likely more: and most of these in the last five years . . . rather like collecting stamps, I suppose.'[34] While recalling five different lovers in as many days, including 'a trade boy', Vidal observed 'October is almost over and with it my N.Y. season. Ballet, dinners, balls, bars, trade and conversation.'[35] Melcarth does not appear in the published memoirs of either Williams or Vidal. However, both were acquainted with the artist and with the aforementioned Painter, one of Melcarth's closest friends and himself no mean photographer. These men swapped photographs and contacts in the 1940s and 1950s.

We are talking here of a hazy world of . . . well . . . traded sex, involving a host of men valued for their working-class masculinity: those loosely described as hustlers certainly, but also seamen, soldiers, gangsters, including the Puerto Rican New York gangs, musclemen, and many others.[36]

Times Square was packed with young men who traded their bodies occasionally or part time – some employed, some not. Strictly speaking, a hustler is a male prostitute, nearly always to men, someone who makes his body available in exchange for cash, but many men who traded on their looks or physical attributes did so for food, drink, clothing, or a room. Some young men were casually instrumental about bodily matters. Oral sex might be received purely for pleasure's sake, without any monetary barter – though if there was also profit so much the better. The irony of these exchanges is that the allure for homosexuals was 'heterosexual' sex. When the hustler or, say, sailor was paid in cash or kind for sex with men, it was as a heterosexual that he was desired. As the writer Edmund White put it, 'We wanted a real man, a heterosexual man.'[37] A gay man, interviewed by the historian George Chauncey for his book *Gay New York* (1994), contrasted the world of the 1930s and 1940s with that of the 1960s and 1970s where the heterosexual–homosexual divide was far more pronounced:

> Most of my crowd [in the 1930s and 1940s] wanted to have sex with a straight man . . . And a lot of straight boys let us have sex with them. People don't believe it now. People say now that they must have been gay. But they weren't. They were straight.[38]

Although the men who had sex with these male heterosexual ideals considered themselves to be homosexual (or queer), their sexual milieu was far more ambivalent.[39]

Venues involving muscularity and bodily display attracted male admirers and the temptation of prostitution. Coney Island, New York's seaside playground, was a major site for Melcarth and Painter (see Figure 11). The frequent subject of Melcarth's art and photography, including some beautiful photographs of working-class women (see Figure 12) and the aforementioned painting purchased by Vidal, Coney Island was an ideal cruising ground for Painter and his friends in the 1940s and 1950s, when they photographed and had sex with young men encountered on the beach, in bars, and at the baths. The *mise-en-scène* of Melcarth's Coney Island photography, as we will also see with his untitled painting of a beach scene at Coney Island, captures the very essence of the sexual mix of the heterosexual and homosexual that so fascinated the artist (and his buyers): the same-sex appeal of opposite-sex interaction and the allure of homosexually available heterosexual men.

Melcarth's art is saturated with hustler imagery (see Figure 13). He used hustlers and trade as models, helpers, and sexual partners (he did not distinguish between the roles): the labour for the Guggenheim sunglasses

11 Edward Melcarth, Coney Island trade, photograph 1950s. Collection of Richard Taddei. Gifted to Edward Melcarth Collection, Archives of American Art, Smithsonian Institution.

12 Edward Melcarth, A woman and sleeping child under the boardwalk at Coney Island, photograph *c.* 1950. Edward Melcarth Collection, Archives of American Art, Smithsonian Institution.

13 Edward Melcarth, Leather-jacketed assistant, photograph 1960s? Collection of Richard Taddei. Gifted to Edward Melcarth Collection, Archives of American Art, Smithsonian Institution.

was provided by this very source. That sex was expected from the male models of artists and photographers is apparent from a description on the back of a Painter drawing from December 1946 depicting a model: 'It was of a boy we picked up in the Square [Times Square] who was amazed to discover we really simply wanted him to pose, as we had said. His big brother was tailing him (a fact we had noted) . . . but we kept to the pure artist line.'[40] The model's surprise indicated the anticipated norm. Photographs were frequently of past (or future) sexual contacts. Melcarth's student and friend, the artist Richard Taddei, has said that Melcarth's form was to photograph his pick-ups the morning after. One of Melcarth's planned works, which does not seem to have survived though it was described to Kinsey in a letter from Painter, was of a union picket portrayed as the fallen Christ, modelled on a sailor whom the artist had picked up. Trade as Jesus Christ is an interesting juxtaposition that provides an added dimension to American socialist art (as previously mentioned, Melcarth was a communist).[41]

The dying Melcarth reminisced with Vidal in 1972 about trade he had known: Jimmy S. who was 'given to complaining that I wasn't taking full advantage of opportunities', and New York Eddie, a heroin addict, 'who responded like a flash to "do you want to take care of business?" Instant response even when at the end it was all free. What I could contribute was not even worth picking up off the night table with a $150 dollar a day habit.' 'I have finally contracted the holy bonds of labor or indentured lovers', he reported from Venice, 'a certain Sergio . . . The perfect model *and* the perfect foundryman . . . I am not sure whether he thinks I am God (not just a god) or thinks he is really taking me, or both.' Melcarth bemoaned his inability to make the most of the situation sexually even though the relationship was clearly good for his work.[42]

Much of Melcarth's work belongs in the tradition of the masculine imaginary of what Weinberg has termed the 'homosexuality in the art of . . . the first American avant-garde'.[43] 'The Man in Uniform' and 'I Want Muscle', two of the chapter headings in his book *Male Desire* (2004), indicate the centre of this attention.[44] Cadmus's sailor trilogy, *The Fleet's In!* (1934), *Shore Leave* (1933), and *Sailors and Floozies* (1938), his *Y. M. C. A. Locker Room* (1933); Demuth's watercolours *Dancing Sailors* (1917 and 1918), *Two Sailors Urinating* (1930), *Three Sailors Urinating* (1930), *Three Sailors on the Beach* (1930), and *On 'That' Street* (1932), the more sexually overt – all watercolour and pencil on paper – intended only for private viewing; and Hartley's semi-naked, muscular, and sometimes hirsute prize-fighter, lumberjack, and fishermen (circa 1938–41), including his *Christ Held by Half-Naked Men* (1940–41): all imagine male-to-male sexualised interactions that vary in their explicitness yet share a clear homoeroticism and a privileging of men valued for their masculinity and perceived attraction to women.[45] Hartley's uniformed army of shirtless, hulking men in trademark blue trousers and hats invoke working-class masculinity, even down to their perfectly chiselled chests rendered in glowing tones of pink, orange, and brown. The massively proportioned bodies, with exaggerated trunk-like arms and legs, are at odds with their squat heads, and the emotionless faces incongruous with the tragedy of the scene. Even Christ's face is abbreviated into a generic bearded mask. And Christ's dead body mirrors their ideal proportions in a world where identity rests in the masculine group, the community of perfectly formed bodies.

Physically potent and sexually available working men and sailors feature strongly in Melcarth's work as well. This is certainly true of the Leslie–Lohman Gallery's collection of his frank drawings of male–male, sado-masochistic sex involving weights, harnesses, bondage, and whips, including one sketch of a loosely bound, hatted sailor being fellated on a bed under a wall hanging that says 'Bless Our Home'.[46] But desirable and obtainable males populate his less overt work too. Melcarth forcefully draws our eyes up the raking bodies of men standing on street corners, sitting on boardwalks, looking from balustrades, waiting on staircases, and gazing out of windows. Such works insistently thematise not just the act of viewing but also the drama of being viewed, from above, below, obliquely, from close up or far away. The dramatic viewpoint in an untitled beach scene, probably set at Coney Island, is enhanced by the unusual (for Melcarth at least) vertically thrust canvas (see Figure 14). The viewer is positioned lying down at the beach, looking up at a woman who is shown from behind, drying herself off. The prominent positioning of the backside is common in Melcarth's works, and one he apparently used to erotic ends. As part of his research on sex in art, Kinsey consulted with Melcarth on the erotic elements of his work, and annotated drawings with a series of categories based on their relative eroticism, for example, 'x Er' (not erotic), 'Er' (erotic), 'Er v' (very erotic), followed by a cursory keyword explanation of what makes them erotic. In several cases it is the 'butt' (and in one case a 'large butt') that makes them so.[47]

Such comment is not confined to images of men; the back view of a fully clothed woman is thus labelled: 'Er . . . fucking over-ripe and great avail [availability].' But the erotic stimulus in Figure 14 extends further up the canvas, where the viewer's eyes are guided through this female figure to the underside of a boardwalk and then the two men displaying themselves on it: a sailor in uniform, his collar drawn up, his legs bent with his backside sticking out, one foot on the railing; he inclines his gaze and open body towards a man seated on a bench with similarly open body language. This interchange is highly erotic, as again the annotations of comparable drawings underscore. Kinsey carefully notes that Melcarth considers images of sailors sitting and waiting for sex as 'Er'. What makes them erotic is their 'avail' (availability), 'when people lean and stick their butts out', when they are shown 'in uniform', and even because the sailor's collar is pushed up to 'hide identity'. The viewer's eyes are pushed up through a series of erotic stimuli: the woman's backside, the pushed-out 'butt' of the sailor, and the open legs of the other man. The oblique angles and hidden faces operate to enhance the eroticism of the work.

The erotics of Melcarth's drawing of a couple in flagrante are similarly ambiguous in a scene where the eroticism is figured in implied rather than explicit sexual imagery (see Figure 15). The viewer's entry point is from the top of a bed that spreads across the horizon of the picture plane; we see a sailor, identified by his hat, from above and behind, shown sprawled out with one knee bent, his hand covering himself, his head angling to look at

14 Edward Melcarth, *Untitled (bather)*, oil on canvas, 72 x 25.5 in. The Forbes Collection, New York.

15 Edward Melcarth, Drawing of sailor and woman. The Forbes Collection, New York.

the open door. As erotically charged and 'available' as the male body is that of his female companion who lunges towards him, her arms outstretched and torso twisted to enhance the focus on her breasts and lower abdomen. Melcarth accentuates the curves of her body, drawing attention to an erotic area that he pointed out to Kinsey in other works as the 'abd-hip line'. The erotic potential is not just in the viewer's gaze at the bodies but also in the representation of the couple being discovered in the act. Both the sailor and the woman look towards an open door, where two men stand, the central one (perhaps the woman's – or man's – boyfriend) shown in the act of walking through the doorway, mouth open in shock. The woman's horrified open mouth echoes his. Thus despite the centrality of the reclining sailor, and the knowingness associated with the very figure of a sailor, any sailor, the implied viewer seems to be expected also to find erotic potential in his disrupted coupling with a woman.

If the iconography of gay visual culture can be divided into the classical and that of 'the rougher physical types', then Melcarth combined categories.[48] Melcarth was preoccupied with the classical potential in the visual beauty of trade.[49] His large (40 x 144 inch) painting *Last Supper* has hustlers and trade as Christ and the Apostles at a bar or counter at a diner or cafeteria (a hustler hang-out?) and Judas as a busboy or waiter (see Figure 16).

16 Edward Melcarth, *The Last Supper*, 1967, oil on canvas, 40 x 144 in. Private Collection, New York. Photographer: Camerarts, Ali Elai.

Although it is by no means clear which of the young men is the Christ, presumably an intentional ambiguity, he is certainly one of these desired, homosexually available heterosexuals.

Melcarth appears to be invoking and subverting traditional Last Supper iconography, with references to both Leonardo's iconic version (1495–98) in the tripartite division of space in the background and to the earlier tradition of positioning Judas on the opposite side of the table from Christ and the other apostles. The focus on tableware is also a point of comparison with Leonardo's rendition, although here we find frosted drink bottles, sugar jars, and long glasses of tea with straws, an upturned mug and a bowl of rolls. The movement, both depicted and implied in the electrifying brushwork, resonates with Veronese's and Tintoretto's handling of the same subject. However, unlike traditional imagery, the men represented here are all beardless and youthful, with taut muscles and tousled hair. The most forcefully positioned body is that of Judas, his serpentine body whipped into a curve to draw attention to his chiselled arms, slung hips, and rounded behind. The erotic charge of Judas's 'butt sticking out' and prominent muscles would not have been lost on Kinsey, who also records that 'big biceps' and 'big arms' are 'erotic' elements of Melcarth's works. A patch of flesh around Judas's waist is revealed, too, and strong black underdrawing, swift brushstrokes, and impastoed highlights draw particular attention to these areas.

Melcarth's pictorial arrangement of male bodies is intimated in his photographs, which do not appear to have been exhibited in his lifetime, or posthumously. Indeed his photography deserves a study in itself. There are a number of photographs taken at Coney Island, which have been dated to the 1950s, now in the Smithsonian, of men sunbathing. Instead of the physique magazine look of full-frontal, directly lit flesh, Melcarth is interested in the weight and volume of bodies in space, bodies that twist and show both tension and relief, bodies that are on display but also seemingly caught unaware, bodies that are partially lit and also draped in shadows. Often the faces are covered in shadows, making recognition difficult (and apparently heightening the erotic charge, as with the sailor's disguised face in Figure 14), as for example in an image of a man standing on a crowded beach. Here, a shadow drips down to his chest, a shadow that draws especial attention to his well-defined upper torso and his gleaming white swimsuit. The deportment of the body is at angles, open and closed, in a way that invites and evades the eye. But critically, there is no eye contact between the subject and viewer; the viewer is positioned as an anonymous observer. Behind the standing man, a slew of bodies can be seen, including a figure

17 Edward Melcarth, Coney Island sleeping man, photograph 1950s. Edward Melcarth Collection, Archives of American Art, Smithsonian Institution.

directly behind the central figure of a man with his legs opened. While the standing figure is the focus of Melcarth's attention, a female figure, shown from the back, is positioned on the right. The addition of this figure reminds us of the bikini-clad woman in Figure 14 and, as a topos in his work, the inclusion of a female seen from behind provides a greater range of potential visual desire beyond homosexuality.

The tactility and volume of Melcarth's photographs are further apparent in an image of a man lying on a beach (see Figure 17). Taken from a standing position nearby, Melcarth has captured the man sleeping, picturing him enveloped by a sea of footprinted sand that seems to mimic the undulations of the body. Gazing upon a vulnerable, sleeping figure was seen to be potentially erotic, as Kinsey notes in a Melcarth drawing of a sleeping male nude.[50] The planes of the body are carefully rendered through close attention to the way that light is hitting the body, the viewing angle, and the positioning of the body, one arm outstretched and one knee bent. Again, the face is bathed in shadows while the bare torso catches light, concentrating our attention on the chest and reinforcing the visual parallels with the indented sand around him. The subject's vulnerability also seems to echo the sand around him, which has been touched, and his prone, seemingly asleep body seems to invite similar contact.

Melcarth's photographs of hustler-conquests in New York and Venice reveal some comparable treatment of light and volume (see Figure 18), but his subjects are generally shown in frontal positions and more uniformly lit than the male subjects he photographed outside. Some are far more overtly sexual than his works in other media, including full-frontal nudity in some cases (see Figure 19). In fact Painter claimed that Melcarth was less motivated by art than sexual commemoration in these works, and Painter saw their potential also as instigators for solo sexual satisfaction; he owned copies of some of these, and commented on their erotic possibilities.

Indeed photographs had an erotic potential and function of a sort more palpable than in painting (see Figure 20). Painter was quite explicit about this to Kinsey and his co-researchers, explaining how the photographs of hustlers and trade were availed for their masturbatory/fantasising promise. Painter even rated the relative success of the images in aiding masturbation: 'Successful about three times'; 'This picture has been successful a good dozen times both with it at hand and remembering it.'[51] He described what he found erotic in them for Kinsey in accompanying inscriptions on the photographs.

> This boy was a working boy . . . Comes to the studio and strips, naked (I picture the process, especially the final act, removal of the drawers. I half imagine *myself* doing it, and *myself* sitting down and posing, legs apart, for the camera). Ordinarily he is clothed. (So I picture him). But this guy from New York wants his body, his naked body . . . I look at his bare thighs and especially the heavy muscular part between the legs below and around the testicles. It is *naked*. Stripped. Stark naked. He doesn't care [there follows other discussions of how he fantasizes about the pictures] . . . I do not imagine having sexual intercourse with the picture or even stroke or caress him. I am amazed (or *allow* myself to be 'amazed' despite my sophistication) at their abandon, etc. I interweave projecting myself into them wholly; reading their thoughts; and just plain objective contemplation, *about* them. The circumstances of the picture, the relation with the taker, the mental attitude of the subject, the degree of naturalness or 'posing' are all important. That is why I prefer these more casual, snap-shot-like things to a whole naked homosexual orgy or a hundred posed 'art photos' by the greatest professional beauties.[52]

The real or imagined (it scarcely seemed to matter) generation of the photograph was as important as its actual imagery, the context as vital as the captured moment.

What kind of sex is being visualised in this homoerotic art? Although we have discussed the role of trade and analysed images that involve both

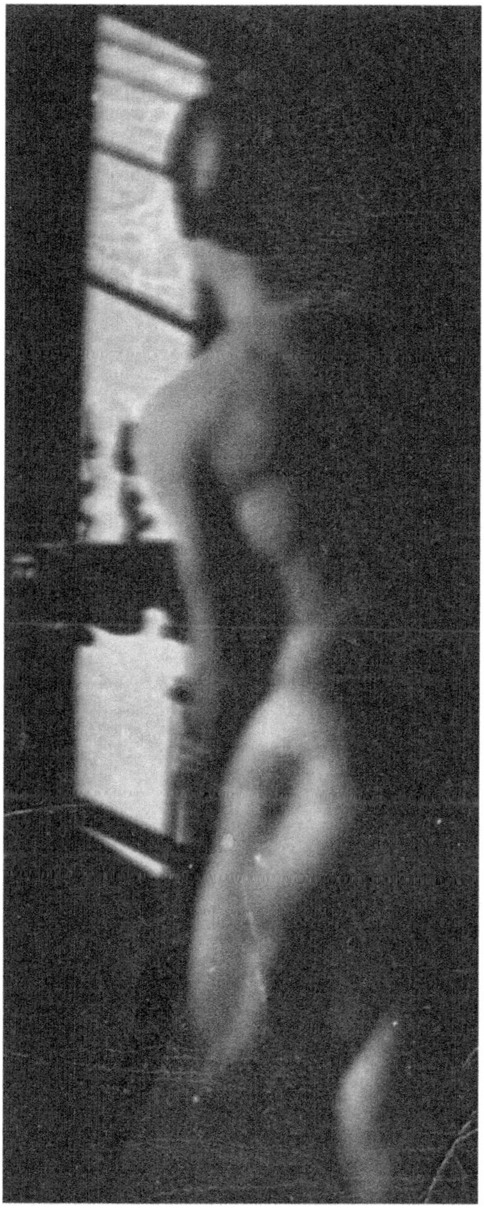

18 Edward Melcarth, Model by window in Venice, photograph 1954.

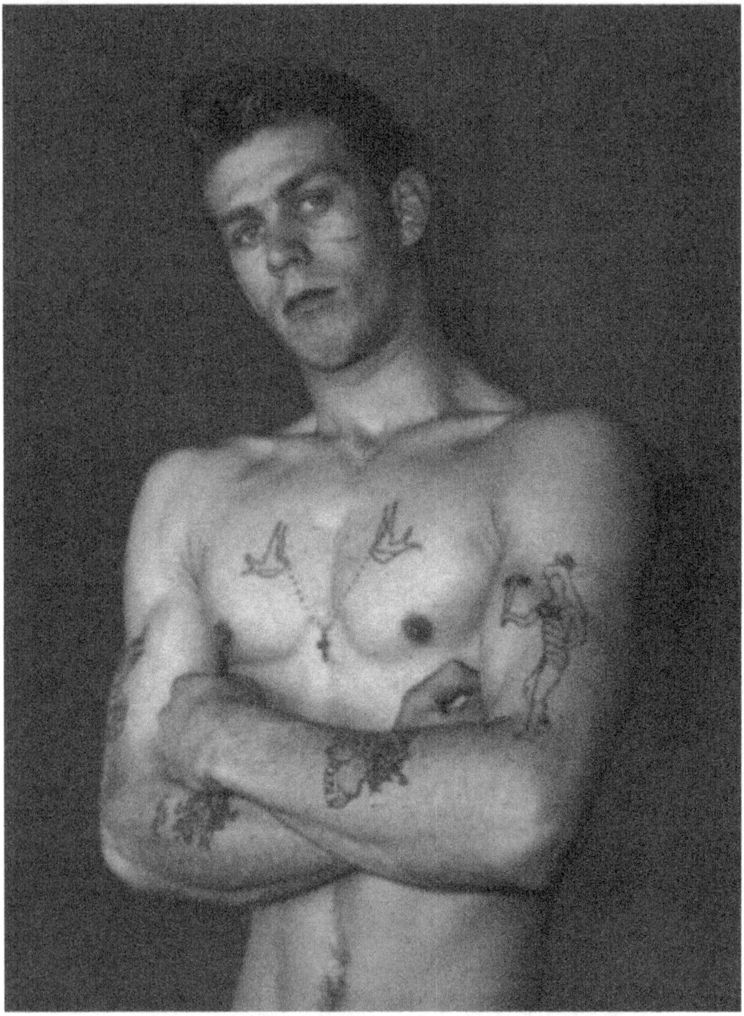

19 Edward Melcarth, Hustler with tattoos, photograph 1950s/1960s, Collection of Richard Taddei.

same- and opposite-sex erotic interchanges, it is important to explain how we depart from convention. Elizabeth Lee's analysis of the iconography of the sailor in post-war America refers to the 'sailor's ability to cross sexual boundaries'.[53] Her fine reading of Norman Rockwell's *Tattoo Artist* cover on *The Saturday Evening Post* (1944) teases out the homoerotic nuances

20 Thomas Painter, Hustler, 1953. Copyright © 2017, The Trustees of Indiana University on behalf of the Kinsey Institute. All rights reserved. Painter took many pictures of this subject. He was also photographed by Melcarth and features in Henry Faulkner's albums (see Figure 7).

of an ostensibly 'heterosexual' image, and she cleverly subverts one of the quintessential images of male-to-female romance, Alfred Eisenstaedt's 1945 *Life* magazine photograph of a sailor and a female nurse kissing in Times Square on V-J Day. Yet despite her claim that the sailor is 'a doubly coded figure with a complex sexual identity', Lee fails to grasp the sexual intricacies of post-war America.[54] Mike Miksche, a commercial artist and Kinsey-recorded practitioner of S/M, is described by her as 'a closeted gay man', and his 1950s painting, *Sailors Kissing*, based on an explicit 1940s photograph of the same subject, is interpreted, somewhat innocently, as 'a tribute to same-sex love'.[55] Lee's sailors 'simultaneously appear gay and straight', and are part of a 'gay culture' mobilised by war, indeed situated 'within the context of gay service in the Second World War'.[56]

This is to impose a distorted sexual polarity on a world that was far from divided into heterosexual and homosexual, especially in the sexual culture of seamen and sailors.[57] Painter provided an account of the morality of an ex-sailor whom he picked up in 1949 in a hustler bar. Painter offered him $5 to go home with him and he did. Over the following weeks he lived with Painter, worked for Melcarth, posed naked for a photographer friend, and was fellated by yet another of Painter's associates, for $50 a week 'plus entertainment'. The former seaman enjoyed being blown, although he thought it 'dirty' and preferred frictation (rubbing) because it was less 'queer'. The young man, who insisted that he was heterosexual, was married but separated, talked incessantly about women, and went out 'cunt hunting' with a friend. 'Sees nothing at all wrong, shameful or deplorable about the homosexual. Just less fun, that's all.'[58] The figure of the sailor was the iconographic epitome of polysexuality. The poet W. H. Auden, no stranger to such subjects, wrote: 'It is not an accident that many homosexuals should show a special preference for sailors, for the sailor on shore is symbolically the innocent god from the sea who is not bound by the law of the land and can therefore do anything without guilt.' Like Genet's *Querelle de Brest*, he is 'sexually promiscuous in every sense'.[59] Thus Melcarth's beautiful photograph of two sailors at Coney Island was no mere photograph of two sailors (see Figure 21). There was no such thing as an unfreighted image of a sailor.

We dwell on the homosexually active, heterosexual sailor because even the most astute commentators present too stark a contrast between sexual alternatives. Weinberg's Demuth 'thought of homosexuality as an alternative to heterosexuality'.[60] Meyer's Cadmus is 'undoing heterosexuality'.[61] Although acknowledging a 'complex knot of desire' (that of the women, the sailors, and the homosexuals) in Cadmus's *The Fleet's In!* (1934), Meyer's

21 Edward Melcarth, Sailors at Coney Island, photograph 1950s/1960s. Collection of Richard Taddei.

Outlaw Representation is about 'the representation of homoerotic desire by artists who identified themselves, with varying degrees of explicitness, as homosexual'.[62] The art that he discusses is specifically homosexual and he employs the categorisations of homosexual versus heterosexual. As he writes of *The Fleet's In!*, 'heterosexual pairing seems to drive figures apart, while same-sex touching drives them together'.[63]

Katz has recently attempted an art history that operates outside the 'gay/straight dichotomy'. He writes, moreover, of 'a world not yet divided between homosexuals and heterosexuals'.[64] However, there is a tension between the 'Hide' and the 'Seek' in the title of his co-authored book: '*Hide/Seek* features straight artists representing gay figures, gay artists representing straight figures, gay artists representing gay figures, and even straight artists representing straight figures (when of interest to gay people/culture).'[65] He is critical of readings that impose modern binaries on a time and culture where such sexual categories did not exist, yet seems unable to extricate himself from the languages of such imposition.[66]

Our approach is different. The 'homosexuality' that we discuss is by no means closeted. Identities – even of some supposedly 'gay' artists and certainly of their subjects – are not fixed: their homosexualities cannot be constrained under the label 'gay'. Their heterosexualities are not straight. The sailor, far from reinforcing arguments for a revealed essential gayness, speaks, in fact, to polymorphous sex.

In Cadmus's *The Fleet's In!*, for example, the sailor can be viewed as a nexus for a complex range of sexual desires. If polymorphous sex found a visual embodiment in images of the sailor, the tugs and thrusts of the sexual encounter found a metaphor in the lacing of bodies together across a picture plane. Cadmus's long canvas is strewn with figures that push in and pull out of the picture, bent knees, tensed buttocks, jutting hips, straddled legs, all wrapped into each other. Weinberg has distinguished the 'heterosexual encounters' from the 'homosexual' character on the left who offers a cigarette to a sailor.[67] This figure, though the only man without a naval uniform, may conform to an iconography of the effeminate 'homosexual', though it is worth noting that his body is visually dominated by the woman who leans in front of him, her buttocks strongly emphasised. The same woman is also engaged visually with the sleeping sailor, whose legs are straddled suggestively towards her.

The insistent rhythm of buttocks, male and female, unbelievably rounded and carefully modelled by Cadmus, suggests a far greater range of sexual desire and pleasure than traditional categories of heterosexual and homosexual would imply. The two sailors on the right, for example, seem to show sexual interest in the sinuous women walking by, but equally the backside views they offer to the viewer open further possibilities for other types of desire. The physical push and pull between the figures operates on the level of sexual impulse for the viewer as well, who is offered sexually potent male and female bodies. The in-and-out rhythm of the composition is mirrored in the eyes and minds of the viewer. It is revealing, then, that no reference to homosexuality was made in the outraged responses to the picture in 1934, which saw it more generally as a depraved scene that did not properly represent the navy.[68]

Melcarth revels in similarly disruptive imagery, as we saw in his untitled Coney Island scene (Figure 14), where the viewer's visualisation of the male-to-male exchange above the boardwalk is mediated by an erotically charged view of a curvy woman's backside in the foreground. Melcarth's drawing of the sailor and woman caught having sex similarly revolves around compet-

22 Edward Melcarth, *Rape of the Sabines*, 1967, oil on canvas, 85.5 x 60 in. The Forbes Collection, New York.

ing gazes; in fact the man shown in the doorway seems to concentrate his eyes not on the woman but on the reclining sailor (Figure 15). However, it is unclear whether he is focusing on his male lover who has cheated on him or spotting the man whom his female lover has taken behind his back. The orgy of bodies is echoed in the violent thrusts of his *Rape of the Sabines* (1967), a work of brutal force (see Figure 22). A trio of men in leather jackets and with switchblades savage a group of men and women, hurling the men to the ground and thrusting the women into their arms, breasts and legs bare, mouths open with fear. In the foreground are the prostrate bodies of men, including one whose arm is being twisted while the central 'raping' figure pulls his knife back as if ready to penetrate him. Some of the sub-categories used in Kinsey's code for the erotic elements in Melcarth's art focus on sexual violence: 'corpse', providing a very erotic image; 'pseudo-rape'; 'bite'; 'SDM – killing six objct at cli [sadomasochism – killing sex object at climax]'. Notably, the latter three sub-categories are all used to describe images of opposite-sex couples having sex.

Melcarth's portrayal of violent heterosexual sexual activity was not dissimilar to the pornographic material available commercially and used to stimulate both heterosexual and homosexual longings: the homoerotic potentials of masculine violence towards women were shared by pornography and art. Arthur Lewis's crude pornographic drawings of heterosexual

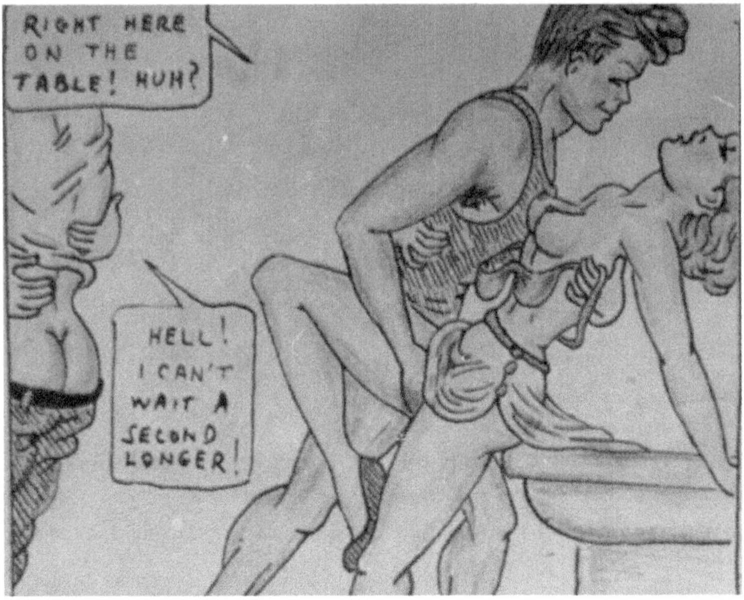

23 Arthur Lewis, artwork for sex comics, 1940s–1950s. From the Collections of the Kinsey Institute, Indiana University.

rape (and male bonding) were used to stimulate the street youths whom he then photographed for homosexual delectation. Both his drawings (a form of *Tijuana Bible* erotica) (see Figure 23) and the photographs are in the Kinsey archive. Painter admired Lewis's depictions of group sex and attempted, unsuccessfully, to imitate them. The Kinsey archive also contains his awkward efforts and his explanation that the men in the rape scene (Puerto Rican gang members) aroused him.[69]

The pose of the figure in *Rape of the Sabines* recalls a pose in one of Melcarth's drawings, with Kinsey's notes informing us that the figure is in a position of 'power and stimulation'.[70] The sexual potency of Melcarth's painting, moreover, extends beyond the homosexual or heterosexual rape theme. We are reminded of the notes Kinsey recorded on Melcarth's drawings, of the erotic potential of the 'butt', the biceps, of figures who are ripe and available. Melcarth's explanation to Kinsey of the erotic elements in some of his drawings suggests that they both saw art as not simply reflecting but physically inviting the erotic, whether imagined or acted-out. The relative eroticism of an image was categorised in a number of visual ways, the appearance of a subject (most significantly its pose but also a generic

24 Edward Melcarth, wall paintings at Rotunda, Hotel Pierre, 1968.

idea of physical attractiveness), the presumed sexual availability of the subject, often communicated by pose (from behind), or attire (sailor's uniform).

Melcarth's prestigious commission for the Pierre Hotel dictated a different treatment of the erotic, but these murals also stage mixed-sex, sexual availability (see Figure 24). The *trompe l'oeil* murals invite comparisons to Veronese's work at Villa Barbaro (1560–61), with Melcarth similarly mirroring the structure of the room and audience for the murals and inviting views through the Villa d'Este-like architecture into the Italianate landscape beyond. Echoing the round room with its grand double staircase, the scene is built around a parallel staircase with couples positioned on the balustrade at the top. Another classical balustrade is fantastically positioned above this magical open-aired palazzo, with further multiple layers of balustrades furnishing infinite possibilities for displaying oneself and being viewed. With their coiffed hair and fashionable dinner dress, people who must have resembled the high-flying Pierre Hotel set position themselves around the staircase to best advantage. Single women are posed at the top of each staircase, mediating our view down the balustrade to groups of men and women. At the base of the staircase, reclining marble statues of a Poseidon and Aphrodite, fictively classicising, similarly pose to advantage.

Male–female correspondences appear elsewhere, too, in the marble busts above the doorways (also by Melcarth).

Baroque fountains with nude statues of Poseidon (with a mermaid) and Aphrodite (with a merman) similarly mediate the vistas opposite the grand staircase, where couples are viewed through illusionistic Corinthian columns. Some figures interact in the distance, while others pose provocatively beside a column, including male figures whose positioning recalls the open-stanced availability we have seen in Melcarth's hustlers. One man hangs suggestively from a tree, his rough trousers an erotic contrast to his bare, muscular chest (Melcarth explained this to Kinsey as an erotic element in other works) (see Figure 25). The couple who excite this hustler-like figure are a man and a woman. The gentle caress of the woman's hand against the man's cheek as he hands her a flower may be at odds with the violence of Melcarth's other groupings, but the insistent focus on looking and catching people unaware is not. Single figures of women, too, position themselves strategically, one in a low-cut gown up close to a column, another shown from the back suggestively holding an apple. The temptations that lurk in the murals are clearly sexual, and Melcarth's iconography of visual pleasure encompasses desire for both the male and female body, for the gaze of both male and female viewers.

25 Edward Melcarth, detail from Rotunda, Hotel Pierre. Photographed by authors, 2010.

Our aim in this chapter has not been to pluck Edward Melcarth from obscurity – though that is an acceptable outcome – but rather to use him, and his world, to rethink the art history of homoeroticism in modern America.

Clearly we are critical of the role of the closet as a heuristic device in art history (indeed any history). The point about the imagery of straight masculinity, we argue, is the absence of any encoding. There was no erotic content to be 'kept in check'.[71] It was there for all to see.

We also depart from the default position of male effeminacy in the history of homosexual art, a tendency, one of us has argued elsewhere, commonplace in American society throughout the period covered in this piece: the homosexual as fairy.[72] This is 'gay art' as camp.[73] For although Butt claims the indeterminacy of the sexual categories of his period of interest, the homosexuality of his inquiry is predominantly exaggerated effeminacy: 'camp talk and the art of Larry Rivers', Warhol and the 'swish', and Warhol as fairy.[74] Our focus, in contrast, is on an all-too-obvious masculinity captured in the multi-medium endeavours of Melcarth and other American artists, professional and amateur. If the effeminacy of James Bidgood's 1960s photography and cinematography adheres less to the actual bodies of his subjects – often hustlers who would not have been out of place in the physique magazines for which Bidgood was commissioned as a photographer in the late 1950s – than in each image's *mise-en-scène*, the diaphanous clothing and the colours of warm pink, flesh, violet, purple, and rich blue, Melcarth's *mise-en-scène* forcefully focuses on real bodies while also rooting them art-historically, with serpentine poses, dramatic Rubensian compositions, scintillating brushwork that recalls Tintoretto and Veronese, and carefully modelled drawings embedded in academic tradition. Melcarth's world is no awkward pastiche but rather an insistently modern arena of masculinity proclaimed on a daily basis in the streets and at work, in parks and apartments, on beaches and in bars.[75]

Moreover, the *mise-en-scène* explored in this chapter – Melcarth's milieu – consisted of interaction and sexual contact, both forced and consensual, involving various combinations of male-to-male and female-to-male. In his discussion of Jasper Johns, Butt broaches the subject of paraded masculinity, the role of physique photography and allied art in what he calls 'the troubling effect of instilling a potential homoerotic gaze within the phantasmatic scene of heterosexual interpellation itself'.[76] The subject of our chapter is indeed this homoerotic gaze but we have argued that it was actual rather than potential and that thinking of 'heterosexual interpellation' – or what Butt terms 'established icons of straight male identification' – assumes a sexual fixity that simply did not exist.[77]

Notes

1 G. Butt, *Between You and Me: Queer Disclosures in the New York Art World, 1948–1963* (Durham, NC, 2005), p. 5.
2 K. E. Silver, 'Modes of disclosure: the construction of gay identity and the rise of Pop Art', in R. Ferguson (ed.), *Hand-Painted POP: American Art in Transition 1955–62* (Los Angeles, 1992), pp. 179–203 (esp. pp. 181–8).
3 Silver, 'Modes of disclosure', pp. 184, 185.
4 Ibid., p. 179.
5 J. Katz, 'The art of code: Jasper Johns and Robert Rauschenberg', in W. Chadwick and I. de Courtivron (eds), *Significant Others: Creativity and Intimate Partnership* (London, 1993), p. 189.
6 Interview in 1990, quoted in ibid., p. 190.
7 Ibid., p. 197.
8 J. Weinberg, *Speaking for Vice: Homosexuality in the Art of Charles Demuth, Marsden Hartley, and the First American Avant-Garde* (New Haven, CT, 1993), p. 108.
9 Ibid., p. 24.
10 E. M. Kornhauser (ed.), *Marsden Hartley* (New Haven, CT, 2002), pp. 27, 207.
11 R. R. Griffey, 'Encoding the homoerotic: Marsden Hartley's late figure paintings', in Kornhauser (ed.), *Marsden Hartley*, p. 214.
12 Ibid., p. 215.
13 R. Tripp Evans, *Grant Wood: A Life* (New York, 2010), pp. 10 (the 'artist's multiple closets'), 198 ('closeted sexuality'), 209 ('He needed cover'), 236 ('a closeted man'), 283 ('his closeted status'), 313 ('Wood's closet'). For over-interpretation, see, for example, pp. 53 (a cow's ear as a phallus), 125 (a plum as penis), 134 (ejaculatory corn sprouts), 158 (phallic women's necks), and 119 (a woman's close-fitting necklace as a cock ring).
14 Butt, *Between You and Me*, p. 8.
15 Ibid., p. 77.
16 Ibid., p. 113.
17 J. D. Katz and D. C. Ward, *Hide/Seek: Difference and Desire in American Portraiture* (Washington DC, 2010). This book is the companion volume to the exhibition that ran from 30 October 2010 to 13 February 2011.
18 J. Boda, 'Edward Melcarth: an essay on an enigma', *The Archive: The Journal of the Leslie/Lohman Gay Art Foundation*, 29 (2008), 15–16.
19 Weinberg, *Speaking for Vice*; J. Weinberg, *Male Desire: The Homoerotic in American Art* (New York, 2004); R. Meyer, *Outlaw Representation: Censorship and Homosexuality in Twentieth-Century American Art* (Boston, MA, 2002).
20 Katz and Ward, *Hide/Seek*. See note 17 above.
21 '19 Young Americans', *Life*, 20 March 1950, pp. 82–93.
22 The best source on Melcarth's career is Archives of American Art, Smithsonian

Institution, Washington DC, Edward Melcarth Papers [henceforth Melcarth Papers]. Among the many boxes are sketchbooks, correspondence, photographs of paintings, reviews and other clippings, Melcarth's own scrapbooks, and legal documents around his estate.

23 Kinsey Institute, University of Indiana, Bloomington (hereafter, KI), the Thomas Painter Collection (hereafter, Painter), Series 2, Vol. 3: Index of Names G–N.

24 The declassified files, obtained in 2010, provide little of substance other than information about Melcarth's international travel, employment details, membership of the Communist Party, the National Maritime Union and the American Labor Party, and attendance at various May Day Parades in 1946. See SAC (Special Agent in Charge), New York (100–88442) to Director, FBI, Subject: Edward Melcarth; and WFO (Washington Field Office), Washington, DC (100–27652) to Director, FBI, Subject: Edward Melcarth. However, the FBI files do include a report that Melcarth refused in 1953 to allow FBI agents to enter his Sixth Ave apartment, 'stating he had nothing of interest to discuss with the FBI'. The memorandum continues: 'The subject refused to answer any questions concerning his CP affiliations, stating his political beliefs are his own business, and that he considered the FBI investigation as harassment upon a private citizen': SAC, New York (100–88442) to Director, FBI, 30 November 1953, Subject: Edward Melcarth.

25 KI, Art and Artifacts Collection, Edward Melcarth file.

26 For this planned project, see J. Crump, 'The Kinsey Institute archive: a taxonomy of erotic photography', *History of Photography*, 18:1 (1994), 1–12. The Kinsey Institute sponsored volume, *Studies in Erotic Art*, drew on Kinsey's collection of erotic art but does not include any of the Melcarth-like material: T. Bowie and C. V. Christenson (eds), *Studies in Erotic Art* (New York, 1970).

27 KI, Kinsey Correspondence Collection, Kinsey to Melcarth, 14 January 1947.

28 'In Virgil Thomson's Rooms', *The New York Times*, 16 April 1972.

29 Boda, 'Edward Melcarth', p. 16.

30 He was married to Hansi Joan Beer for five years (1939–44). See Melcarth Papers, undated typed entry for *Who's Who in American Art*, presumably completed by Melcarth himself; and the FBI files referred to above. The FBI files claim that she was an Austrian refugee 'salesgirl-model' whom Melcarth married in Paris to provide a US visa.

31 Painter, Series 2, Vol. 4: Index of Names O–Z, entry for Fred R., one of the 'muscle boys who was with Edward [Melcarth]'.

32 Painter, Box 1, Series 2, C. 1, Vol. 6: Painter Letters: 5 March 1949; Box 1, Series 2, C. 1, Vol. 10: 5 July 1953.

33 Painter, Index of Names G–N, entry for Edward Melcarth.

34 Houghton Library, Harvard University, MS Am 2350 (2879): Gore Vidal Papers, Diary, May–September 1949: Journal 2 (no pagination), May 1949. These journals are restricted but viewed by permission of Gore Vidal.

35 Gore Vidal Papers (2880), Diary, September–November 1949: Journal 3 (no pagination), September 1949.
36 For these worlds, focusing respectively on New York (Chauncey and Reay) and Chicago and San Francisco (Spring), see G. Chauncey, *Gay New York: Gender, Urban Culture, and the Making of the Gay Male World, 1890–1940* (New York, 1994); B. Reay, *New York Hustlers: Masculinity and Sex in Modern America* (Manchester, 2010); J. Spring, *The Secret Historian: the Life and Times of Samuel Steward, Professor, Tattoo Artist, and Sexual Renegade* (New York, 2010).
37 E. White, *My Lives* (London, 2005), p. 109.
38 Chauncey, *Gay New York*, pp. 21–2.
39 Argued by Reay, *New York Hustlers*.
40 KI, Art and Artifacts Collection, Thomas Painter Drawings, 1945–50.
41 Painter, Box 1, Series 2, C. 1, Vol. 6: 27 February 1949.
42 Gore Vidal Papers (1665), Edward Melcarth Letters 1950–73, Edward Melcarth to Gore Vidal, 12 March 1972.
43 Weinberg, *Speaking for Vice*.
44 Weinberg, *Male Desire*, chs 2 and 3.
45 For these artworks, see Weinberg, *Speaking for Vice*; and Weinberg, *Male Desire*. For trade and its aesthetic, see Reay, *New York Hustlers*, esp. ch. 6: 'Hustler hustled'.
46 Available on their online collection: see http://leslielohman.pastperfect-online.com/34216cgi/mweb.exe?request=keyword;keyword=melcarth;dtype=d (last accessed 26 April 2018).
47 KI, Art and Artifacts Collection, box of photographic reproductions of Melcarth's drawings with Kinsey's notes (hereafter, Melcarth drawings); the drawings are not individually labelled.
48 For the two types, see J. A. Suárez, *Bike Boys, Drag Queens, and Superstars: Avant-Garde, Mass Culture, and Gay Identities in the 1960s Underground Cinema* (Bloomington and Indianapolis, IN, 1996), p. 157.
49 For twentieth-century homosexuality's use of classical Greek and Roman imagery, see A. Richlin, 'Eros underground: Greece and Rome in gay print culture, 1953–65', *Journal of Homosexuality*, 49 (2005), 421–61.
50 Melcarth drawings.
51 Painter, Box 16, Series 4, A. 1. c., box 1, A2 (1949), A4 (1949).
52 Ibid., A4 (1946). He writes about this image in Box 1, Series 2, C. 1, Vol. 3: 17 September 1946.
53 E. Lee, 'When sailors kiss: picturing homosexuality in post-world war II America', *The Journal of American Culture*, 32:4 (2009), 318–31, quote at 323.
54 Ibid., 324.
55 Ibid., 319, 329.
56 Ibid., 320, 323, 327.
57 Explored further in Reay, *New York Hustlers*.

58 Painter, Box 1, Series 2, C. 1, Vol. 6: 14 January, 17 January, 29 January, and 21 June 1949.
59 W. H. Auden, *The Enchafèd Flood* (New York, 1950), p. 146.
60 Weinberg, *Speaking for Vice*, p. 89.
61 Meyer, *Outlaw Representation*, p. 43.
62 Ibid., pp. 8, 42.
63 Ibid., p. 42.
64 Katz and Ward, *Hide/Seek*, pp. 15–16.
65 Ibid., p. 15.
66 See, for example, his analysis of Demuth's sailors: Katz and Ward, *Hide/Seek*, p. 24.
67 Weinberg, *Speaking for Vice*, p. 35.
68 On the reception and fate of the picture, see ibid., pp. 37–8.
69 KI, Painter, Box 26, nos 374–8 and 399.
70 Melcarth drawings.
71 Kornhauser (ed.), *Marsden Hartley*, p. 316.
72 See Reay, *New York Hustlers*, ch. 5.
73 P. Gefter, 'Off to camp: the photographs of James Bidgood', *aperture*, 191 (2008), 62–5.
74 Butt, *Between You and Me*, p. 14, and chs 3 (Rivers) and 4 (Warhol).
75 For Bidgood, see the lush images in J. Bidgood and B. Benderson, *James Bidgood* (Cologne, 2009), and Gefter, 'Off to camp'.
76 Butt, *Between You and Me*, p. 147.
77 Ibid., p. 148.

3

Autoarchivism: Alfred Kinsey's informants

The work of Alfred Kinsey is indelibly associated with quantification – counting orgasms was how he charted America's sexual past in the famous 1940s and 1950s reports on male and female sexuality and his recognised affirmation of same-sex desire and activity.[1] The essayist Lionel Trilling noted that it was symptomatic of American culture that 'the community of sexuality requires now to be established in explicit quantitative terms'.[2] Kinsey was a professor of zoology at the University of Indiana in Bloomington, an expert on gall wasps who turned his scientific inquiry to humans, from wasps to WASPs, as I am sure someone has said.[3] His colleague Wardell Pomeroy's description of him as a collector is totally appropriate.[4] He was an obsessive collector, collating data on sexual behaviour, starting, interestingly enough, with his students. Although most of his publications were in the 1940s and 1950s, the sexual histories that he amassed went back to the beginning of the century in terms of their remembered sex. The team's technique was to gather case histories – as many as possible – through interviewing. Their first book on the male (1948) was based on the sex histories of 5,300 men. The next book, on the female (1953), was based on interviews with nearly 6,000 women. The central core of four men in his team interviewed a total of about 18,000 people over the years – a massive research base of sexual histories. Kinsey also answered letters from men and women seeking sexual advice; there are about 15,000 of these on file in the Kinsey archive. And there are photographs, an estimated 75,000 to 80,000, focused on recording the range of sexual acts that so fascinated Kinsey and his team. James Crump, a curator at the Kinsey Institute, described Kinsey's goal as collecting 'photographic representation of *every* form of sexual behavior' – in multiple examples, of course.[5] Ironically, and counter-intuitively given the projects discussed in this chapter, the photographs' origins and historical contexts were sacrificed for the classification of their represented acts: from ANL HT (anal intercourse, heterosexual) to Z (zoophilia).

As Pomeroy put it, the sexual histories' data came from a list of occupations that 'began with bootleggers and ended with women's-club leaders. Thieves and holdup men were cheek by jowl with YMCA secretaries; lawyers and male prostitutes were joined snugly in alphabetical sequence.'[6] So the informants were a rather eclectic bunch, even if their files were later sorted into groups according to education, sex, age, and so on. Sarah Igo has noted how eager people were to cooperate with the study, partly because Americans had become used to social science surveys and public opinion polls, so that a sex survey was almost a logical step in modern attitudes, but also because many found it therapeutic and wanted to place themselves in a sexual spectrum or to be reassured that their practices and desires were not abnormal.[7]

In the late 1930s Kinsey had discovered a vibrant male homosexual culture in Chicago, his excitement palpable in a letter to a close friend: 'You are among the *very, very* few individuals to whom I can ever tell *all* of the story – the part that has too much dynamite to get into even the most objective scientific print.' He wrote of individuals who had had 2,000 to 3,000 same-sex sexual contacts each. 'Have been to Halloween parties, taverns, clubs, etc. which would be unbelievable if realized by the rest of the world . . . Why has no one cracked this before?'[8] Then in the 1940s he gained an introduction to New York's sexual scene. It was there that he met Herbert Huncke, Thomas Painter, Edward Melcarth, and others in this book. The Kinsey archive holds a returned letter to Kinsey from an address in West 48th Street, unsurprising given Huncke's shiftless existence. The researcher had thanked Huncke for providing his history, with the obvious hope that, in what researchers now call snowball sampling, the hustler and Beat would provide other contacts. 'It was a most unceremonious way in which to approach anyone who was a stranger', he wrote; 'I must admit this has happened so often, however, and I have so many good friends out of such procedures, that I was not hesitant in trying it with you.'[9] Huncke had clearly been suspicious when first approached (he said as much in later reminiscences), so Kinsey was reassuring: 'I felt confident that you became convinced by the end of our interview that I objected to nothing, and that I had no interest in attempting to redirect anybody else's behavior. Your history, on the contrary, contributed definitely to my own education, and for that I am deeply grateful.'[10]

The core of this research, then, was the questionnaire, the case history, sexual histories of tens of thousands of subjects. Kinsey took pride in wielding his numbers. In an early article in the *Journal of Clinical Endocrinology* he took on hormonal explanations of homosexuality by challenging not only the researchers' method of sampling but also their very categories. 'More basic than any error brought out in the analysis of the above data', he wrote, 'is the assumption that homosexuality and heterosexuality are two mutually exclusive phenomena emanating from fundamentally . . . different types of individuals. Any classification of individuals as "homosexuals" or "normal" (= heterosexuals) carries that implication.'[11] And he proceeded to relay his early findings (it was 1941) of varied homosexualities (men with 'as many as fifteen or twenty thousand homosexual contacts', including a 29-year-old with 15,000 homosexual and 4,200 heterosexual contacts), and provided a graph of combinations of heterosexuality–homosexuality, 'showing every gradation between exclusively heterosexual and exclusively homosexual experience'.[12]

'Kinsey profoundly shook up the way we understand sexuality', writes the modern critic Elizabeth Grosz, and 'he did so through the credibility of science; he wrapped this subterranean, private activity in the cloak of a disinvested knowledge, through a pure neutral search for truth. He was arguably the last and greatest contributor to the impulse to generate a *scientia sexualis*, a science of sexuality.'[13] At the time of the publication of *Sexual Behavior in the Human Male* (1948), Trilling too had thought it significant that 'our society makes this effort of self-enlightenment through the agency of science'.[14] But Grosz is critical of Kinsey's approach, especially when it came to female sexuality. Though aware of the limitations of the statistical method and the importance of the qualitative, Kinsey was nevertheless imprisoned by counting, 'dazzled by numbers', and, as a result, 'lost what is sexual about sexual behavior'.[15] The solution, Grosz argues, would have been less counting and classifying and more 'qualitative immersion', *ars erotica* rather than *scientia sexualis*.[16] Tim Dean has similarly invoked the formulations of Michel Foucault to criticise Kinsey. Kinsey's informant Samuel Steward, one of the subjects of what follows, was the famous sex researcher's pornographic unconscious. 'Whereas Kinsey struggled to segregate the scientific from the pornographic, Steward worked to mingle them, contaminating the would-be purity and objectivity of scientific research with his particular desires.' Steward's archive was the *ars erotica* to Kinsey's *scientia sexualis*.[17] Long before Grosz and Dean, Georges Bataille had made an analogous point about Kinsey's method.[18] 'It is possible for me to regard the study of man's sexual behavior with the interest of a scientist who observes almost absently the play of light on the flight of a wasp', Bataille began his essay on Kinsey, picking his simile carefully; 'Of course, human conduct can be the object of scientific study: it is then observed with no more humanity than if it were an insect's.'[19]

It is true that Kinsey proclaimed scientific neutrality, dispassionate observation. *Sexual Behavior in the Human Male* bills itself as 'an attempt to accumulate an objectively determined body of fact about sex which strictly avoids social or moral interpretations of the fact'.[20]

> No preconception of what is rare or what is common, what is moral or socially significant, or what is normal and what is abnormal has entered into the choice of the histories or into the selection of the items recorded on them . . . This is first of all a report on what people do, which raises no question of what they should do, or what kinds of people do it. It is the story of the sexual behavior of the American male, as we find him.[21]

Yet it would be careless to mistake strategy for method. Janice Irvine has explained that, however naïve Kinsey's claims to objectivity might now seem, in the context of his time they were 'a careful presentation of self'.[22] For it is clear from his writings (and all his associates knew) that he had a far more radical agenda. 'When Kinsey proclaimed his "objectivity"', writes Irvine, 'he was eschewing both the moralism of religion and the pathologizing tendency of the social sciences.'[23] Trilling had also referred to the *Male* book's 'pledge of indifference to all questions of morality at the same time that it patently intends a moral effect'.[24] Kinsey's was a reformist, strategic neutrality. He stressed the naturalness of sex against those who wanted to control or condemn certain types of sexuality. As he once wrote to a Chicago graduate student, 'I am absolutely tolerant of everything in human sex behavior.'[25]

Kinsey did not moralise. 'Whatever the moral interpretation', he wrote, 'there is no scientific reason for considering particular types of sexual activity as intrinsically, in their biological origins, normal or abnormal.' 'Present-day legal determinations of sexual acts which are acceptable, or "natural", and those which are "contrary to nature"', he continued in his discussion of an individual's total sexual outlet (sum of their orgasms), 'are not based on data obtained from biologists, nor from nature herself.'[26] The historian James Gilbert has noted the 'tone of celebration' in Kinsey's presentation of graphs and figures in what amounted to an 'unmistakable assault upon the vocabulary of normalcy'.[27] In his private communications he certainly stressed his progressive attitudes. Whether it was trying to persuade the physique photographer Lon Hanagan to provide copies of his homoerotic body images or the writer Julian Green to deposit his French homosexual diaries, his credentials were the same: 'we hope that as a result of our study there will be more tolerance in general on a wide variety of sex behavior'; 'We believe that the world would be a better place if people learn to take human nature as it is and to sympathetically understand it is as we find it.'[28]

Kinsey was always interested in the qualitative as well as the quantitative, erotica as well as scientia. Indeed, following a lengthy discussion of the collection of the case histories, interviewing techniques, coding, and statistical problems, *Sexual Behavior in the Human Male* has a section called 'Supplementary Data' which refers to additional source material from longer-term associates. This includes research material generated over a number of years, extending way beyond the initial sex history, including socialising, contact with friends and cultural networks, extensive correspondence and 'day by day records of their activities, and of their thinking on various aspects of sex', as well as photographic collections and scrapbooks. There is specific mention of two cases where such material amounts to over a thousand pages, and reference to the manner in which this kind of information informed not the 'statistical tabulations' but, as the book states, 'a considerable portion of the detail which is given in this volume on the physical nature of sexual arousal and of orgasm, and of the psychologic and social concomitants of sexual behavior, particularly in relation to the factors which motivate and control the activities'.[29]

We have to remember too that *Sexual Behavior in the Human Male* and *Sexual Behavior in the Human Female* (1953) were but the first of several planned studies (we referred to another on sex in art in the previous chapter). Kinsey's ambitious programme was terminated by his early death in 1956. It may well have been that the considerable, and ever-growing, archive of 'Supplementary Data' generated by the men discussed in the pages that follow would have contributed, say, to the projected volumes on 'Prostitution' or 'The heterosexual–homosexual balance'.[30] Grosz might have a point about Kinsey and female sexuality – though the jury is still out on that issue, pending forthcoming studies by Judith Allen – but as far as sexual behaviour in the human male was concerned, as evidenced by the archives of the research informants whom we are about to discuss, the thick description was very thick.

Kinsey became a kind of custodian of sex for America. The former collector of gall wasps collected not just sexual histories but all the artefacts of sex. Various police departments sent him confiscated pornographic material on the understanding that the source of such material would never be publicly acknowledged. Literary and artistic figures gave him erotic material for safekeeping.[31] In a revealing page in his memoirs, Pomeroy observed that Kinsey's possession of the nation's sexual secrets gave him a sense of power. Pomeroy said that in Indiana University alone there were twenty professors with homosexual histories unknown to their colleagues and employer.[32] The writer Glenway Wescott claimed later that because he had taken sexual histories in the nation's capital Kinsey 'knew of homosexuality in high places, which of course he kept mum about'.[33]

To say that there was openness about sex in the research would be an understatement. After Kinsey died, an associate found a container that he assumed was a recording of a lecture and sent it to a colleague, a folklorist, to have it transferred to tape. When it was returned, he played it, and it began, 'This is a recording made secretly of a daisy-chain [group sex]. The assorted sighs, grunts, and groans you will hear . . . etc.'[34] Kinsey also arranged for the filming of sexual activity in New York and of more selective interactions in Bloomington. A letter to an associate, C. A. Tripp, in 1948 refers to motion pictures of masturbation, with the researchers paying models $3 per orgasm or $6 for a pair of performers – as well as a cryptic reference to 'when we do them of ourselves'.[35] Pomeroy mentions the filming of 'twenty homosexual couples, ten heterosexual couples and about twenty-five males and females engaged in masturbation'.[36] Given the archival inaccessibility of the originals, the precise figures are uncertain; Kinsey's biographer Jonathan Gathorne-Hardy refers (hesitantly) to thousands.[37] This filming was not widely known at the time, carried out secretly in the knowledge that it would have given wonderful ammunition to his critics, and several of the Kinsey team were involved in these demonstrations of practical sex.[38]

Apart from his counting, Kinsey cultivated some long-term suppliers of sex-related material in the form of letters, journals, mementos, artwork, and photography. His research agenda included amassing a vast archive of qualitative material, dependent on the participant research of favoured collaborators. And this highly colourful sexual archive informed his project, both before and after *Sexual Behavior in the Human Male*. This chapter focuses on two of these collaborators, two autoarchivists, archivists of the self: Thomas Painter, who pioneered the use of the famous Kinsey Scale through his recorded, decades long sexual interactions with hustlers; and Samuel Steward, who provided practical and archival evidence of America's BDSM culture and the sexual aspects of tattooing. This chapter examines their place and role in the Kinsey project.

While we will be focusing on two of these 'unofficial collaborators', there were others, including the notorious 'Kenneth S. Green' (or Braun) who provided information on pre-adolescent sex and whose diaries are not available for viewing at the Kinsey Institute, though Gathorne-Hardy has seen them.[39] Thomas Waugh has discussed the films of Otis Wade, a contact in Los Angeles, who destroyed much of his work after Kinsey had copied it.[40] Kinsey maintained contact with Louise Lawrence, a trans woman, who provided him with an autobiography and the autobiographies of others, clippings, transcriptions of (to use the terminology of the time) transvestite erotica, contacts for interviewing, and a general introduction to the worlds of cross-dressing and transsexuality.[41] The photographer George Platt Lynes, a friend of Steward, was another associate. Kinsey watched him having sex in New York at a specially arranged sex party and praised his skill in a letter to Steward: 'He made love better than anyone I have ever witnessed!'[42] The Kinsey Institute is a major repository for Platt Lynes's work, with 600 photographs and 2,300 negatives.[43] Ned Rorem, the composer, recalled talking at length to Kinsey about musicians for the researcher's project on sex in the creative arts (the previously mentioned sex in art was part of this programme): 'In the forties one could make the following generalizations: organists ninety-five percent homosexual, violinists one percent, pianists fifty percent, cellists and violists zero, harpists less than we might think . . . composers approximately fifty percent . . . And I gave Kinsey my reasons as much as I could figure them out.'[44] The 'goodies' were all there in the archives in Bloomington.[45]

Kinsey knew the avant-garde film-maker Kenneth Anger and got him to locate in Sicily some classic erotic photographs by Wilhelm von Gloeden (1856–1931), one of the first photographers of the male nude. Anger was in Taormina in December 1955 and located 100 of von Gloeden's prints to ship to Kinsey (see Figure 26). Anger combined work and pleasure, for he also sent Kinsey a map with a list of his sexual contacts marked in blue: '18 years of age in a ruined house'; '16 years, 4 nights (near the Madonna della Rocco)'.[46] Kinsey was in Sicily later that same month and noted that he had located the remains of von Gloeden's collection of 1880s and 1890s nude males. Much of the original collection, believed to be 10,000 negatives, had been destroyed by the Fascists, but 3,000 were left: 'The town is filled with older men who are the boys photographed by the Baron. They will tell of their contact with the Baron.'[47] The Institute now has 250 original prints by von Gloeden.[48]

One of Kinsey's most fascinating informants was a European businessman called Sixt Kapff – known as R. J. by Pomeroy and Gathorne-Hardy, and as Mr. 'X' by Martin Duberman.[49] Encouraged to count and record by his mentor, Kapff had sex with nearly 28,000 different men in a thirty-five-year period, providing detail first to Kinsey and then to another associate, C. A. Tripp, whose files (including copies of the Kinsey correspondence) now reside in the archives of the New York Public Library.[50] Ranging from Morocco to Mumbai and from Naples to New York, it was a quantitative

26 Alfred Kinsey and Kenneth Anger, 1955. © Bettmann: Getty Images.

and qualitative cornucopia of homosexual sex with heterosexuals that meshed perfectly with Kinsey's work on the USA. Kapff wrote of the possibilities of sexual contact in Indian trains and at religious festivals, in the stalls at the Italian Opera, in restrooms worldwide, outside Italian brothels at closing time with men who were waiting for sex with women, in Italian and New York porn theatres, including (especially) those showing heterosexual porn; in the street, in taxis, and when tradesmen visited, in labourers' encampments, in the fields in Italy where heterosexual couples went; and with policemen, soldiers, sailors, hotel lift operators and bell-hops, and hitch-hikers.[51] Post-Kinsey, he went on carefully calculated, two-week sex holidays to North Africa from 1962 to 1976, allocating $300 a trip to cover '120 to 130 contacts'.[52] He visited the famous club The Mineshaft (mentioned several times in this book), but it was too much for even this most accomplished sexual adventurer. Fisting: 'It's a medical operation, you know, it's not a sexual act for me.' Urine play: 'Phil, that is too much, that is too much.'[53]

Italian men told Kapff in the 1950s that they really did not care whether it was a man or woman masturbating them or giving them head, or that men were more skilful providing such service, and that anal was preferable to vaginal sex. Soldiers in Milan would pay for oral sex from a female prostitute, yet expect to be paid themselves if a man provided it: Kapff called it a 'switch over'.[54] He reported on the sexual availability of the sailors in Naples, and his general theme, with many specific examples of sexual contact with married men and men with girlfriends, was of the homosexual availability, for money, of a very heterosexual community ('in the outlook of life of the Napolitan [Neapolitan] the woman is just as important as the spaghettis').[55] Kapff wrote to Kinsey that the more data that he collected, the more he questioned the hetero/homo division, or, as he put it in his often faltering English, 'the public sin of formulating here heterosexual [t]here homosexual'.[56] He wrote similarly to the novelist Rodney Garland in 1954: 'You . . . can meet among 100 Italians 80 who go to bed with you. But maybe one of them is queer.'[57]

Advised by both Anger and Kapff, Kinsey recorded his own observations while on the European trip referred to earlier (we know this from the notes of his presentations to his team). Like most tourists in Rome he visited the Colosseum and the Spanish Steps, but was more interested in sex than architecture. It could almost have been Kapff writing:

> I saw a great deal of male prostituting. Every person I talked to says every male has homosexual activity and this is true of married as well as unmarried and pre-adolescent as well as adolescent, with emphasis on the fact that you very seldom find an exclusively homosexual male. It was perfectly apparent from what I saw that most of the males who were out looking for sex would have accepted it from either female or males except they would be paid for it if they were brought to climax by males but would pay for it if brought to climax by females. Consequently they would go looking for males first and then go out and have it with a girl and since the girl would cost less than he had been paid by the male, he would still make a profit.

Kinsey noted centres of sexual activity in the passages and niches of the Colosseum, recording thirty couples engaged in activity ranging from embracing to – one can almost hear his technical voice – 'completed sexual activity'. 'We [he was with Anger on this particular outing, though Clara Kinsey, Mrs Kinsey, accompanied him to Europe] watched a couple [for] about 40 minutes; there was no disrobing but she ultimately opened his trousers and masturbated him to orgasm.' The Colosseum was a centre for both homosexual and heterosexual activity. He said that he 'went into one of the blind alleys in the Colosseum and found two soldiers masturbating each other. This is not necessarily homosexual but were unable to get other contact.' 'I saw a priest whom I watched on and off for two hours who was certainly cruising the Colosseum.' Kinsey explained too that the fields around Rome were 'filled with copulating couples both homosexual and heterosexual'.[58] Again, it was an interesting supplement to the homosexual–heterosexual regime that, as we will see, his collaborators found in Chicago and New York.

The title of this book, *Sex in the Archives*, might be said to apply most to Samuel Steward, for he literally had sex in the archives at the Kinsey Institute; not merely filmed S/M interactions with Mike Miksche (part of the filmed research previously mentioned) but, according to Steward, off-screen, spontaneous sex on the library floor with the same film partner after reading some of its erotic holdings.[59] Steward was a university academic, tattooist as Phil Sparrow, artist, and, as Phil Andros, pioneering 1970s homosexual pornographic writer. He is the subject of a biography by Justin Spring, who, in an impressive work of historical detection, assembled a dizzying range of material generated by Steward, a scattered archive partially represented in the Kinsey Institute in copies made specifically for the sex researcher, and partly held in the Beinecke at Yale University.[60] The complete tattoo diaries, for instance, are only available at the institute, given that Steward's copy was 'inadvertently destroyed', though there are some extracts in the Beinecke.[61] Since Spring's biography, Steward has achieved retrospective fame, with the publication of ephemeral writings and a collection of academic essays dealing with his life and work – though to describe him as 'a major figure in twentieth-century gay history and literature' may be exaggerating his importance somewhat.[62]

As explained in an earlier chapter, Spring rescued Steward's personal archive and ensured its survival in the Beinecke, where the Stud File, a boxed card-index of Steward's many sexual contacts, can now be viewed. It is a sexual archive of a man whose life spanned the history of homosexuality almost from the time that it was named: friend of the genteel Gertrude Stein and Alice B. Toklas, visiting them in France from the 1930s; English professor at Loyola and DePaul universities; occasional sexual partner of Thornton Wilder; friend of the photographer Platt Lynes, with whom he shared erotica and sex partners; Kinsey Institute informant and filmed sexual performer; contributor to the homophile magazine *Der Kreis*; translator of Jean Genet's *Querelle de Brest* (1947); early practitioner of Chicago BDSM; tattooist of Chicago sailors and then Oakland Hells Angels; and writer of gay pornography, often based (Spring reveals in his biography) on actual people and personal encounters. He was also an early exploiter of Polaroid technology – the Beinecke archive holds hundreds of black-and-white photographs of physical sex.[63] As the old saying goes, if Steward had not existed it would have been tempting to invent him . . . but would anyone have had the imagination!

Steward was an educated man who quoted André Gide to Kinsey, knowing that he would approve: 'In the name of what God or what ideal do you prohibit me from living according to my desires? . . . My normal is your abnormal, and your normal is my abnormal.'[64] He gave Kinsey a copy of his 1950 Paris journal, which recounted failures as well as successes:

> In the evening to a gathering of 9 French pédès . . . in a depressing stuffy little apartment. We worked around to taking off our clothes and sucking cocks here & there in a smelly pile of perspiring bodies on a scratchy sofa – all in all a most depressing partouzie. Still we can put it down as an experience in Paris.[65]

He unselfconsciously recorded masturbatory activity, 'hand-rape' while reading Genet, and a sketch of himself 'making myself at home, which turned out not *too* bad, and then I *did* make myself at home'.[66]

He provided elegant and often humorous accounts of his encounters, writing of San Francisco's Embarcadero YMCA, in about 8,000 closely typed words of described sexual manoeuvres and short sexual histories, that it was a 'Christian brothel, a lupanar. Here, under the paternal and indulgent eye of the YMCA, more sins are committed per minute than were in the palmiest days of ancient Rome.' 'Life here like a virus, a disease', he continued; 'When you get away from the place, you keep thinking: "Jesus, I ought to get back." Like life on the needle.'[67] In a letter to Platt Lynes, Steward explained that Kinsey had described it as the 'most notorious Y in the States' and that Steward had specifically taken 'elaborate notes' for 'him and myself on the activity'. 'It's called the Armed Services Y – and cockfull (make that chockfull – Freud pushed my finger) of sailors, soldiers, marines, and flyboys, but mostly sailors . . . I don't know when I've had a more sucksexful summer.'[68] There are drawings, too, in the Kinsey Institute, representing sailor sex (see Figures 27–8).

Steward's is what Jennifer Burns Bright has termed a 'lived archive' of sadomasochism.[69] His tattoo journals, kept at his mentor's request, provided graphic details of BDSM, with, in just one recorded incident, whips, paddles, tweezers, a white rat, vibrator, douche tube, industrial tape, blindfold, cold-cream, grease, and handcuffs.[70] In 1959 there were two new entries for the nation's sexual secrets. One was about a defrocked priest; 'We handcuffed him to the wall, and beat him until he hollered. Then we put him down on the floor, and *used* him, for about everything we could think of.'[71] The other was the director of a museum of art, a distinguished

27 Samuel Steward, Embarcadero, 1953. From the Collections of the Kinsey Institute, Indiana University. Permission the Estate of Samuel Steward.

28 Samuel Steward, stained glass window, 1951. From the Collections of the Kinsey Institute, Indiana University. All rights reserved. Permission the Estate of Samuel Steward.

art historian, who showed Steward some crudely sadistic art that seemed to shock even him: 'These are rather poorly executed, but do have a pretty fair impact.'[72] He witnessed and recorded what he described as the transformation of Chuck Renslow – owner of Kris Photographic Studio and Triumph Gym and future Chicago sex entrepreneur and founder of the Leather Archives & Museum – from a 'theoretical sadist', a 'butch-type homosexual', into a 'forthright, complete, and all-absorbed sadist . . . and it was astonishing'. Steward called it 'one of the major sexual events of the summer'.[73]

Steward was skilled with the telling vignette: the religious hustler who would tell his customers how sinful they were while they went down on him; the bodybuilder, Mr Illinois no less, who called off one appointment because he had just had 'pussy', and another because he slept in, 'but you forgave him a lot of things for the perfection of his body'.[74] During one of their sessions Steward told Mr Illinois that he was a masochist and asked the perfect-bodied-one to beat him; '"Oh I couldn't do that!", he said, "I don't know you well enough."'[75] The Kinsey Institute's informant extolled the virtues of self-pleasuring, describing masturbating while wearing a blue worker's cap, leather jacket, dungarees, and with a purple light on his cock! 'I should begin to talk about the superiority of masturbation, . . . you can have the world's pick if you just use your head.' This was after he had masturbated under the same purple light while admiring his own rose tattoo.[76]

While keeping the journal, Steward was writing pornography, and it is difficult, apart from the dates and real names, to tell one from the other – *scientia sexualis* certainly blended with *ars erotica*. The detail and elegance (and sexual explicitness) of the original bears no resemblance to the condensed, choppy, published version *Bad Boys and Tough Tattoos* (1990), with its Foreword by Pomeroy.[77] Steward must have spent many hours actually crafting the original document. As he observed in 1955, knowing of course that Kinsey would read it,

> Spent two hours or more getting caught up on this damned journal, which takes an unconscionable amount of time. Once started, however, it's semi-narcotic for me, and I suppose I shall keep on with it. I hope Prok [Kinsey] appreciates it, But I imagine I would continue for myself, even if he didn't want to see it.[78]

The necessary detachment of his actual sexual encounters, given their quantity, contrasted with the attachment and permanency of his cataloguing. He kept samples of the pubic hair of many of his lovers, DNA reminders on the back of filing cards in his Stud File, and in the jar which seems no longer to exist. Dean has argued that these were precious material traces of erotic bodily contact, representing cultural memory – 'a memorializing of same-sex relations', an archive of queer history – as much as an erotic reliving of a personal past.[79] Moreover, most of these tricks are named in this voluminous file, from anonymous to Thornton Wilder, with coded details of the precise sexual acts and the number of encounters (see Figure 29).[80] Recall too that many of his encounters are pictured for posterity in the Polaroid collection: Steward blowing 'trade' (masculine, sexually accessible heterosexuals), group sex, S/M, bondage, masked shots anticipating the artist David Wojnarowicz's work, and sailor-themed material.[81] As he wrote in a ledger summary of his contacts for 1951, 'Great leap after March partly due to purchase of Polaroid camera . . . Word to the lonely: Buy a Polaroid.'[82] A year later he was reporting to Platt Lynes that he was recording the group sex encounters: 'when it gets well under way I'll do what I always do – memorialize the event with my polaroid camera'.[83] His is a very personal, and extensive, archive of casual sex.

Steward redoubled his archiving efforts after he had encountered Kinsey, but he was already a recorder and a collector. Kinsey recognised the potential.

> The thing that amazed him most of all was that he found I was a 'record-keeper' – something all too rare, he said. But I had an accurate count on the number of persons I had been to bed with, the total number of times of 'releases' (as he termed them) with other persons, number of repeats, and all the usual statistical information, taken from the 'Stud File' that I had kept . . .[84]

Given that opportunity and the agreed archiving of the sexual aspects of tattooing, Kinsey made sure that Steward fulfilled his autoarchival promise, encouraging him in a letter of early 1950 – 'It was very good of you to have been so generous in giving us the material and your very important record' – and reinforcing his importance to the project in another dated 1951:

> The photographs add greatly to the material in our file on you . . . You have a hundred or more things up there that Bill [Kinsey's photographer William Dellenback] should photograph . . . Now that we have started accumulating a full record on you, we must not fall short of anything but the full record.[85]

At Kinsey's urging, and assuring discretion, Steward purchased handcrafted, S/M implements, a strap, whips, paddle, presumably duplicates of those now in the Beinecke; 'I would say', he wrote to their new owner, 'that you now have an implement for any mood, and one that would offer

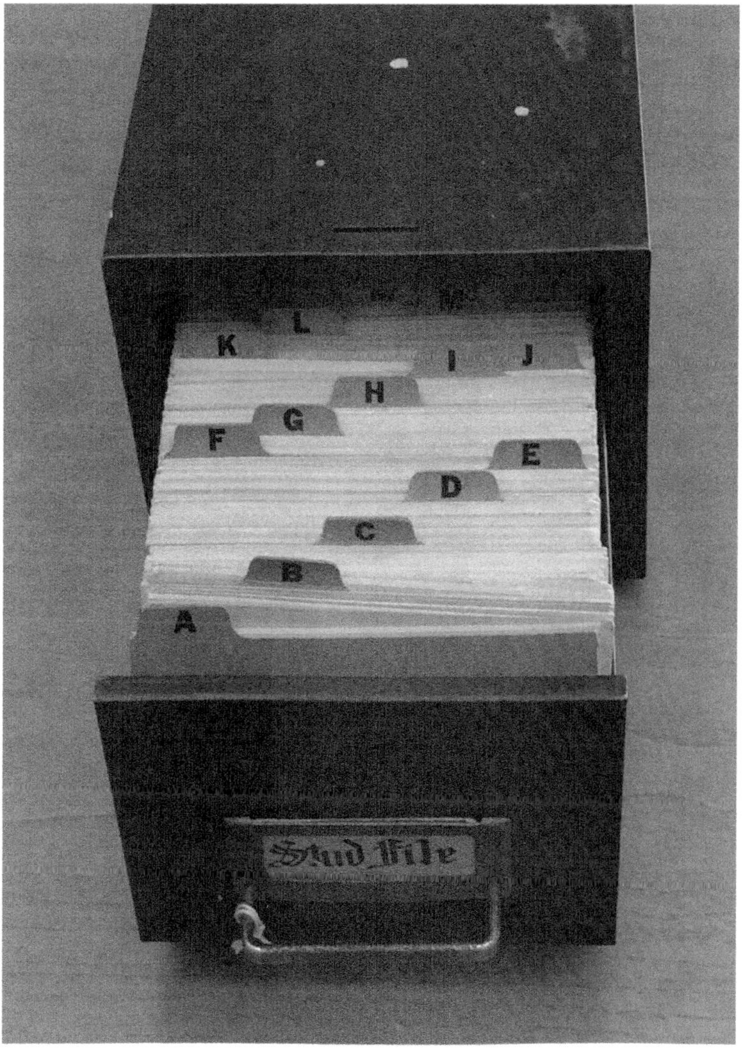

29 Samuel Steward's Stud File, Beinecke Rare Book and Manuscript Library, Yale University. Photograph by author, 2016. Permission the Estate of Samuel Steward.

sufficient variety to satisfy most general tastes' (see Figure 30).[86] There is an intriguing reference to a 30-foot-long rope of hair – current whereabouts unknown.[87] Dellenback took pictures of Steward's apartment, a homoerotically designed living (and playing) space with its trade and sailor-sex murals,

30 Samuel Steward's S/M implements, Beinecke Rare Book and Manuscript Library, Yale University. Photograph by author, 2016. Permission the Estate of Samuel Steward.

some of which reappear in his Polaroids of sex with real trade and sailors.[88] Though Kinsey certainly encouraged Steward's sexual archiving, there was more to it than sexual research. As already intimated, these were mementos of pleasure, and Scott Herring has linked Steward's later elderly hoarding to these earlier remnants of a rich sexual history.[89] As Herring intuited, Steward himself wrote perceptively of the role of reminders of the past.

> The 'Stud File' is full of cards and names and bits of coded information. The glass jar is packed with snippets of crinkly hair taken from my favorite persons, for when I was seventeen I knew I was going to be seventy. And there were going to have to be tangibles to which the imagination and memory could be tied, devices to stimulate nostalgia and the remembrance of things past.[90]

Even if we disregard his Proustian claim to a precocious prescience, his justification is part of a moving reflection on a life lived through detachment as a means of self-preservation (he referenced the poet John Keats's concept of negative capability), while preparing for a transition from a life of sexual excess to one of ageing and sexual privation. *Thinking*, the activity of the mind, the 'wildest and most passionate activity known to man', was still available, but to indulge in that required 'a treasury of memories'. And it was there that the mementos came in. 'Since our emotional lives are fragmented, we should have a vast stock of tangible things to invest our love in: mementos, memorabilia, photographs . . . anything which can stimulate us, can make us remember.'[91]

Given the sexual volume and variability of Steward's history, it is debatable whether the metaphor of the 'closet', which clearly informs his biographer's account, is at all appropriate.[92] Steward himself said in 1983 that he had never really been in any closet.[93] Nor is this history necessarily best described as a 'secret' history. True, Steward's life story was not published when he was living it, but a life that intersected with so many other lives, that straddled the emerging worlds both of heterosexuality and homosexuality, and that left so many traces in such multiple and varied media, was hardly secret.

I have written about our other Kinsey informant Thomas Painter elsewhere, but it is worth encapsulating some of the main details.[94] This chronicler of New York hustlers from the 1930s to the 1960s provided material to the Kinsey Institute until the early 1970s (after Kinsey's death): his entire life record in the form of letter-journals, about a thousand photographs, fiction, and drawings (see Figure 31).[95] Throughout the war and post-war period, Painter regaled Kinsey with detailed accounts of sex involving hustlers, servicemen, bodybuilders, and gangsters, mostly handwritten letters that were later transcribed in typewritten form by Clara Kinsey for filing in the archive. 'With your utterly incredible voracity for detail, I thought it might amuse you to know *just* what I do when I "cruise"', he wrote in 1946, before

31 Thomas Painter and friends at the New York apartment he shared with Edward Melcarth (who probably took the photograph), 1940s.

embarking on a thorough account of said activity.[96] Pomeroy has described the Painter archive as 'probably the most complete record of human sexual life ever compiled'.[97] Painter also provided contact with further informants. By 1949 Kinsey and Pomeroy had interviewed the whole of his circle, seventeen named associates, but there was the lure of still more connections.[98] One of Painter's companions, a New Jersey gangster and communist merchant seaman, promised in 1948 to introduce Kinsey to these twin aspects of his existence, and the sex researcher responded positively.

> We would be delighted to get his underworld group some time . . . As for our $4.00 going to the Communist Party, that is his business and theirs, not ours. It is of no concern to us whether the money that we give is spent for wine, women, or song, or whether that song be red or white. They would be helping the research and that is the important thing.[99]

Pomeroy thought that the correspondence between Kinsey and Painter read like 'one insider talking to another'.[100] 'Dear Doctor', Painter wrote in 1953 during the 'hullabaloo' over the publication of *Sexual Behavior in the Human Female*, 'They complain you say girls fuck too much. I remarked you pointed out they hardly fuck at all. I presume it all depends on one's frame of reference.'[101] Painter certainly felt comfortable enough (knowing that Clara Kinsey transcribed his communications) to relay rumours about his patron's sexuality; a friend of a friend had told him that 'he "carried on" with you, not once but frequently'.[102] He was also confident in providing novel ideas or new sexual information: 'I don't believe that you or I or even [Magnus] Hirschfeld has a name for this', he wrote after describing masturbating with his head near a man's penis, 'but there you are. Let's call it pornophilia.'[103]

Kinsey's informant provided a more substantial form of Gavin Butt's 'whispering in the archives', the gossip and queer disclosures referred to earlier in this book.[104] He sent amusingly voyeuristic (and somewhat grainy) snaps of the physique photographer Lon photographing and then picking up young men on the beach in 1949: the captions were 'As Photographer' (see Figure 32) and 'As Escort' (see Figure 33). However, the information

32 Thomas Painter, Lon 'As Photographer', 1949.

33 Thomas Painter, Lon 'As Escort', 1949.

was sometimes of such a confidential nature that it would be inappropriate to reveal it, even now: the New York chaplain who groped a hustler in the confessional; the high-ranking US war politician who was interested in 'any boys that may be about . . . I pass this on for what it is worth'; the named famous bodybuilders who were available for the right price; the film stars who started their careers as hustlers; the celebrated songwriter who attended mass fellatory parties; the heiress and patron of the arts who shared rough trade with a New York artist; the future Hollywood actor, sexually available to pretty much anyone with enough money or influence, but 'too beautiful to fuck'; the well-known young writer who (like Painter) preferred frictation (rubbing) as his main form of sexual release; the European aristocrat who lived at the Waldorf Astoria but who 'cruised the Bowery and fellated bums in alleys and doorways . . . and had a chain, several yards long, of woven human hair – pubic hair – one from each man he had fellated', an interesting echo of Steward's hair fetish; an early television teen idol who was, 'to put it bluntly, a cocksucker, but also liked to be fucked in the ass' (a publicity interview referred to there being 'no Mrs [teen idol] in his near future', to which Painter had added 'he being queer as a kite').[105] This was insider gossip that Kinsey and his team probably could not have accessed from many other sources.

Painter sent detailed summaries of his responses to movies, including how he (psychologically) identified with Marilyn Monroe in *Bus Stop* (1956) and that he went to see the film, drawn both by the body of the male star, Don Murray, and by the director Joshua Logan, who seemed to populate his filmography with 'great muscular young beauties'; 'Logan's tastes are broadly similar to mine, I have discovered, and he shows it (as Tennessee Williams' plays show him).'[106] Presumably Painter would have known that the film was based on two plays by William Inge, so that may have been another motive, given that trade featured in much of that playwright's work.[107] More predictably, he reported back on Tab Hunter in *Battle Cry* (1955), 'a very sexy movie – as evinced by the parade of the leather jacket set', and reflected on the heterosexual–homosexual mix of such films and about whether or not the industry was trying to cater for varied tastes:

> It would be interesting to know who (or whom, I guess) the 'cinemogula' . . . think they are arousing by this shirt removal business – and the back stroking routine. Do you know? According to us (you and I) we (I and my fellow homosexuals of various sorts) are the only ones interested – not the bobby socksers [soxers], who only drool about how cute his face is (which it indeed also is), not his torso. Is Hollywood conscious of this and consciously catering to our some six million (4% of 150 million), or are they just ignorant about women – or do they disagree with you or never read your book?'[108]

Painter was capable of substantial reflection and sexual analysis. I have written elsewhere of his early formulation of the Kinsey Scale and of his sophisticated pressing of Kinsey on some of his sexual categories and definitions.[109] His 1941 proposal of the categories of true heterosexual, predominantly heterosexual, heterosexual/bisexual, true bisexual, homosexual/bisexual, predominantly homosexual, and true homosexual are remarkably similar to Kinsey's 0–6 classification from exclusively heterosexual to exclusively homosexual (Kinsey would have disapproved of the mention of bisexual).[110] Donna Drucker has argued that Kinsey was influenced by prior work by Katherine Davis and discussions with a graduate student in 1940, so 1941 may seem slightly late to have been the deciding inspiration that I initially claimed.[111] But it is certainly possible that Painter was an influence during this early formulation.[112] It is also a reminder – and such reminders are necessary – that qualitative evidence could inform quantitative classifications; they were not hermetically sealed entities.

We saw in the previous chapter how Painter was willing to engage in analysis of the masturbatory role of photographic imagery. He wrote at length about the erotic potential of some of Henry Faulkner's pictures, in this case 'one of the few top pictures in successful arousal of my eroticism':

> Because these boys, here posing for Faulkner and some friends, are ordinary proletarians picked up, who obligingly strip naked for the queers to have their fun, and let them take pictures of them. As they are completely devoid of beauty of physique (but at the same time not repellent) they are totally 'naked', in no degree 'nude'. Their self-conscious giggling increases this effect . . . Next the queers suck their cocks, right there in front of each other. As the boys are in contact it also gives a contact fillip. On the right is Faulkner himself posing with, I believe, the one with this hair hanging in the left picture. It is obscene and erotic for his, naked, to pose with Faulkner clothed and thus fondling him.[113]

He knew that Faulkner habitually photographed his young models, often sailors, either just before or after sex – in other words that the pictures were indexically linked to sex acts. Painter had not been there at the time (despite living with Faulkner in New York in the 1940s), but he knew his friend's mode of operation and part of the attraction anyway was the fantasy about the circumstances of their taking. As he wrote on the back of another picture, 'since I did not take them and the subjects are unknown to me, the erotic content is high'.[114] 'My masturbation over obscene pictures is a very important part of my sex life', he clarified to the Kinsey Institute in 1961.[115]

When Kinsey told Painter that he had helped 'materially' in the making of *Sexual Behavior in the Human Male*, he was probably referring to his brokering of subjects for interviewing.[116] However, the informant also played an ethnographic role. 'I feel an increasing indebtedness to you for continuing this record. It is a magnificent lot of material', Kinsey wrote in 1948. 'I have been seeing a good many diaries in the last few years, and there are only three or four which would be worth our keeping. Yours is one of the best two from any scientific standpoint.'[117]

It is true that Painter's reports were shaped by his class, race, and personal preferences.[118] He could be dismissive of his sexual partners, observing of one that he thought that America was discovered by Napoleon and had never heard of Julius Caesar; he did know of Judgement Day, for the young man's mother had taught him about that – though, as Painter put it sardonically, 'fortunately she taught him nothing about sex'.[119] Painter was not generally attracted to African Americans, so descriptions of Harlem bars, while they exist, are rare. Un-muscular hustlers did not affect him. He hated effeminacy, which excluded a whole sexual category from his portfolio, apart from mocking comments. He was well aware that his research was not impartial, joking that it should have been called 'Professional Heterosexual White Male Prostitution of a Specific Age Group in New York, with Notes on Allied Phenomena, perhaps adding . . . A Subjective Approach.'[120] Presumably Kinsey and his associates were aware of this perspective (something perhaps not recognised by later critics), for they received long reflective letters from their informant about this very issue: 'I am a very queer sort of queer.'[121] In any event, these lenses do not make Painter's observations any the less pertinent – especially since cross-class attraction was the very point of the sexual interactions that were being mapped out.[122]

The urge to count was shared by Kinsey's informants, and, curiously, as touched on in the following chapter, by generations of same-sex cruisers. Contemplating his own sexual history, Painter noted that he was 'a promiscuous fellow . . . I must have had sex with a thousand different persons.'[123] He classified many of his sexual contacts according to the Kinsey Scale, ranking them 0–6.[124] Steward's journals and index cards are also a relentless tallying. During the aforementioned 42-day visit to San Francisco in 1953, recorded in detail for Kinsey, Steward had 63 sexual contacts with 38 different people.[125] In 1954, at the age of 45, he calculated from his file that he had had 1,100 sexual contacts up to the age of 38 and exactly the same number in the mere seven years since then.[126] Years later the total approached nearly 5,000, with over 800 different sexual partners.[127]

Individual index cards in Steward's Stud File list daily or thrice weekly blowjobs, over years, at $3 each, from a toothless provider, with breaks only when that supplier was in jail. Steward had regular sex with hustlers and bodybuilders provided by Kris Studio and Chicago's Triumph Gym (a fact that was also recorded meticulously), $5 and $10 a time with one favourite, costing some $4,000 in four years.[128] Even the 29 daisy chains were quantified, the participants named, the events dated in precise detail, from 16 September 1949 to 24 September 1957.[129] And then there was the key to the bodily dimensions of his partners (long, short, medium, thick, thin, circumcised, clean, bent, very small, not hard, huge, average, Negro, Jew, melon, beautifully shaped) and the type of sexual activity engaged in (piss, spit, feet, trade, mutual, several mutual, was browned, 50–50 browned, done, browned one, brown & suck, jackpot, love & kisses, rub, nothing, masturbated, whips & sadism, ropes, games, gamahucher, standing or kneeling over).[130] Huge, long, thick was his coded assessment of one professional wrestler 'courtesy Kris Pimping Service. $5. Big white skinned . . . completely stupid, but nice.'[131]

Yet it was to the qualitative rather than to the quantitative that Painter and Steward made their contributions. The pre-Stonewall period explored – lived – by these Kinsey informants, and which had so enthused Kinsey when he first encountered it in Chicago in 1939, was one that Steward was almost nostalgic about from the perspective of the 1980s. 'Well it was fun', he said of the world that he had lost when interviewed by a representative of the new identity politics of the world that he had gained.

> You see, we had this lovely protective umbrella of ignorance over it. This was especially true during the '30s and '40s. No one knew anything about homosexuality and if they did know anything . . . they thought it happened only in the wicked cities of Europe or maybe New York or somewhere, but certainly not in Chicago which was the City of the Big Shoulders, and Hog Butcher to the World. So under that umbrella of ignorance, we lived and went our ways and had our apartment parties and gatherings and wild orgies . . . and that sort of thing.[132]

He then proceeded to talk about daisy chains in his Chicago apartment and of the recordings of them that he made for Kinsey. Steward also clarified, in a section not used in the published version of the interview, that this was in the years before S/M was codified and ritualised, with safe words and 'consensual agreements', when practitioners were never sure whether or not they might be killed; 'it was completely dangerous'.[133]

He resisted the efforts of several interviewers to force him into a post-Stonewall straitjacket. Where were the bars that 'gay people' gathered in? 'Gay people just didn't gather yet.' Was there a 'homosexual identity'? 'I wasn't particularly aware of that because . . . ah . . . it didn't matter to me.'[134] A few years earlier he had told Winston Leyland, changing his metaphors, that 'We all let a little fog rise around us, to conceal us – and thus not categorized, not pigeonholed, not stereotyped – we enjoyed a really perfect form of freedom.'[135] Whether he was a man, then, who, as his biographer puts it, 'literally spent his whole life pondering the nature of his sexual identity', is debatable.[136] He seems to have been too involved in acts to worry about identities.

The emerging worlds of heterosexuality and homosexuality revealed in the qualitative evidence provided by Kinsey's two informants intersected and overlapped: notions of isolated and separated sexual spheres are highly misleading.[137] They involved heterosexual homosexuals and homosexual heterosexuals, men who went from man to man and from man to woman. As Steward later elucidated, 'it didn't matter a whole hell of a lot whether it was male or female. A man enjoyed a good blow job just as much as he did a good screw.'[138] Despite Steward's talk of umbrellas of ignorance and fog, it was not a totally unknown world. Albert Ellis recognised it in an article on sexual promiscuity, written on the very eve of Stonewall: 'Not only are literally hundreds of thousands of Americans promiscuously homosexual but many basically heterosexual individuals now actively seek occasional homosexual encounters as well.'[139] But no one described it as vividly and exhaustively – and from the perspective of participant research – as did Kinsey's two collaborators.

Kinsey wrote to Painter in 1945 that his project was a protracted one and that there was another twenty years of research before he was ready to 'generalize on many aspects of our problems'. 'Even in New York there is a tremendous variety of types', Kinsey wrote, as if thinking out loud.[140] It is a pity that Kinsey never lived to see his projects realised and for us to see how he would have made use of all the work of his participant researchers and autoarchivists. Sammy Steward and Thomas Painter were central to this project – both *ars erotica* and *scientia sexualis*.

Indeed, Thomas Waugh long ago detected the 'collaborative dynamic' in Kinsey's project, 'in which knowledge and desire inextricably interplay'.[141] Since this chapter began by invoking Foucault, perhaps it should end by taking seriously (like Waugh and Dean) the great philosopher of sex's recognition that *ars erotica* might be inherent in *scientia sexualis*, in the 'multiplication and intensification of pleasures connected to the production of the truth about sex'.[142] Though there is no mention of Kinsey in the *History of Sexuality*, the man whom Steward once described as a voyeur and an auditeur, it would be difficult to identify a greater contributor to what Foucault termed the 'great archive of the pleasures of sex'.[143]

Notes

1 For Kinsey and counting, see D. J. Drucker, *The Classification of Sex: Alfred Kinsey and the Organization of Knowledge* (Pittsburgh, PA, 2014).
2 L. Trilling, 'The Kinsey Report', in his *The Liberal Imagination* (New York, 1951), pp. 223–42, quote at p. 223.
3 For the best biography of Kinsey, see J. Gathorne-Hardy, *Sex the Measure of All Things: A Life of Alfred C. Kinsey* (Bloomington, IN, 1998); and for the best

short accounts of Kinsey's project, see P. Robinson, 'Alfred Kinsey', in his *The Modernization of Sex* (New York, 1976), ch. 2; R. M. Morantz, 'The scientist as sex crusader: Alfred C. Kinsey and American culture', *American Quarterly*, 29:5 (1977), 563–89.

4 W. B. Pomeroy, *Dr. Kinsey and the Institute for Sex Research* (New York, 1972), p. 16.

5 J. Crump, 'Archiving sexuality: the photographic collection of the Kinsey Institute', in J. P. Witkin (ed.), *Harms Way: Lust & Madness, Murder & Mayhem* (Santa Fe, NM, 1994), no pagination. Emphasis in original.

6 Pomeroy, *Dr. Kinsey*, p. 109.

7 S. E. Igo, *The Averaged American: Surveys, Citizens, and the Making of a Mass Public* (Cambridge, MA, 2008), pp. 267–80.

8 Letter to Ralph Voris, 1939, in D. J. Drucker, '"Building for a life-time of research": letters of Alfred Kinsey and Ralph Voris', *Indiana Magazine of History*, 106:1 (2010), 71–101, quotes at 97–8. Emphasis in the original.

9 Kinsey Institute, University of Indiana, Bloomington (hereafter, KI), Kinsey Correspondence Collection, Letter to Herbert Huncke, 26 January 1943.

10 Ibid.

11 A. C. Kinsey, 'Criteria for a hormonal explanation of the homosexual', *Journal of Clinical Endocrinology*, 1:5 (1941), 424–8, quote at 425.

12 Ibid., 427, 428.

13 E. Grosz, *Time Travels: Feminism, Nature, Power* (Durham, NC, 2005), p. 204.

14 Trilling, *Liberal Imagination*, p. 224.

15 Grosz, *Time Travels*, pp. 205, 209.

16 Ibid., p. 209.

17 T. Dean, 'Sam Steward's pornography: archive, index, trace', in D. A. Moddelmog and M. J. Ponce (eds), *Samuel Steward and the Pursuit of the Erotic: Sexuality, Literature, Archives* (Columbus, OH, 2017), ch. 1, quotes at p. 34.

18 Trilling, *Liberal Imagination*, p. 231; G. Bataille, 'Kinsey, the underworld and work', in his *Death and Sensuality: A Study of Eroticism and the Taboo* (Salem, NH, 1984 [1962]), pp. 149–63.

19 Bataille, *Death and Sensuality*, p. 149.

20 A. C. Kinsey, W. B. Pomeroy, and C. E. Martin, *Sexual Behavior in the Human Male* (Philadelphia, PA, 1949), p. 5.

21 Ibid., p. 7.

22 J. M. Irvine, *Disorders of Desire: Sexuality and Gender in Modern American Sexology* (Philadelphia, PA, 2005 [1990]), p. 21.

23 Ibid., p. 20.

24 Trilling, *Liberal Imagination*, p. 224.

25 Pomeroy, *Dr. Kinsey*, p. 78.

26 Kinsey, Pomeroy, and Martin, *Sexual Behavior in the Human Male*, p. 202.

27 J. Gilbert, *Men in the Middle: Searching for Masculinity in the 1950s* (Chicago, 2005), pp. 84–5.
28 KI, Kinsey Correspondence Collection, Letter to Lon Hanagan, 23 October 1943; Letter to Julian Green, 17 October 1952.
29 Kinsey, Pomeroy, and Martin, *Sexual Behavior in the Human Male*, p. 74.
30 Mentioned in ibid., p. 7; and in Pomeroy, *Dr. Kinsey*, pp. 446–8.
31 T. Waugh, 'Knowledge and desire: Dr Kinsey as arbiter of the homoerotic imaginary', in J. Murray (ed.), *Constructing Sexualities* (Windsor, ON, 1993), pp. 63–87; J. Crump, 'The Kinsey Institute archive: a taxonomy of erotic photography', *History of Photography*, 18:1 (1994), 1–12; C. Johnson-Roehr, 'From visual data to fine art: photography collections at the Kinsey Institute', *Visual Resources: An International Journal of Documentation*, 25:3 (2009), 259–80.
32 Pomeroy, *Dr. Kinsey*, p. 107.
33 G. Wescott, *A Heaven of Words: Last Journals, 1956–1984*, ed. J. Rosco (Madison, WI, 2013), p. 150.
34 KI, Kinsey Correspondence Collection, Letter from Paul Gebhard to Glenway Wescott, 12 March 1959.
35 KI, Kinsey Correspondence Collection, Letter to Clarence Tripp, 3 November 1948.
36 Pomeroy, *Dr. Kinsey*, p. 177.
37 Gathorne-Hardy, *Sex the Measure of All Things*, pp. 307–8, 483, n. 60.
38 Ibid., pp. 333–8.
39 Discussed in ibid., pp. 220–5, 478, n. 78. Waugh also mentions some of the main collaborators: Waugh, 'Knowledge and desire', pp. 71–4.
40 T. Waugh, *Hard to Imagine: Gay Male Eroticism in Photography and Film from Their Beginnings to Stonewall* (New York, 1996), pp. 332–6.
41 For Lawrence, see J. Meyerowitz, 'Sex research at the borders of gender: transvestites, transsexuals, and Alfred C. Kinsey', *Bulletin of the History of Medicine*, 75:1 (2001), 72–90. See also KI, Kinsey Correspondence Collection, Louise Lawrence.
42 E. H. Brown, 'Queering glamour in interwar fashion photography: the "amorous regard" of George Platt Lynes', *GLQ*, 23:3 (2017), 289–326, quote at 319.
43 https://iucat.iu.edu/kinsey/13540183 (last accessed 26 April 2018). For a sample of Platt Lynes's work, see J. Crump (ed.), *George Platt Lynes: Photographs from the Kinsey Institute* (Boston, MA, 1993).
44 W. Leyland (ed.), *Gay Sunshine Interviews: Volume Two* (San Francisco, 1982), 'Ned Rorem', pp. 191–218, quote at p. 214.
45 Ibid., p. 215.
46 KI, Kinsey Correspondence Collection, Letter from Kenneth Anger, 2 December 1955.
47 KI, Kinsey, Box 1, Series 1. B. Folder 2: 'Notes on European Trip of late 1955, dictated by Dr. Kinsey at Staff Meetings'.

48 For the role of von Gloeden in homosexual historiography, see J. Goldman, '"The golden age of gay porn": nostalgia and the photography of Wilhelm von Gloeden', *GLQ*, 12:2 (2006), 237–58.
49 Pomeroy, *Dr. Kinsey*, p. 402; Gathorne-Hardy, *Sex the Measure of All Things*, p. 426 (and with a photograph of him, Plate 41); M. Duberman, *About Time: Exploring the Gay Past* (New York, 1991), pp. 194–215.
50 The New York Public Library, Humanities and Social Sciences Library, Manuscripts and Archives Division, MSS Col 23206, C. A. Tripp Papers.
51 See ibid., Box 3, Correspondence between Alfred Kinsey and Sixt Kapff, 1950–55; Box 4, Correspondence with Sixt Kapff, 1971–2003.
52 Ibid., Box 4, Folder 9, Transcripts of Philip Nobile's interview with Sixt Kapff, NYC, November 1982.
53 Ibid., Box 4, Folder 7, Transcripts of Philip Nobile's interview with Sixt Kapff, NYC, November 1982.
54 Ibid., Box 3, Folder 2, Sixt Kapff to Alfred Kinsey, 11 January 1952.
55 Ibid., Box 3, Folder 3, Sixt Kapff to Alfred Kinsey, 4 January 1953.
56 Ibid., Box 3, Folder 5, Sixt Kapff to Alfred Kinsey, 22 May 1954.
57 Ibid., Box 3, Folder 6, Sixt Kapff to Rodney Garland, 28 November 1954.
58 KI, Kinsey, 'Notes on European Trip of late 1955'. The trip is also discussed in Gathorne-Hardy, *Sex the Measure of All Things*, ch. 22.
59 S. M. Steward, 'Dr. Kinsey takes a peek at S/M: a reminiscence', in M. Thompson (ed.), *Leatherfolk: Radical Sex, People, Politics, and Practice* (Boston, MA, 1991), pp. 81–90, at p. 89. Of course Steward was a skilled pornographer so he may merely have been following a trope in the retelling.
60 J. Spring, *Secret Historian: The Life and Times of Samuel Steward, Professor, Tattoo Artist, and Sexual Renegade* (New York, 2010).
61 Yale University Library (hereafter YUL), Beinecke Rare Book and Manuscript Library, General Collection of Modern Books and Manuscripts, GEN MSS 987: Samuel Steward Papers, Box 5, Rough Draft of Autobiography, p. 197.
62 J. Mulderig (ed.), *Philip Sparrow Tells All: Lost Essays by Samuel Steward, Writer, Professor, Tattoo Artist* (Chicago, 2015), p. xiii, for quote; Moddelmog and Ponce (eds), *Samuel Steward and the Pursuit of the Erotic*.
63 Spring, *Secret Historian*, p. 129. For some exhibits, see J. Spring, *An Obscene Diary: The Visual World of Sam Steward* (North Pomfret, VT, 2010).
64 YUL, Samuel Steward Papers, Box 5, Rough Draft of Autobiography, p. 183. This passage was only partially quoted in the printed version, S. M. Steward, *Chapters from an Autobiography* (San Francisco, 1981), p. 99.
65 YUL, Samuel Steward Papers, Box 9, Travel Diary 1950.
66 Ibid.
67 KI, Samuel Steward Collection, Series 2, D, Diary 1953–4: 'The Embarcadero Y'. See also, YUL Samuel Steward Papers, Box 4, 'The Embarcadero Y'.
68 YUL, Samuel Steward Papers, Box 3, Letters to George Platt Lynes, 18 October 1953.

69 J. B. Bright, 'Queerest of the queer: why Samuel Steward's masochism matters', in Moddelmog and Ponce (eds), *Samuel Steward and the Pursuit of the Erotic*, ch. 7, quote at p. 144. Strangely, Bright does not use the unpublished material discussed below.
70 YUL, Samuel Steward Papers, Box 1, 'Pages from Tattoo Journal, Kinsey Archives', pp. 575–6.
71 Ibid., p. 590-A. Emphasis in original.
72 Ibid., p. 597.
73 Ibid., pp. 590-A, 611. For Renslow, who clearly fell out with Steward, see T. Baim and O. Keehnen, *Leatherman: The Legend of Chuck Renslow* (Chicago, 2011). Spring discusses him too: Spring, *Secret Historian*, Index: Renslow, Chuck.
74 YUL, Samuel Steward Papers, 'Pages from Tattoo Journal', p. 616.
75 Ibid., p. 620.
76 KI, Samuel Steward Collection, Series 2, F, S.S. 1955 Diary, 25 January 1955, 25 April 1955.
77 S. M. Steward, *Bad Boys and Tough Tattoos: A Social History of the Tattoo with Gangs, Sailors, and Street-Corner Punks, 1950–1965* (New York, 1990).
78 KI, Samuel Steward Collection, Series 2, F, S.S. 1955 Diary, 25 April 1955.
79 Dean, 'Sam Steward's pornography', pp. 27, 43.
80 YUL, Samuel Steward Papers, Box 25, The Stud File.
81 YUL, Samuel Steward Papers, Box 14 and Box 16: Polaroid photographs. They are reproduced in Spring, *An Obscene Diary*.
82 YUL, Samuel Steward Papers, Box 32, Ledgers compiling information from the Stud File, 1950–2, Summary for 1951.
83 YUL, Samuel Steward Papers, Box 3, Letters to George Platt Lynes, 3 November 1952.
84 Steward, *Chapters from an Autobiography*, p. 96.
85 KI, Kinsey Correspondence Collection, Letters to Samuel Steward, 14 February 1950 and 6 November 1951.
86 KI, Samuel Steward Collection, Series 1, A, SS to K[insey] 1950–55, Letter from Samuel Steward to Kinsey, 21 June 1951.
87 Ibid., 1 January 1951.
88 Spring, *Secret Historian*, Plates between pp. 238–9.
89 S. Herring. 'On late-life Samuel Steward', in Moddelmog and Ponce (eds), *Samuel Steward and the Pursuit of the Erotic*, ch. 3.
90 Steward, *Chapters from an Autobiography*, p. 129.
91 Ibid., pp. 140–1.
92 Spring, *Secret Historian*, pp. 211, 410.
93 Gay and Lesbian Historical Society of Northern California [later the Gay, Lesbian, Bisexual, Transgender Historical Society] (hereafter GLBT Historical Society), San Francisco, Oral History Collection, 83–06: Samuel Steward.

94 B. Reay, *New York Hustlers: Masculinity and Sex in Modern America* (Manchester, 2010), Index: Painter, Thomas.
95 Henry Minton has also written about Painter: H. L. Minton, *Departing from Deviance: A History of Homosexual Rights and Emancipatory Science in America* (Chicago, 2002), chs 6–7.
96 KI, the Thomas Painter Collection (hereafter Painter), Box 1, Series 2, c. 1, Vol. 3: 30 July 1946. Emphasis in original.
97 Pomeroy, *Dr. Kinsey*, p. 169.
98 KI, Painter, Box 1, Series 2, c. 1, Vol. 6: 20 May 1949.
99 KI, Kinsey Correspondence Collection, Alfred Kinsey to Thomas Painter, 21 January 1948.
100 Ibid.
101 KI, Painter, Box 1, Series 2, c. 1, Vol. 10: 26 August 1953.
102 KI, Painter, Box 1, Series 2, c. 1, Vol. 9: 28 January 1952.
103 KI, Painter, Box 1, Series 2, c. 1, Vol. 6: 7 February 1949.
104 G. Butt, *Between You and Me: Queer Disclosures in the New York Art World, 1948–1963* (Durham, NC, 2005).
105 These are all examples from KI, Painter.
106 KI, Painter, Box 1, Series 2, c. 1, Vol. 13: 13 October 1956.
107 Reay, *New York Hustlers*, pp. 199–200.
108 KI, Painter, Box 1, Series 2, c. 1, Vol. 13: 23 January 1956.
109 Reay, *New York Hustlers*, pp. 137–40.
110 KI, Thomas Painter, 'Male Homosexuals and their Prostitutes in Contemporary America', New York, 1941, Vol. 1: 'American Homosexuals', p. 131.
111 Drucker, *Classification of Sex*, p. 136.
112 Henry Minton has suggested this as well: Minton, *Departing from Deviance*, pp. 139–40.
113 KI, Painter, Box 16, Series 4, A. 1. b., box 1, # 47.
114 Ibid., #1.
115 KI, Painter, Box 1, Series 2, c. 1, Vol. 18b, 18 July 1961.
116 KI, Kinsey Correspondence Collection, Alfred Kinsey to Thomas Painter, 9 January 1948.
117 Ibid., 30 May 1948, 14 October 1948.
118 See Y. Zikratyy, 'Interviewing hustlers: cross-class relations, sexual self-documentation, and the erotics of queer archives', in A. L. Stone and J. Cantrell (eds), *Out of the Closet, Into the Archives: Researching Sexual Histories* (Albany, NY, 2015), ch. 12.
119 KI, Painter, Box 1, Series 2, c. 1, Vol. 6: 17 January 1949.
120 A letter dated 2 September 1962, pasted into the front of the book: KI, Thomas Painter, 'Male Homosexuals and their Prostitutes in Contemporary America', New York, 1941, Vol. 2: 'The Prostitute'.
121 For example, KI, Painter, Box 1, Series 2, c. 1, Vol. 18a, 27 May 1961; Box 1, Series 2, c. 1, Vol. 18b, 22 August 1961, for quote.

122 As discussed in Reay, *New York Hustlers*.

123 KI, Painter, Box 3, Series 2, D. 2., Folder 1, Autobiographical Sections, # ix (1971–2); Box 1, Series 2, c. 1, Vol. 18b, 'Moral Code Essay, Summer 1961', for quote.

124 Reay, *New York Hustlers*, pp. 112–14.

125 Spring, *Secret Historian*, p. 178.

126 Ibid., p. 203.

127 Ibid., p. 380.

128 YUL, Samuel Steward Papers, Box 25, The Stud File. The $4,000 estimate comes from YUL, Samuel Steward Papers, Box 5, Rough Draft of Autobiography, p. 211. For further quantification of Steward and his hustlers, see Spring, *Secret Historian*, p. 284.

129 YUL, Samuel Steward Papers, Box 25, The Stud File.

130 Ibid.

131 Ibid.

132 T. Kissack (ed.), 'Alfred Kinsey and homosexuality in the '50s: the recollections of Samuel Morris Steward as told to Len Evans', *Journal of the History of Sexuality*, 9:4 (2000), 474–91, quote at 482.

133 GLBT Historical Society, San Francisco, Oral History Collection, 83–06: Samuel Steward.

134 YUL, Samuel Steward Papers, Box 1, Interview with Samuel Steward by Gregory Sprague, 20 May 1982.

135 Leyland (ed.), *Gay Sunshine Interviews: Volume Two*, 'Samuel Steward', pp. 219–42, quote at p. 242.

136 Spring, *Secret Historian*, p. xiii.

137 For other discussions of this sexual milieu, see C. Heap, *Slumming: Sexual and Racial Encounters in American Nightlife, 1885–1940* (Chicago, 2009); D. Romesburg, '"Wouldn't a boy do?" Placing early-twentieth-century male youth sex work into histories of sexuality', *Journal of the History of Sexuality*, 18:3 (2009), 367–92; Reay, *New York Hustlers*; C. R. Johnson, *Just Queer Folks: Gender and Sexuality in Rural America* (Philadelphia, PA, 2013).

138 Kissack (ed.), 'Alfred Kinsey and homosexuality in the '50s', 487.

139 A. Ellis, 'Sexual promiscuity in America', *Annals of the American Academy of Political and Social Science*, 378 (1968), 58–67, quote at 60.

140 Quoted in Pomeroy, *Dr. Kinsey*, p. 170.

141 Waugh, 'Knowledge and desire', p. 83.

142 M. Foucault, *The History of Sexuality: Volume 1: An Introduction*, trans. R. Hurley (London, 1978), pp. 70–1, quote at p. 71.

143 Ibid., p. 63. For Steward, see Steward, *Chapters from an Autobiography*, p. 99.

4

Promiscuous intimacies: rethinking the history of American casual sex

Casual sex – uncommitted, fleeting, non-romantic sexual encounters, sex for sex's sake – has become something of a cultural commonplace in the late twentieth and early twenty-first centuries. 'For me', observes a female character in a Jennifer Egan novel, 'the sexual act had nothing to do with love, or rarely. On the contrary, the less I cared for or even knew a man, the more easily I lost myself in his physical company.'[1] This is the kind of sex central to the high-rating TV series *Sex and the City*, with the four, Manhattan-based female characters who, one academic commentator has calculated, had some 130 different sexual contacts in the show's first four seasons: 'Who would have thought an island so small could hold all of our boyfriends?'[2] Before *Sex and the City* there was the massively successful, 1990s, nine-season *Seinfeld* that was also about (among other things) friendship and casual sex.[3] And there is the brilliant Lena Dunham, whose film *Tiny Furniture* (2010) (who could forget the sex in a pipe in Brooklyn!) and HBO series *Girls* (2012–17) provide the knowingness that discomfits in ways that her predecessors never did.[4] Uncommitted sex, though it may lead to less transitory contact, is simply assumed in Dunham's New York.

Cultural ubiquity is not normally conducive to good history, however. For one of the weaknesses of contemporary analyses of casual sex is that they read as though their subject is without any precedent. This is especially true of casual sex's most recent iteration, hooking up. The word 'history' occurs only once in *Hooking Up, Hanging Out, and Hoping for Mr. Right* (2001), the study by Norval Glenn and Elizabeth Marquardt.[5] A literature review of 'sexual hookup culture' that argues for its emerging normativity has but one short paragraph dealing with 'cultural shifts in dating'.[6] This elision of the past is true of even the more astute academic commentators. *Hooking Up*, Kathleen Bogle's well-received 2008 study of college student casual sex, moves too quickly through the sexual culture of the period before her study commences.[7]

Presumably the practice of uncommitted sex was not an invention of modernity, but what was the thing before it was identified as casual sex or hooking up? The aim of this chapter, with a focus on twentieth-century American sexual history, is to begin to rethink modern casual sex. It draws on two important sexual archives: the University of Chicago Library's holdings of the work of 1920s sociologists on sex in Chicago, and the New York Public Library's collection of moral reformers' reports on casual sex in New York in the early twentieth century. It is not intended as the total history of a concept, but rather a reflection on particular historical moments as a way of reconsidering a concept's claimed novelty. This exploration has been prompted less by current academic interest in non-monogamous sex – much of which seems far too organised and emotionally committed to be considered casual – and more by the thematic and historical silences in accounts of what has been termed a 'new sexual script'.[8]

We are concerned with both the name and the behaviour. We can date the advent of the actual term 'casual sex' fairly precisely. Promiscuity was the nomenclature favoured initially. When in 1968 Albert Ellis wrote about what he termed 'sexual promiscuity' in an article for the American Academy of Political and Social Science, he named his subject variously as 'plural sexuality', 'nonmonogamous indulgence', 'sex-love affairs', 'sexual varietism', 'those who have many sex partners', 'sexual experimentation', and 'promiscuous sex-love affairs'. Such were the practitioners and practices of what Ellis called 'sex affairs on a rather casual basis'. His article was published at the historical moment – significantly the late 1960s – when promiscuity was becoming casual sex, and the latter term occurs only once in his analysis.[9] Ellis was a liberal supporter of what he termed 'sex relations without love': 'I can and have spent a LITTLE time with many girls with whom I had common sex and cultural but little love interests.'[10] His colleague Ira Reiss, on the other hand, was more sexually conservative, clearly favouring what he categorised as 'person-centered' sex or 'permissiveness with affection', premarital sexual interaction in the context of a perceived stable relationship, and which he contrasted with what would later be called casual sex but what he then referred to as 'body-centered' sex or 'permissiveness without affection'.[11] In 1957 Ellis and Reiss used the terms 'coitus without affection' and 'sex without love' when they debated the justification of uncommitted sex, but not the ascription 'casual sex', though this is indeed what they were dealing with.[12] Neither man referred to 'casual sex' in their discussion until they edited their correspondence in the 2000s.[13]

So the term, if not the practice it named, was new to post-war America. Indeed *The New York Times* provides a rough guide to educated usage. The words 'casual sex' were not employed before the 1960s. Thereafter, the decade with the most frequency was the 1980s, the initial era of AIDS, when the virus was popularly associated first with homosexual and then (when AIDS 'went heterosexual') with heterosexual promiscuity. By the 1990s much of the referencing of casual sex related to same-sex activity. What began as a marker of heterosexual promiscuity in the so-called sexual revolution of the 1960s and 1970s became closely associated with the transmission of a virus and homosexual sex. More recently, as already hinted, the term has become linked with a form of heterosexual sex known in the US as hooking up, more of which later.[14]

But we are interested in the described behaviour as much as the named term, and its practices were not so novel. Meanings were slippery. One of Reiss's major academic contributions was to show that what many contemporaries took to be sexual promiscuity among the unmarried in the 1950s was actually rather conventional sexual behaviour: 'premarital coitus . . . which accepts intercourse as a right . . . when strong affection, love, or engagement is present'.[15] In other words, it was sex in anticipation of marriage, a traditional form of sexual interaction in the history of European culture.[16] This was in contrast to the unnamed (and Reiss argued rare) casual sex, sex without affection.[17]

Michael Schofield's 1970s working definition of casual sex or promiscuity was numerical: those who had intercourse with more than one person in the space of a year.[18] This is a characterisation that would surely seem to set the level rather low by certain contemporary standards, though, as we will see, is not too dissimilar to the sexual culture of hooking up in the 2000s. Ellis, on the other hand, thought that 'two dozen or more' sexual partners in an 'entire lifetime' indicated promiscuity.[19] Schofield was amusingly aware that individual criteria differed: 'One girl was most indignant when her doctor said that she was promiscuous because she had slept with fifteen men in the last year. She insisted that she was not promiscuous because she never went to bed with a man on her first date.'[20]

Alfred Kinsey's discussions of premarital intercourse had stressed variation: males who had sex only with the woman they planned to marry; those with scores of partners. 'In some cases, lower level males may have intercourse with several hundred or even a thousand or more girls in premarital relations.'[21] Women ranged from the 1 per cent who had more than a hundred petting partners to the majority (53 per cent) who had experienced premarital sexual intercourse with only one man. The sex surveyors were agreed on the gender pattern: 'In all of these types of relationships, few females have anywhere the number of partners that many a promiscuous male may have.'[22] (A more recent survey of American premarital sex found that for young women, a 'working definition' of 'too many' was ten or more sexual partners – reaching double digits.)[23]

Definitions of casual sex were diverse, then. Kinsey and his team wrote that they had encountered

> many males in the upper level who develop a fine art of achieving orgasm by petting techniques which avoid intercourse. The youth who may have experienced orgasm scores or hundreds of times in petting, and who may have utilized every type of petting technique, including mouth–genital contacts, still has the satisfaction of knowing that he is still a virgin, as his level defines virginity. There are even cases of males who effect genital union; but because they avoid orgasm while in such union they persuade themselves that they are still virgins.[24]

Petting's historical importance suggests that casual and non-casual sex cannot be confined to coitus. Kinsey and his collaborators noted that for their 1940s subjects, petting was often 'an end in itself' and that for generations of sexually active women from the 1900s through to the 1940s petting was 'the most widespread type of pre-marital heterosexual activity'.[25] Ninety per cent of their female sample had experienced premarital petting, and nearly 40 per cent had achieved orgasm by this means.[26] According to the Kinsey sexual histories, over a third (35 per cent) of married women had engaged in petting with over ten different males before they married, but only 5 per cent admitted to premarital intercourse with as many different partners. Promiscuous petting contrasted with more restrained coitus.[27] Reiss used the work of Kinsey to argue that even women who abstained from sexual intercourse could have 'considerable experience in sexual behavior', coining the term the 'promiscuous virgin'.[28]

Academic observers in the 1950s and 1960s agreed that unmarried sexual intercourse was more likely at the working-class level. Another Reiss, Albert, referred to lower-status girls justifying premarital sex as 'fun' and middle-class girls explaining it in terms of 'love'.[29] Kinsey found that heterosexual, working-class men were more likely to have had intercourse than to have indulged in kissing or petting: 'Many a college male will have kissed dozens of girls, although he has had intercourse with none of them. On the other hand, the lower level male is likely to have had intercourse with hundreds of girls, but he may have kissed few of them.'[30] The Kinsey researchers reported that they had encountered working-class communities where it was impossible to find a male who had not 'had sexual relations with girls by the time he was 16 or 17 years of age' – such inexperienced males were considered mentally deranged, homosexual, or college-bound.[31]

Without entering the zone of celebrity sex (e.g. Mick Jagger's alleged 4,000 women), we need also to consider sex in far greater numbers than Schofield's more-than-one-partner-a-year subjects.[32] The 1963 diary of the writer Leonard Michaels chronicles a friend:

> The compulsive fucker . . . A scholar, he read voraciously. With books as with girls, insatiable devourer. I was horrified by the girls. Could they be like Horton, shamelessly bestial? Horton said he 'serviced' them. Two a day sometimes, and never showered in between. I was horrified, angry, envious.[33]

For another generation, there is Brett Easton Ellis's archetypal novel of sex and drugs and youthful ennui in Los Angeles. Casual sex, though never named as such, takes on a new indifference in *Less Than Zero* (1985):

> And somewhere along the line, Blair leaves with Rip or maybe with Trent, or maybe Rip leaves with Trent or maybe Rip leaves with the two blond girls sitting next to Trent or maybe Blair leaves with the two blond girls, and I end up dancing with this girl and she leans over to me and whispers that maybe we should go to her place.[34]

The various, indistinguishable characters sleep with each other in bewildering combinations of sexual orientation and gender and no one seems certain of who has fucked or been fucked by whom. 'Blair thinks about it for a moment and then says slowly, evenly, "If Cliff slept with Didi, then he must have slept with . . . Raoul." "Who's Raoul?" Alana and Kim ask at the same time. I open my menu and pretend to read it, wondering if I slept with Raoul. Name seems familiar.'[35]

Historically, then, American casual sex encompassed a range of behaviour and attitudes from rather non-casual, marriage-predicated courtship practices to less committed sex. It also included same-sex activity, and commentators are agreed that even allowing for stereotypes about male homosexual promiscuity, the rates of casual sex among gay males have been higher than for lesbians and the heterosexual population.[36] *The Joy of Gay Sex*, a 1970s classic, consciously validated gay sex, 'whether it be between lovers or strangers'.[37] The Kinsey Institute's 1978 survey of the San Francisco Bay Area reported that 28 per cent of the white homosexual males in the study claimed 1,000 or more homosexual sexual partners during their lifetimes and 60 per cent reputedly had had 250 or more partners.[38] In terms of their sexual history during the year before the survey, 28 per cent reported more than 50 sexual partners.[39] Most of these contacts were with strangers and were one-off episodes – archetypal casual sex.[40] (In comparison, the heterosexual averages could be counted on the fingers of one or two hands.)[41] As the authors of *The Joy of Gay Sex* expressed it, 'Sex is one of life's chief pleasures, and gay men have gained the reputation of being extraordinarily sexually active.'[42]

While it is not the focus of this chapter, it is essential to note that morality and practice changed over time. To return to heterosexual practices, Martin King Whyte's 1984 Detroit area study found that the cohort of women married between 1925 and 1944 said that (on average) they had dated 4–7 males, the baby boomers married from 1945 to 1964 had dated 10–14 males, and the youngest cohort of 1965–84 estimated 12–15 potential premarital sexual partners.[43] Those who were calculated to have had sex before marriage ranged across the cohorts from 24 per cent (1925–44) to 72 per cent (1965–84). But if finer subdivisions are made in the last cohort, it goes to 56 per cent (1965–69), 67 per cent (1970–74), 85 per cent (1975–79), and 88 per cent (1980–84):

> In other words, according to our estimates, it is probably the case that less than 10% of those women in the Detroit area who were marrying in the mid-1980s were still virgins. Clearly a sexual revolution has taken place. From a situation in which 'nice girls don't' we have moved to a new era in which 'most girls do'.[44]

Whyte drew on Kinsey to point out that, traditionally, most of this premarital sexual activity was with the man who became the woman's husband, but that this was changing. Those who had sexual partners other than their eventual husband rose, across the cohorts, from 3 per cent to 17 per cent to 33 per cent, and in the refined breakdown of the last category, from 17 per cent (1965–69) to 51 per cent (1980–84).[45] Given these trends, Whyte argued for what he termed an 'intimacy revolution' rather than a sexual revolution. 'For the vast majority of young people, intimacy in the dating stage serves simply as a further preliminary to the selection of a mate.'[46] The study certainly errs on the side of sexual respectability: only a little over half of his subjects were poor or working class, and he only interviewed the married.[47] But even allowing for this bias, the indication of change seems clear.

Beth Bailey's examination of courtship conventions from 1900 to the 1960s also demonstrates shifting patterns. Dating, which as an actual word can be traced precisely to the 1910s, and to which money became central in ways that will be explored in this chapter, became 'an American Institution' by the 1930s.[48] In the late 1940s and early 1950s, 'going steady' replaced the casually competitive dating.[49] Michael Moffatt's ethnography of college life at Rutgers in the late 1970s and 1980s found that (at the very time that Bailey was publishing her findings) students there were engaging in both casual sex and more durable relationships. Over two-thirds of his sexually active female informants, whom he trusted more than the males, admitted to at least one case of casual sex.[50] Bogle has detected hooking-up culture (including the actual use of the term) in campuses by the 1980s.[51] By the end of the 1990s, of course, conservative commentators were bewailing the end of courtship, the ubiquity of marital infidelity and 'pre-marital promiscuity', and the influence of an elite 'who lack a cultural script whose denouement is marriage'.[52]

Although we could start the history of casual sex earlier than the twentieth century, the intention of this chapter is to provide historical depth to the ahistorical assumptions of some recent studies, so we can begin the prehistory of casual sex in the early twentieth century while still providing the required perspective. Indeed the 'promiscuous intimacies' of this chapter's title comes from the work of the 1920s sociologists of the Chicago School who certainly located uncommitted sex in the communities that they studied as they mapped the sexual potentials of the anonymity and freedom of the furnished rooms' district of Chicago.[53] 'Such is the world of furnished rooms', wrote Harvey Warren Zorbaugh in 1929, 'quick and intimate relationships spring up in the most casual way, and dissolve as quickly and as casually.'[54] 'I am no longer lonely', one of Chicago's North Side's inhabitants told the sociologist,

> I am surprised to find that I can actually enjoy the girls I pick up at public dance halls, at restaurants, along the lake front, in the park. I know a great many of them now – many of them pretty and clever, and good companions for a night. I no longer go with prostitutes . . . For the city is full of women who are just as lonely as I was, or who draw on their sex as I would on my bank to pay for the kind of clothes they want to wear, the kinds of shows they want to see. Then, too, there are the 'emancipated' women, who don't want to marry, who are not 'gold diggers', but who feel the need of a man and a normal sex life.[55]

This was the world of the taxi-dance halls, where, as the name implies, women were hired by the dance: 'Like the taxi-driver with his cab, she is for public hire and is paid in proportion to the time spent and the services rendered.'[56] We know a great deal about this site of casual sex because it was a focus of attention in the early part of the twentieth century. The New York

34 Reginald Marsh, *Ten Cents a Dance*, 1933. Whitney Museum of American Art, New York; Felicia Meyer Marsh Bequest. © Reginald Marsh/ARS. Licensed by Viscopy, 2017.

artist and illustrator Reginald Marsh produced *Ten Cents a Dance* (1933), now in the New Whitney Museum of American Art, a lush, colourful painting of ample-bodied, gold and crimson, satin-clad women, gathered at the balcony of the dance hall, exhibiting fleshly promise – perhaps a visual rendering of the fantasies of many a male patron (see Figure 34).[57] The writer Henry Miller's second wife June was a taxi dancer, and he wrote in *Tropic of Capricorn* (1939) about a visit to the Roseland Dance Hall in the 1920s, 'sizing up the taxi girls all diaphanously gowned, powdered, perfumed, looking fresh and alert but probably bored as hell and leg weary. Into each and every one of them, as I shuffle about, I throw an imaginary fuck. The place is just plastered with cunt and fuck.'[58] He continued: 'This is no harmless recreation . . . this is serious business. At each end of the floor there is a sign reading "No Improper Dancing Allowed". Well and good . . . In Pompeii they probably hung a phallus up. This is the American way. It means the same thing.'[59] There was not much sign of 'cunt and fuck' when the Roseland women were photographed ten years later in a series of pictures capturing the lives of taxi dancers. They all looked rather desultory (see Figure 35).

35 Roseland Dance Hall, New York, 1937. © Bettmann: Getty Images.

The moral reformers of New York's Committee of Fourteen were particularly interested in taxi dances. One investigator reported his interactions at the Melody Gardens Dance Hall at West 23rd Street in 1928, the very time that Miller was writing of, and he was excitedly repetitive about the sexual contact involved in such venues:

> During the time I (#5) was dancing with Mitzi she danced very close and would stand for a period of two or three minutes violently rubbing her sexual parts against my body. She also did this with other men she danced with (on 3 or 4 occasions, but for a longer period than with me) . . . The procedure is for the girls to stand at the entrance of the dance floor and to solicit men to dance. Two ticket takers are also on the dance floor at convenient places to collect tickets and in such a position where they can easily observe all couples dancing. We observed during all these dances that five or six of the couples would dance to the far right hand corner of the dance hall which was slightly darker than the other part. They would remain there throughout the entire period of the dance, standing in one position and rubbing their sexual parts violently against each other. Two of these couples in particular were observed to dance most indecently. The men would bend the girls far over and hold her in a steady position for nearly 3 or 4 minutes while both of them would violently rub their parts against each other. This was in plain view of the manager who occasionally came to the rail and could easily observe what was going on.[60]

'Taxi-Dance Hall', one of the sketches that Marsh did for *The New Yorker* in 1931, could almost have been of these 'rubbing' interactions, for the couples are intertwined in a clearly suggestive manner – right under the sign 'No objectionable dancing allowed' (see Figure 36).

One of the Chicago School's best studies was devoted to this very subject; the taxi dance, wrote Ernest W. Burgess, was 'organized to exploit for profit a situation of promiscuity', and promiscuity, he explained, was 'intimate behavior upon the basis of casual association'.[61] The *raison d'être* of the taxi dance was fleeting sexual contact, either in the form of the momentary spells of dancing (and possible erotic contact in the form of that genital rubbing) or the longer-term arrangements of a 'date' after closing.[62] (Taxi dances were closed to female customers and also to African American men.) Its attraction for its patron was that 'it offers him certain pleasures to be enjoyed without disclosing his identity and without the need for becoming involved with those met'.[63] The fact that, like all casual sex environments, sex might or might not eventuate, or that such contacts might lead to more permanent arrangements, did nothing to negate the importance of the dance hall as a site for what Paul Cressey called 'promiscuous intimacies'.[64]

This world of casual sex clearly merged with the demi-monde, and the investigators' reports for New York's Committee of Fourteen archive the sexual possibilities from the 1900s to the 1930s. Although twenty-first-century definitions of casual sex do not usually include paid sex – as contact is predicated on mutual desire rather than monetary exchange – this was clearly not the case in the early twentieth century, when paid sex was a form of this yet-to-be-named casual sex. Hotels provided suggestive entertainment and permitted open sexual interaction among patrons.[65] Restaurants were eateries by day and clubs by night. The Pepper Pot at 146 West 4th Street in 1927 offered prostitution, by both women and fairies (exaggeratedly effeminate homosexuals).[66] The waiter at the Golden Gate, another restaurant on West 4th Street, 'offered to procure one of the girls in the place to perform an act of perversion in the lavatory'.[67] Frances Donovan, who wrote a remarkable piece of participant sociology working as a waitress in a variety of restaurants, tea rooms, and cafes in Chicago in 1917, referred to what she termed the 'Sex Game', where 'the man is the one pursued, the woman the pursuer'.[68] Sometimes sex was promised but withheld: 'I always keep two or three fellows on the string and I get all I can out of them. I never "come through" unless I have to.'[69] Sometimes it was delivered: 'A pretty girl was telling how much she had made that day in tips and someone said, "Tell us how you do it Daisy". "I do this to them under the table", answered Daisy, making a suggestive movement.'[70]

36 Reginald Marsh, 'Taxi-Dance Hall', *The New Yorker*, 13 February 1932. © Reginald Marsh/ARS. Licensed by Viscopy, 2017.

And the taxi dances were but one category of such entertainment; Cressey identified fourteen different types of dance establishment in Chicago before 1932.[71] He was keen to preserve the special status of his subject, but there was considerable slippage between forms. The Strand Roof Garden Dance Restaurant in New York admitted both male and female patrons, mainly book-keepers, clerks, stenographers, and those involved in the music business on Broadway, but also employed male and female instructors. Two of the male coaches were said to be 'assiduous date-makers and go the limit'.[72] Then there were the 1920s dancing studios where sex could be purchased: 'I am supposed only to instruct you, but if you want me to make you come you will have to pay me extra', which was $10 in the bathroom.[73] A woman at the Martha Dancing Studio offered the investigator relief for the same sum: 'let me open your pants and I'll jerk it off'.[74] The instructress at Remenyi's Dancing School on East 84th Street wanted '$3 for a straight lay and $5 for French'.[75] One of the women at the Adele Studio claimed that she made as much as $80 in tips from just rubbing up against men and was not interested when asked for 'a little party' (that is private sexual intercourse).[76]

Moral investigators found what were known as 'charity girls', young women who worked by day in factories, hotels, stores, and offices, and who engaged in what was interpreted as casual prostitution at night, though they did not see it as such:

> [a] large number of girls and young women who sin sexually in return only for the pleasures given or the company of the men with whom they

> consort . . . They have no ethical standards and believe that they have as good a right, as it is generally supposed men have, to lead a double life; that they have a right to the pleasure they can gain from their bodies if they can do so without exposure.[77]

A 1914 study of working-class, Irish-American, West Side Manhattan wrote of young factory girls who worked from 7 a.m. to 5.30 p.m. and then danced several nights a week to 2 a.m. or 3 a.m. Budgets were tight and clothing was often on instalment, but if a young woman walked to work she could save the car fare to the dance and its entrance fee; then, if she met a man, he would pay for her fare back home – 'a "pick-up" is easy to acquire'.[78]

'Treating', sponsorship by men in return for anticipated sexual favours, reflected a culture where sex was seen as part of a commercial transaction, and many young women were adept at negotiating their way through this combination of sexual pleasure and danger.[79] A Committee of Fourteen undercover investigator encountered the environment of the charity girls at Corso's Cabaret on East 86th Street in New York in 1929, a place with tables, an orchestra, and dancing. A waiter told him that most of the girls who came to the cabaret were 'servants, chambermaids and working girls. They all are out for the purpose of meeting men with whom they would like to have sexual intercourse if they like them.' The waiter explained that it was cheaper to get a 'lay' from the women at the cabaret than the hostess/prostitutes in the speakeasies or other clubs. They had to be plied with drink and then paid for sex, whereas the women in his cabaret (charity girls) made do with a dance or two, a few drinks, and 'the price of a pair of shoes or a hat'.[80]

The investigators were knowledgeable about this sexual culture. One, who visited a dance hall on Flatbush Avenue in Brooklyn where 'charity girls' met their men, implied that the young women sought the safety of numbers, going out in pairs or groups. They were not 'professional prostitutes' – though 'would probably accept money if it would be given to them' – but rather out for 'a good time'. The men whom they went out with were of modest means; they would take them to a cabaret, 'buy the girls sodas or ice cream, dance with them, then take them to a chop suey restaurant'. Then on the way home afterwards, they might 'have intercourse'. 'I was told that most of the girls in here will do anything for a man that they go out [with] and who is a good sport.'[81]

It is clear from the various reported interactions that we should not assume that the endpoint of such casual heterosexual sex was always sexual intercourse. (We should recall the earlier discussion about petting.) The Strand Roof Garden clientele – male and female – were referred to as 'salamanders', or fireproof; 'they will go all the way up to the limit, but they do not often overstep that mark'.[82] More than one Committee of Fourteen undercover investigator went through the hopeful scenario outlined above, feeding and entertaining a date without the desired outcome. One, who met his contact at the Diana Dance Hall where she worked as an instructress, said that she had 'offered to go out for a good time (sexual intercourse)'. She suggested going to a restaurant and then said that she had been kidding about the intercourse but had a friend who might have sex with him for money. The friend arrived and suggested that they go to a movie, which they did. Then they returned to the restaurant and the first woman went to work and the second had a meal and then proposed going to a cabaret. The investigator said that that was not what he had in mind but she said that she did not know him well enough and promised to call him at his hotel the next day. There was no call.[83] These men were being played. Such interactions were prolonged negotiations, a sounding out, with the man implying that he would pay for sex, and the woman resisting any commitment on that front while extracting a long night out from him, at his expense.

Cressey described the taxi-dance hall as the site of a mutual struggle between male and female:

> The dominant scheme of life for both patrons and taxi-dancers grows out of the combined commercial and romantic interests and the necessary casual intimacies with many patrons. It is represented in the motive of exploitation toward the other sex, prominent in the minds of most seasoned taxi-dancers and of not a few patrons.[84]

Female success was suggested by the glossary of words indicating susceptible males ('fish', 'fruit') and advantageous economic arrangements ('paying the rent', 'buying the groceries', 'playing').[85] One woman, who worked in a dress shop by day and partied by night until 5 a.m., told a New York investigator that she was not 'afraid of men. I know how to take care of myself.' She said too that she 'came into contact with all kinds of girls and women, learn a lot, see a whole lot and never follow their footsteps'.[86] But the dangers were clear too: a 'line-up' indicated not necessarily consensual group sex involving several men and a woman.[87]

The scenarios varied. As described above, women might meet men and go with them for an evening, the man paying for entertainment in return for company and possibly sex of some kind. Or women would go steady with a man (or several men) for a period of time with much the same arrangements. One such man told Cressey about a rather open arrangement with a taxi dancer:

> Ann wasn't what you'd call promiscuous. She had an understanding with four fellows by which she'd restrict herself to us four. She picked us out and then invited us into the arrangement. We each contributed something. Two of us paid her rent, another paid her groceries, and the fourth fellow bought some of her clothes. There was never any jealousy among us. Often we'd meet at her apartment and sit around together. It got to be quite a joke who'd get to stay . . . As far as any of us ever knew she was faithful to this arrangement as long as it lasted – for over four months.[88]

Sometimes sex was merely a lure. In his novel *Sexus* (1950), about life in New York in the 1920s, Miller wrote of

> old men, nice old men . . . at the dance hall. What they wanted was to have the company of a beautiful young girl – someone they could eat with and take to the theater. They didn't really care about dancing – or even going to bed with a girl. They wanted to be *seen* with young women.[89]

His wife June supported Miller in his early years through the generosity of the various wealthy men whom she strung along.

While the moral commentators said that such women had no ethics, Elizabeth Clement has argued that they had a clear morality. Treating fell between the traditional sexual culture that permitted courting couples to have intercourse when the declared intention of such courtship was marriage, and (on the other hand) the culture of prostitution. It was a 'moral middle ground'.[90] The charity girls distinguished themselves from prostitutes in that they exercised more choice than merely exchanging sex for money and that acceptance of kind rather than money meant that they were not for hire.[91] The 1917 investigator of the earlier-mentioned Chicago waitresses, who in effect operated as charity girls, observed that their activity 'borders upon prostitution' but they were not prostitutes because they earned their living by their waiting rather than by any extra activities. 'The girl earns her own living but the man takes her to places of amusement where she has the opportunity to wear her clothes. He may also give her money or articles of wearing apparel but these are in the nature of a gift rather than in payment of a service rendered.'[92] When asked, some charity girls said that they also did it for the sex: as one Chicago woman put it, 'Frankly, I like intercourse.'[93] Taxi dancers referred to the thrill and excitement of the dance hall life. 'I know all men are deceitful, but I still can't get on without them. It used to be that one man at a time was enough, but now since I'm married I've got to have several.'[94]

We should also consider the clubs and nightlife in Harlem and elsewhere, including the buffet flats, small clubs in private houses or apartments, usually run by women, where alcohol and gambling and sex were available. The African American singer Bessie Smith's niece Ruby Walker gave a good description of one in Detroit that they attended in the 1920s, where there were live sex performances involving two men (in one act) and (in the other) a woman with a lighted cigarette and a Coca-Cola bottle – 'she could do all them things with her pussy – an educated pussy, you know'. As Ruby put it, 'It was nothing but faggots and bulldykers, a real open house. Everything went on in that house – tongue baths, you name it. They called them buffet flats because buffet means *everything*, everything that was in the life.'[95]

The Digital Harlem Project has charted the leisure venues in Harlem in the 1920s: the speakeasies (bars with entertainment) and nightclubs, as well as the buffet flats.[96] It shows impressive coverage but was just the tip of the iceberg, in the sense that these are only the ones that left some historical imprint. These venues, potential sites for fleeting sexual contact, were not confined to Harlem but were all over Manhattan. In the West Village in 1931, around 18th and 19th Streets, near the docks, there were 75 speakeasies for each block. Sometimes called smoke joints, they were modest venues, with a sitting room and beer. There were 1,000 such places on the Bowery in the Lower East Side.[97]

There were also what were called rent parties, occasional affairs where residents helped to pay their rent (hence the name) by charging admission (25 cents) to what was in effect a party, with drink, food, music (usually a piano player), and dancing provided, either as part of the deal or for extra cost. The point was to raise money. The black writer Wallace Thurman wrote in 1927 that rent parties were 'Harlem institutions'. He counted twelve in one block and five in one apartment house with forty flats. 'The music will be barbarous and slow. The dancers will use their bodies and the bodies of their partners without regard to the conventions. There will be little restraint . . . Here "low" Harlem is in its glory, primitive and unashamed.'[98]

Nor was this leisure and sexual culture limited to New York. Cynthia Blair has discussed an identical milieu in Chicago's South Side Black Belt, from 22nd to 55th Streets, with its commercialised and sexualised leisure – theatres, nightclubs, cabarets, buffet flats, saloons, live sex shows, dancing, blues, jazz, and prostitution – what she calls black women's 'sex entrepreneurship'.[99]

It is also worth noting that the physical contacts crossed the boundaries of heterosexuality and homosexuality – if we can even talk of such boundaries at that time. Ruby Walker's reference to 'in the life' hints at this sexual world. The reports of the Committee of Fourteen on speakeasies and nightclubs provide many examples from the 1920s. There are references to 'Pussy Parties' ('a party where various forms of sex perversions are committed') and 'Bushers' (men who perform oral sex on women).[100] One investigator was taken in 1928 to an apartment at 108 West 137th Street

> by a casual who wanted to show him a 'Woman's Party', as he called it. At the time of the visit there were 15 women and 7 men, all colored, present. Women were dancing with each other imitating the motions of sexual intercourse and the men were dancing with each other, all indecently. Some of the women had their dresses pulled up to their thighs. The madame said 'This is a freakish party. Everyone in here is a bull dagger or faggot.' One of the women solicited investigator for prostitution for the sum of $5 to be committed in her room at this place. One of the men present also solicited investigator for an act of perversion.[101]

Finally, we should note the sexually abandoned world outlined in George W. Henry's *Sex Variants* (1941), a snapshot of New York in the 1920s and 1930s.[102] As one might expect, Henry's 'bisexual' cases recorded a labile sexuality as well as considerable promiscuity. Donald H. described mutual masturbation and sex between the thighs with sailors, and sex with a man and his wife (sodomising the man while he had intercourse with his wife). He had group sex with two young hoboes and three nurses – what he called 'normal sexual relations'. Though married, he took up with a 'very masculine looking' former gangster who alternated between fairies and women.[103] This practitioner of polymorphous sex thought that he was being unfaithful to his wife when 'a cunt' was involved but not when he was having sex with a man – 'I am better able to satisfy my wife if I have a man every now and then.'[104] We might also anticipate a fluid sexuality in the cases classified as 'narcissistic' (another of Henry's categories). Max N., who claimed that some weeks he had a 'new boy every night', was attracted both to virile men and the 'obviously effeminate', but had also participated in 'mass sex relations', 'parties in which both men and women took part'.[105] Several of those whom Henry talked to referred to group sex:

> Once I saw three men and three women lying crosswise of the bed. They were all having normal sex and they wanted me [a cross-dressing male prostitute] to get in on it. There were six or seven of both sexes watching, laughing and drinking. Some of them were show girls.[106]

A woman would arrange for men to have sex while she watched.[107] One of Henry's 'homosexuals' (his final category) mentioned 'a daisy chain', in which women might well take part.[108] So there is frequent reference both to group and serial sex, of a somewhat casual character. Another 'homosexual' told his classifier that he had had sex with many 'homosexual men, most of them pick-ups', but was also going out with women; 'In the past ten years it's been about the same. I have spasms now and then with men or women but mostly with men. This last week I slept with a different person every night. Some of them were women and none of them interested me.'[109]

Henry's bisexual women also indicate a sexual flexibility and multiplicity of partners. Pearl M., an African American singer, remained with her second husband but had had sexual relations with women, including one 'who sought both men and women'.[110] Molly N., who had been married twice, was quite graphic in her descriptions of the sexual practices of those she had been involved with, outlining oral, anal, and group sex as well as various sado-masochistic practices. 'I think I'm bisexual but I prefer women', she explained, 'I'm not so much thrilled now with a man.' She recounted an incident when her mother had walked in on her after she had had sex with a female lover and the lover was 'performing fellatio on a young man who was present'.[111] Roberta H. was another woman who was kept by men but involved with women. 'Her penchant is for women but except for two instances her relationships with them have been casual, fleeting, and purely for sensation. Her economic needs are cared for by men and she does not hesitate to exploit her attraction for them to earn an easy living.'[112]

Henry wrote of Fannie E.,

> For two or three years she has lived with men, and she has also engaged in a series of liaisons with women. She spends practically her whole time in the pursuit of such entertainment as is to be had in dingy cafés in the Village and in Harlem where with much drinking she spends days and nights with whatever bedfellow is at hand.[113]

Marian J., a professional entertainer who had a reputation in theatrical circles for her expertise in 'lingual caresses', told Henry 'I'm in the habit of using my mouth and whether it's a man or a woman just depends on my mood.'[114] Another woman described herself as a 'landmark in all the well-known speakeasies, especially those frequented by women. During that time I have been everybody's and anybody's girl.'[115]

Given the silences in studies of hooking up, which are predominantly confined to heterosexual sex, it is important to stress that casual sex is homosexual as well as heterosexual.[116] And, as already intimated, the subject assumes a different dimension when it comes to male homosexuality.[117] Take this description of a bar in Greenwich Village in the 1970s:

> Facing the screen, the crowd of boys was so thick you could scarcely move, the noise deafening, the heat terrible. Behind two or three rows of attentive spectators there was nothing but groping, sucking, or complex fucking, all in the powerful stink of poppers. You couldn't actually stay there very long, for fear of smothering.[118]

The encounter occurs without words, based merely on a smile and eye contact:

> We kissed each other, we pressed close together, and unzipped each other's trousers. I sucked his cock, he sucked mine . . . we kissed on the floor, and could easily have been trampled or smothered. It was very difficult to get back up. Hands from unidentified sources brushed over our chests, our asses, mouths appeared in the vicinity of our cocks.

Then, eventually, the first words occur (with 'our jeans somewhere around our ankles'), 'Let's get out of here for a while.'[119]

Renaud Camus's elegant *Tricks* (1981) dwells on 25 such casual encounters in the space of six months in 1978, not a huge total of sexual contacts one might think, though the number of subsidiary interactions is considerably larger given that these incidents often included group or multiple sex. Intriguingly, as Roland Barthes observed in his preface to the work, its author manages to speak homosexuality without actually speaking about it, and the same could be observed of its casual sex: 'never to invoke, not to let Names into language – Names, the source of dispute, of arrogance and of moralizing'.[120] That is to say, casual sex is described but not named, and male same-sex acts are recalled in detail without any philosophising about their meanings or any attempt at identity-work. (Camus, it should be acknowledged, is perfectly capable of philosophising on other matters.) These encounters led to sex; but it may be more accurate to say that the sex led to an encounter, for the sex was invariably very quick in coming. For there to be a trick there has to be an outcome. These are first encounters. Some were the beginnings of something more, a longer association, perhaps a relationship. But this was never their intent and was unknown when the subject of these recollections, the trick, occurred. 'A trick must be unknown, or almost so. Only first encounters are related here.'[121] Sometimes no words are spoken; no names are exchanged. Of the man known only as 'Plaid Shirt', Camus records, 'He wanted to make me come too, but I had already begun to button up. He did the same. We smiled at each other for the first time, and exchanged a light punch on the shoulder. We had not uttered a single word.'[122] Sometimes the names are given after the acts and in the process of leaving, never to cross paths nor, if paths do cross, to acknowledge one another again. 'Never saw him again' is a common conclusion. The intensity of physical and intimate sex contrasts with the curious lack of intimacy of their verbal interaction, sometimes non-existent as already hinted, occasionally profound, but more often quotidian (if not banal).

One of the intriguing aspects of Camus's sexual stories is that they were by no means tales of success. Whether it was the ennui of excess or merely a refreshing candour, he was remarkably casual about some of his casual sex: 'To tell the truth, I wasn't at all sure I wanted to go home with him, there wasn't much about him that turned me on except the desire he seemed to have for me . . . I touched several bodies, virtually at random. But no one really interested me.'[123] The purity of this casualness could be challenged. There was nothing especially random about the rituals of cruising, the chosen venues (bars, parks, clubs, movie theatres, porn stores), the sartorial themes of denim and corduroy and repetitive codes of grooming (the ubiquitous 1970s moustache), the muscularity of bodies. *The Joy of Gay Sex* warned that one of the risks of one-night stands was compulsivity: 'Everything about your sex life, including you, becomes routinized.'[124] Some of Camus's men were already known by sight or even by name, so contact was neither strictly anonymous nor arbitrary. A few, as already implied, would lose their trick's status through familiarity and repetition: 'Perhaps he will be more than a trick. But at the moment of writing, Wednesday, he can still be considered as such.'[125]

Steven Seidman has discussed the ambiguities of such homosexual casual sex. It was 'pleasure-centered', act-based, impersonal, and 'any expectations of intimacy, commitment and responsibility are restricted to the encounter'.[126] Yet it was 'not necessarily an emotionally empty, anonymous exchange'.[127] In ways that Camus illustrated, casual sex could be selective, personal, and intimate. The science fiction writer Samuel Delany once referred to long-term 'nonsexual' friendships developing out of casual sex, interestingly comparing them to the sorts of acquaintances that could arise from a conversation in a grocery store or with the postman, as if casual sex was equally quotidian.[128] Even in sites specifically arranged for their impersonality, as Martin Weinberg and Colin Williams found of the gay baths, 'human beings often have a difficult time sustaining complete impersonality'.[129]

One could argue for significant qualitative as well as quantitative differences between some forms of heterosexual and homosexual casual sex. This is exactly what Michel Foucault had in mind in 1982 when he said – in contrast to Giacomo Casanova's observation that the greatest moment in a (heterosexual) love affair is when one is climbing the stairs before the encounter – that for the homosexual 'the best moment of love is when the lover leaves in the taxi'. He elaborated,

> Now, when sexual encounters become extremely easy and numerous, as is the case with homosexuality nowadays, complications are only introduced after the fact. In this type of casual encounter it is only after making love that one becomes curious about the other person. Once the sexual act has been consummated you find yourself asking your partner, 'By the way, what was your name?'[130]

The nature of the sex varied with the site. Tea-room sex, in public restrooms, was invariably impersonal and silent. 'One may spend many hours in these buildings and witness dozens of sexual acts without hearing a word', Laud Humphreys reported. 'Often, in tearoom stalls, the only portions of the players' bodies that touch are the mouth of the insertee and the penis of the insertor; and the mouths of these partners seldom open for speech.'[131] This did not indicate lack of communication. 'No amount of written description can capture the subtle, complex contrapuntal web of communications that take place during tearoom eroticism.'[132] The sociologist Edward William Delph was almost certainly valorising toilet sex, but he was alert to the subtleties of 1970s anonymous sex. Silence focused the sex. 'In the silent face-to-face situation, the participant remains a stranger, albeit a physically intimate one. He is able to focus on sexual activities to a degree that would be much more difficult to do if speech revealed his emotions, ideas, ideals, social status, occupation.'[133] Delph dissected the graduations of impersonality: from the visual anonymity of the glory hole, and the darkened club back-rooms and interiors of parked trucks, to the more visual, but still silent, depersonalised sex of the orgy rooms, bars, baths, and the 'meat racks' found at certain beaches and parks. 'JUST FOR SEX': that was the focus.[134] The tea room was 'the erotic oasis par excellence'; 'the homosexual bath is devoted exclusively to immediate sexual gratification'.[135]

There is no doubting the essential elements of this form of casual sex. Sometimes it was with someone not clearly seen, as in a Los Angeles bath house: 'The Invisible Man tipped Tony over onto his back, raised his thighs and for a long time licked his ass, while behind him, I licked his. Then, kneeling, he fucked Tony. He was kissing him. And I fucked the ass of the fucker.'[136] It was ephemeral, transitory, outside or supplemental to the context of a longer-term sexual relationship; Camus's longer-term partner accompanied him on several of these adventures. It was sex without any necessary emotional commitment. The composer Ned Rorem, more reflective than Camus, told an interviewer in 1973 that

> Anonymity can be so uninhibited, the sex so incredibly fulfilling, that it could never be repeated with the same person, precisely because the next time he would *be* a person . . . Promiscuity does not mean hopeless seeking. Promiscuity means: renewal of perfection under different circumstances. Because perfection, by definition, can't be duplicated.[137]

And, as touched on earlier, it was sex in numbers, quantity, that of itself negated the possibility of any attachment other than that of the intensity of the moment. 'The *thousands* of people I went to bed with!' Rorem recalled of the war years of the 1940s.[138] One of Delph's informants recalled fellating 17 men in the baths one night. He could not remember anything about any of those he was involved with; 'all he recalled was that he did 17 – the number seemingly more important than any of the particulars'.[139] In 1983 a friend who had been researching AIDS told Samuel Delany to forget about press stories of 100 to 300 sexual contacts per year; the men that he knew had a lot more casual sex, 'Three hundred a month *minimum* is a lot more like it.'

> And the straight people who are working with people with AIDS just have no idea what's out there and sexually available in this city . . . it just never occurs to them that this is someone who may have had three sexual encounters in the last 20 minutes on the way to the doctor's office.[140]

The friend was preaching to the converted. In 1984, when he was in his early forties, Delany estimated that he had had ten to fifteen thousand sexual encounters.[141] The gay activist Hal Call, former president of the Mattachine Society, claimed in an interview in 1995 that he had 'probably had sexual contact with more than six thousand males'.[142]

In comparison with Chicago and New York in the 1920s and 1930s and with homosexual casual sex during the 1970s, the forms of heterosexual casual sex that have attracted the most attention seem markedly constrained in their sexualities: recall Reiss's 'permissive' sex in anticipation of marriage. Morton Hunt's survey of sex in the early 1970s detected casual or 'recreational' sex, but saw it as a minor moment in the inexorable quest for romantic commitment: 'Even while it asserts its freedom from marriage, it is an apprenticeship for marriage'. 'Where . . . are those wild teen-agers we have all heard about?'[143] Casual sex at Rutgers in the 1980s existed amid a prevailing sexual conservatism: 'The majority of these self-reporters said they had restricted themselves, by and large, to sex with commitment and to conventional heterosexual practices.'[144]

As Ellis touched on in his 1968 article, casual sex also included 'swinging', less acceptably referred to as 'wife swapping', in vogue in the late 1960s and early 1970s.[145] By 1976 Betty Fang was already able to talk retrospectively about swinging as 'the agreement between husband and wife to have sexual relations with other people, in contexts in which they both engage in such behavior at the same time and usually in the same place'.[146] What distinguished swinging from marital or relationship infidelity (or adultery) was that both partners knew: 'What is crucial to this definition is the mutual consent, knowledge, and approval of the participants.'[147]

The academic commentators of the 1970s were especially intrigued by the ordinariness of this practice, the containment of sexual deviance within conventional structures – the emergence of 'middle-class deviant subcultures' as one study termed it.[148] Swinging was heterosexual (apart from some cursory female–female contact), middle-class, white, suburban, and middle American. Swinging both is and is not casual sex. It is linked to casual sex in that one of its justifications is sex without emotional involvement. However, the description of the practice as 'an institutionalized form of extramarital sex' suggests organisation rather than randomness.[149] Moreover, swinging could result in far from transient relationships, and was indeed justified in terms of increasing rather than ignoring emotional commitment. A more recent account of twenty-first-century swinging insists on its disruptive effects, challenging the assumptions of monogamy, yet still writes in terms of its reinforcement of that very relationship: 'the act of non-monogamy is designed to stimulate . . . additional sexual activity, enhancing a bond with the primary partner, resulting in a more emotionally monogamous relationship'.[150]

Another lure of swinging for the social scientist has been its perceived functionality. A practice that provided the 'experience of impersonal and varied sex in a context which minimises any threats to a conventional marriage and life-style' takes us somewhat away from what most people think of as casual sex.[151] As one of the first studies of swinging pointed out, of all the various ways for husbands and wives to seek sexual variety outside of their relationship, 'mate swapping is the least threatening and the one most compatible with monogamy'.[152] Swinging did (and does) little to challenge the sexual status quo.

Finally, we come to hooking up, the practice presented as archetypal, contemporary casual sex in ways that have prompted this historical inquiry. It too is rather limited in its sexual parameters. On the face of it, the concept seems unproblematic. Hooking up refers to a brief, uncommitted, sexual encounter. However, there are actually many qualifications. What a sexual encounter is varies greatly. It ranges from kissing to full intercourse, but may merely mean spending the night with someone involving companionship, literally sleeping together.[153] Only 30 per cent of participants in a New Jersey study had engaged in hook-ups involving actual sexual intercourse.[154] A mere 4 per cent of those involved in a study of alcohol and 'casual coupling' reported having had sexual intercourse during their reported alcohol-fuelled event. The hooking up in the study's title referred primarily to kissing and (that vague concept) 'making out'.[155] It may include oral sex, although given a culture where oral–genital contact may be explicitly excluded from definitions of sex, one could be pedantic and say that this is not casual *sex* either.[156] It is not only the type of sex but also the reported incidence of hooking up that shows its limitations. One of the common statistics proffered in the literature to argue for its cultural currency is that between '60–80% of college students engage in *at least one* of these encounters' or that 'most studies show that a large majority of undergraduate students will hook up *at least once* while in college'.[157] A 2014 study, employing social survey data, found that over half of the respondents had had only one sexual partner in the previous year and a significant proportion (17 per cent) had experienced no sex at all.[158] (Notably, nearly 40 per cent were against same-sex sex.) The researchers concluded that the stereotype of rampant, uncommitted college sex was highly questionable. The Online College Social Life Survey (2005–11) indicates that the time-honoured, long-term relationship and dating exist alongside the newer hook-ups in campus sex. Only 8 per cent of the surveyed students eschewed the more established forms of sexual contact for an exclusive focus on hooking up.[159] So apart from being predominantly heterosexual in its assumptions – not much gay sex here – and not necessarily involving intercourse, or even more than one sexual encounter, the nature of this form of casual sex is imprecise. In Moffat's 1980s study, one male described mutual masturbation with a girlfriend, fellatio and cunnilingus, 'pseudo sex through the pants', and other genital–bodily contact, yet ended his account with the observation: 'we never did have sex'.[160]

What we do know is that hooking up is depressingly gendered: 'I would never, ever date a girl I banged on the first night.'[161] Males gain status through multiple partners: females lose status. Women want commitment:

men want sex.[162] Despite the professed egalitarian standards of many college students, and even the 'reverse double standards' of some, studies still show the currency of the traditional double standard and the power disadvantages and 'inequitable power dynamics' that mean women are more likely to be pressured into 'unwanted sexual activities' and to subordinate their own sexual pleasure to their male partners.[163]

The casualness of this form of casual sex is also questionable. Many of the hook-ups are with people already known, friends of friends rather than anonymous strangers.[164] Some of the hook-ups are regular, may develop into something more meaningful, indeed for some participants (especially women) may be part of a strategy to form more lasting relationships, and are part of a campus culture based on a shared ethnic, class, and educational background, a sense of community, and the feelings of safety that these shared assumptions bring.[165] Therefore the sex may not be especially sexual; and the casual may be somewhat more prescribed. Those studying hooking up routinely admit the non-representational nature of their studies' cohorts, and even that the incidence and enjoyment of the sexual encounters has been overestimated, but some will still claim it has 'become part of the cultural script' more generally, and that it is 'normative despite widespread student non-participation'.[166]

'Friends with benefits', another newly named script of college sex, where 'friends engage in sexual activity but do not define their relationship as romantic', seems even less casual.[167] Though it is supposedly sex without commitment, it is not casual because – by definition – it involves friendship and an ongoing relationship. In any case, it is by no means clear how common the practice is. Surveys claim that as many as 60 per cent of college students have experienced at least one such relationship, but the imprecision of questioning (confusion between one-off sex with a friend and an ongoing arrangement) does not inspire confidence in these results.[168] However, one (more searching) study of young males found that although they were well aware of the scripts of both hooking up and friends with benefits, few actually conformed to them; their lived sexual experiences were, as the researchers put it, 'a mixture of committed, semi-committed, and nonrelational sexual relationships'.[169]

Casual sex recurred in a variety of cultural mappings during the twentieth century and people certainly engaged in it before it was actually called 'casual sex'. In the early to mid twentieth century, casual sex shaded into prostitution in ways not true of more recent casual sex. The 1940s sex histories of working-class men for Kinsey's study indicate that nearly 75 per cent had experienced sex with prostitutes.[170] Clement is convincing in her argument for a shift in American culture from one where treating, courtship, and prostitution overlapped in a manner unimaginable to contemporary culture, to a situation where dating both replaced and incorporated elements of these earlier forms.[171]

We have seen that before casual sex was named, both 1930s and 1950s sociologists were writing about sex in anticipation of marriage versus sex without commitment, however they chose to term the latter. Indeed Willard Waller's research on the sexual culture of college students in the 1930s anticipated the more recent phenomenon of hooking up when he drew a distinction between courtship, a process 'to induct young persons into marriage by a series of progressive commitments', and dating. 'Dating is not true courtship, since it is supposed not to eventuate in marriage; it is a sort of dalliance relationship . . . dating is largely dominated by the quest of the thrill and is regarded as an amusement.'[172] Waller's dating, then, approaches casual sex. Dating is pleasure-seeking rather than a search for long-term commitment. In Winston Ehrmann's study of late 1940s and early 1950s college students, the name for the subjects of casual sex was 'pick-ups'. A pick-up, he explained, meant 'a person of the opposite sex whom one had known previously only casually or not at all and whom one dated for the sole purpose of having sexual intercourse'.[173]

Yet the history of casual sex should not be limited to college patterns. Elijah Anderson's research into the 1980s sexual culture of inner-city Philadelphia revealed a code that he described as the mating game, where, for young males, sex without commitment conferred status.[174] The culture did not call it casual sex: it was getting 'pussy', getting 'some', 'getting over', 'booty', 'trickin''.[175] But peer esteem came from having sex with as many women as possible. 'The peer group places a high value on sex, especially what middle-class people call casual sex.'[176] (Ehrmann's college males, it is worth noting, tended to date women lower in the social scale when they wanted uncomplicated sex.)[177]

We have seen that the ideology of heterosexual romance and the possibility of more lasting commitment stalk representations of casual sex. Its temporariness can hold the promise of permanency. In Philadelphia's street culture, amid much evidence to the contrary, young women still had hopes of 'playin' house', as those young men attempting to avoid such commitment termed domestic life.[178] The young male university soccer players interviewed for a 2012 study (they were aged between 18 and 22) clung to the ideal of monogamy in their relationships while simultaneously breaching that ideal through sexual cheating – 'At least with cheating there is an attempt at monogamy.'[179] An earlier-referenced qualitative study of hooking up and friends with benefits found that such 'nonrelational sexual relationships' were 'the exception rather than the norm'.[180] This stress on heteronormativity is not to deny the articulated pleasures of one-off sexual encounters, both before and after the naming of casual sex: the appeal of Cressey's 'promiscuous intimacies'; the joys of gay male sex; the pleasure of the young soccer players' monogamy-breaching.

As explained in this chapter's introduction, my purpose has not been a systematic history but rather the employment of particular historical illustrations as a way of rethinking a concept. As will hopefully now be clear, casual sex did not spring fully formed, history-less, in the college culture of the postmodern *fin de siècle*. The examples of opposite-sex interactions in the 1920s and same-sex encounters in the 1970s demonstrate that casual sex has a rich and nuanced past. Thus when Kathleen Bogle compares the increased 'sexual possibilities' of hook-up sex to the assumed restrictive practices of the earlier 'dating era' (*c.* 1920s–1960s), she distorts both the restrictions of the earlier period and the freedoms of the latter.[181]

Notes

1 J. Egan, *Look At Me: A Novel* (New York, 2002), p. 50.

2 Calculation by M. Merck, 'Sexuality in the city', in K. Akass and J. McCabe (eds), *Reading Sex and the City* (New York, 2004), p. 59. The quote comes from the character Carrie Bradshaw: A. Nelson, 'Sister Carrie meets Carrie Bradshaw: exploring progress, politics and the single woman in *Sex and the City* and beyond', in Akass and McCabe (eds), *Reading Sex and the City*, p. 93.

3 I. Hirsch and C. Hirsch, '*Seinfeld*'s humor noir: a look at our dark side', *Journal of Popular Film and Television*, 28.3 (2000), 116–23.

4 See E. Blair, 'The loves of Lena Dunham', *The New York Review of Books*, 7 June 2012.

5 N. Glenn and E. Marquardt, *Hooking Up, Hanging Out, and Hoping for Mr. Right: College Women on Dating and Mating Today* (New York, 2001), p. 59.

6 J. R. Garcia, C. Reiber, S. G. Massey, and A. M. Merriwether, 'Sexual hookup culture: a review', *Review of General Psychology*, 16:2 (2012), 161–76.

7 K. A. Bogle, *Hooking Up: Sex, Dating, and Relationships on Campus* (New York, 2008), p. 8. The historical chapter, 'From dating to hooking up', is a relatively short 13 pages. Since I wrote the original version of this chapter in 2012, more studies – a tiny minority – have discussed the emergence of the practice, but their histories only go back to the 1960s. See, for example, R. Allison, '"It goes hand in hand with the parties": race, class, and residence in college student negotiations of hooking up', *Sociological Perspectives*, 57:1 (2014), 102–23;

C. D. Williams and S. Harper, 'Toward complex and inclusive studies of sex scripts, college students' sexual behaviors, and hookup cultures on US campuses', *MCS: Masculinities and Social Change*, 3:3 (2014), 271–98.

8 For non-monogamies, see C. Klesse, *The Spectre of Promiscuity: Gay Male and Bisexual Non-Monogamies and Polyamories* (Aldershot, 2007); M. Barker and D. Langdridge (eds), *Understanding Non-Monogamies* (New York, 2010). The quote about a new sexual script comes from Bogle, *Hooking Up*, p. 8.

9 A. Ellis, 'Sexual promiscuity in America', *Annals of the American Academy of Political and Social Science*, 378 (1968), 58–67.

10 I. L. Reiss and A. Ellis, *At the Dawn of the Sexual Revolution: Reflections on a Dialogue* (Walnut Creek, CA, 2002), pp. 4, 5.

11 Ibid., p. 1.

12 Ibid., pp. 8, 11, 19.

13 Ibid., p. 1.

14 *New York Times* Digital Archive: keyword search, 'casual sex'. 1961–70: 14 hits; 1971–80: 17 hits; 1981–90: 182 hits; 1991–2000: 140 hits; 2001–7: 102 hits. No hits before 1962.

15 I. L. Reiss, *Premarital Sexual Standards in America: A Sociological Investigation of the Relative Social and Cultural Integration of American Sexual Standards* (New York, 1960), pp. 77–8.

16 For this long tradition, see K. M. Phillips and B. Reay, *Sex Before Sexuality: A Premodern History* (Cambridge, 2011), ch. 2.

17 Reiss, *Premarital Sexual Standards in America*, p. 126.

18 M. Schofield, *Promiscuity* (London, 1976), pp. 37, 46, 130.

19 Ellis, 'Sexual promiscuity in America', 59.

20 Schofield, *Promiscuity*, p. 130.

21 A. C. Kinsey, W. B. Pomeroy, and C. E. Martin, *Sexual Behavior in the Human Male* (Philadelphia, PA, 1948), p. 557.

22 A. C. Kinsey, W. B. Pomeroy, C. E. Martin, and P. H. Gebhard, *Sexual Behavior in the Human Female* (Philadelphia, PA, 1953), p. 683.

23 M. Regnerus and J. Uecker, *Premarital Sex in America: How Young Americans Meet, Mate, and Think About Marrying* (New York, 2011), p. 29.

24 Kinsey, Pomeroy, and Martin, *Sexual Behavior in the Human Male*, p. 379.

25 Kinsey et al., *Sexual Behavior in the Human Female*, pp. 227, 233.

26 Ibid., pp. 233–4.

27 Ibid., pp. 239, 683.

28 Reiss, *Premarital Sexual Standards in America*, pp. 110–11.

29 A. J. Reiss, 'Sex offenses: the marginal status of the adolescent', *Law and Contemporary Problems*, 25:2 (1960), 309–33, quote at 315.

30 Kinsey, Pomeroy, and Martin, *Sexual Behavior in the Human Male*, p. 369.

31 Ibid., p. 381.

32 For Jagger, see K. Von Gilnow, 'Mick Jagger sex life', *The Huffington Post*, 7 November 2012.

33 L. Michaels, *Time Out of Mind: The Diaries of Leonard Michaels 1961–1995* (New York, 1999), p. 32.
34 B. E. Ellis, *Less Than Zero* (New York, 1998 [1985]), p. 120.
35 Ibid., p. 28.
36 The best discussion of this is by S. Seidman, *Romantic Longings: Love in America, 1830–1980* (New York, 1991), pp. 176–91.
37 C. Silverstein and E. White, *The Joy of Gay Sex: An Intimate Guide for Gay Men to the Pleasures of a Gay Lifestyle* (New York, 1977), p. 14.
38 A. P. Bell and M. S. Weinberg, *Homosexualities: A Study of Diversity Among Men and Women* (New York, 1978), p. 308.
39 Ibid., p. 312.
40 Ibid., pp. 308, 309.
41 Seidman, *Romantic Longings*, p. 177.
42 Silverstein and White, *Joy of Gay Sex*, p. 13.
43 M. K. Whyte, *Dating, Mating, and Marriage* (New York, 1990), pp. 22, 24.
44 Ibid., p. 26.
45 Ibid., p. 27.
46 Ibid., pp. 38–40, quote at p. 39.
47 Ibid., p. 266.
48 B. L. Bailey, *From Front Porch to Back Seat: Courtship in Twentieth-Century America* (Baltimore, MD, 1989), pp. 16, 19.
49 Ibid., pp. 49–56.
50 M. Moffatt, *Coming of Age in New Jersey* (New Brunswick, NJ, 1989), pp. 249, 267, n. 4.
51 K. A. Bogle, 'The shift from dating to hooking up in college: what scholars have missed', *Sociology Compass*, 1:2 (2007), 775–88.
52 L. R. Kass, 'The end of courtship', *Public Interest*, 126 (1997), 39–63, quotes at 39, 40.
53 C. Heap, 'The city as a sexual laboratory: the queer heritage of the Chicago school', *Qualitative Sociology*, 26:4 (2003), 457–87.
54 H. W. Zorbaugh, *The Gold Coast and the Slum: A Sociological Study of Chicago's Near North Side* (Chicago, 1969 [1929]), p. 86.
55 Ibid.
56 P. G. Cressey, *The Taxi-Dance Hall: A Sociological Study in Commercialized Recreation and City Life* (Chicago, 1932), p. 3.
57 For Marsh's women, see E. W. Todd, 'Art, the "New Woman", and consumer culture: Kenneth Hayes Miller and Reginald Marsh on Fourteenth Street, 1920–40', in B. Melosh (ed.), *Gender and American History Since 1890* (New York, 1993), ch. 6.
58 H. Miller, *Tropic of Capricorn* (New York, 2012 [1939]), p. 104.
59 Ibid., p. 105.
60 New York Public Library (hereafter NYPL), Manuscripts and Archives Division, Committee of Fourteen Records, Box 37: Investigators' Reports

1927–32, Folder: Dance Halls 1927–30, Melody Gardens Dance Hall, 168 West 23rd Street, 19 November 1928.
61 Cressey, *Taxi-Dance Hall*, pp. xvi–xvii.
62 Ibid., p. 13.
63 Ibid., p. 242.
64 Ibid., p. 258.
65 NYPL, Manuscripts and Archives Division, Committee of Fourteen Records, Box 32: Investigators' Reports 1917–20, Folder: Coney Island and Queens 1918–19.
66 Ibid., Box 37 Investigators' Reports 1927–32, Folder: Night Clubs and Speakeasies, Pepper Pot 146 West 4th Street, 22–29 December 1927.
67 Ibid., Golden Gate 186 West 4th Street, no date.
68 F. Donovan, *The Woman Who Waits* (Boston, MA, 1920), p. 217.
69 Ibid., p. 213.
70 Ibid., p. 218.
71 Cressey, *Taxi-Dance Hall*, p. 19.
72 NYPL, Manuscripts and Archives Division, Committee of Fourteen Records, Box 28: Investigators' Reports, 1905–15, Folder: Strand Cafeteria, Strand Roof Garden, 16 May 1915.
73 Ibid., Box 37: Investigators' Reports 1927–32, Folder: Dance Halls 1927–30, Adele Studio of Dancing, 304 West 71st Street, 30 April 1928.
74 Ibid., Martha Dancing Studio, 33 West 71st Street, 9–10 March 1928.
75 Ibid., Remenyi's Dancing School, 177 East 84th Street, 4 January 1929.
76 Ibid., Adele Studio of Dancing 304 West 71st Street, 31 May 1928.
77 The Newark Vice Commission, 1914, quoted in M. T. Connelly, *The Response to Prostitution in the Progressive Era* (Chapel Hill, NC, 1980), p. 40.
78 R. S. True, *West Side Studies: The Neglected Girl* (New York, 1914), pp. 54–5, 59, 70, 83, quote at p. 70.
79 See K. Peiss, 'Treating and sexuality', in her *Cheap Amusements: Working Women and Leisure in Turn-of-the-Century New York* (Philadelphia, PA, 1986), pp. 108–14.
80 NYPL, Manuscripts and Archives Division, Committee of Fourteen Records, Box 36: Investigators' Reports 1927–9, Folder: 86th–116th Streets, Corso's Cabaret, 205 East 86th Street, 8 February 1929.
81 Ibid., Box 37: Investigators' Reports 1927–32, Folder: Dance Halls, Danse Caprice, 344 Flatbush Avenue, Brooklyn, 2 April 1921.
82 Ibid., Box 28: Investigators' Reports, 1905–15, Folder: Strand Cafeteria, Strand Roof Garden, 16 May 1915.
83 Ibid., Box 37: Investigators' Reports 1927–32, Folder: Dance Halls 1927–30, 'Charity and occasional prostitutes', 19 May 1927.
84 Cressey, *Taxi-Dance Hall*, p. 39.
85 Ibid., p. 35.
86 NYPL, Manuscripts and Archives Division, Committee of Fourteen Records,

Box 36: Investigators' Reports 1927–9, Folder 30th–48th Streets, Hudson Hotel, 102 West 44th Street, 15 June 1927.

87 Cressey, *Taxi-Dance Hall*, pp. 35, 267–8.

88 Ibid., p. 49.

89 H. Miller, *Sexus: The Rosy Crucifixion I* (New York, 1994 [1950]), p. 363.

90 E. A. Clement, *Love for Sale: Courting, Treating, and Prostitution in New York City, 1900–1945* (Chapel Hill, NC, 2006), pp. 47, 69.

91 Ibid., p. 47.

92 Donovan, *Woman Who Waits*, pp. 211–12, 214.

93 J. Meyerowitz, 'Sexual geography and gender economy: the furnished room districts of Chicago, 1890–1930', in B. Melosh (ed.), *Gender and American History Since 1890* (London, 1993), p. 54.

94 Cressey, *Taxi-Dance Hall*, p. 103.

95 Her interview with Bessie Smith's biographer, Chris Albertson, is included on the last of the compact discs in the ten-disc compilation, *Bessie Smith: The Complete Columbia Recordings* (2012); see also C. Albertson, *Bessie* (New Haven, CT, 2003 [1972]), pp. 140, 142.

96 S. Robertson, 'Harlem undercover: vice investigators, race, and prostitution, 1910–1930', *Journal of Urban History*, 35:4 (2009), 486–504; https://digitalharlemblog.wordpress.com/2009/04/17/harlem-undercover-the-maps/ (last accessed 26 April 2018).

97 NYPL, Manuscripts and Archives Division, Committee of Fourteen Records, Box 35: Investigators' Reports 1923–32, Folder: Seaman's Church Institute, 20 May and 29 May 1931.

98 W. Thurman, *Negro Life in New York's Harlem* (Girard, KS, no date), pp. 40, 42–3.

99 C. Blair, *I've Got to Make My Livin': Black Women's Sex Work in Turn-of-the-Century Chicago* (Chicago, 2010), p. 79.

100 NYPL, Manuscripts and Archives Division, Committee of Fourteen Records, Box 37: Investigators' Reports 1927–32, Folder: Speakeasies & Nightclubs, 123 West 138th Street Basement, 25 May 1928; 40 West 132nd Street, 16 June 1928.

101 Ibid., 108 West 137th Street, Apt 2, 25 May 1928.

102 G. W. Henry, *Sex Variants: A Study of Homosexual Patterns*, 2 vols. (New York, 1941).

103 Ibid., vol. 1, pp. 26–37.

104 Ibid., pp. 36–7.

105 Ibid., pp. 408–11.

106 Ibid., p. 446.

107 Ibid., p. 139.

108 Ibid., pp. 141–2.

109 Ibid., pp. 214–15.

110 Ibid., vol. 2, pp. 566–7.

111 Ibid., pp. 644–8.
112 Ibid., p. 653.
113 Ibid., p. 664.
114 Ibid., pp. 724–5.
115 Ibid., p. 978.
116 For exceptions to this focus on heterosexuality (which have been published since I first wrote about hooking up in 2012), see L. J. Rupp et al., 'Queer women in the hookup scene: beyond the closet?', *Gender & Society*, 28:2 (2014), 212–35; A. Kuperberg and J. E. Padgett, 'Dating and hooking up in college: meeting contexts, sex, and variation by gender, partner's gender, and class standing', *The Journal of Sex Research*, 52:5 (2015), 517–31; A. Kuperberg and J. E. Padgett, 'Partner meeting contexts and risky behavior in college students' other-sex and same-sex hookups', *The Journal of Sex Research*, 54:1 (2017), 55–72; S. B. Olmstead, K. M. Anders, and K. A. Conrad, 'Meanings for sex and commitment among first semester college men and women: a mixed-methods analysis', *Archives of Sexual Behavior*, 46:6 (2017), 1831–42.
117 See B. Gove, *Cruising Culture: Promiscuity, Desire and American Gay Literature* (Edinburgh, 2000).
118 R. Camus, *Tricks: 25 Encounters*, trans. R. Howard, with preface by R. Barthes (New York, 1981), pp. 191–2.
119 Ibid., pp. 192–3.
120 Ibid., p. viii.
121 Ibid., p. xii.
122 Ibid., p. 217.
123 Ibid., p. 93.
124 Silverstein and White, *Joy of Gay Sex*, p. 141.
125 Camus, *Tricks*, p. 67.
126 Seidman, *Romantic Longings*, p. 179.
127 Ibid., p. 181.
128 S. R. Delany, *Times Square Red, Times Square Blue* (New York, 1999), p. 123.
129 M. S. Weinberg and C. J. Williams, 'Gay baths and the social organization of impersonal sex', *Social Problems*, 23:2 (1975), 124–36, quote at 134.
130 M. Foucault, *Foucault Live (Interviews, 1966–84)*, ed. S Lotringer, trans. J. Johnston (New York, 1989), pp. 224–5.
131 L. Humphreys, *Tearoom Trade: Impersonal Sex in Public Places* (New York, 1975 [1970]), pp. 12, 13.
132 E. W. Delph, *The Silent Community: Public Homosexual Encounters* (Beverly Hills, CA, 1978), p. 81.
133 Ibid., p. 28.
134 Ibid., p. 127.
135 Ibid., pp. 64, 135.
136 Camus, *Tricks*, p. 237.

137 W. Leyland (ed.), *Gay Sunshine Interviews: Volume Two* (San Francisco, 1982), 'Ned Rorem', pp. 191–218, quote at p. 213.
138 Ibid.
139 Delph, *Silent Community*, p. 28.
140 S. R. Delany, *1984* (Rutherford, NJ, 2000), pp. 13–14.
141 Ibid., p. 213.
142 Gay and Lesbian Historical Society of Northern California [later the Gay, Lesbian, Bisexual, Transgender Historical Society], San Francisco, Oral History Collection, 95–93: Hal Call.
143 M. Hunt, *Sexual Behavior in the 1970s* (Chicago, 1974), p. 154.
144 Moffatt, *Coming of Age in New Jersey*, p. 248.
145 There are several studies but a good early starting point is G. D. Bartell, 'Group sex among the mid-Americans', *The Journal of Sex Research*, 6:2 (1970), 113–30.
146 B. Fang, 'Swinging in retrospect', *The Journal of Sex Research*, 12:3 (1976), 220–37, quote at 220.
147 Ibid., 220.
148 M. L. Walshok, 'The emergence of middle-class deviant subcultures: the case of swingers', *Social Problems*, 18:4 (1971), 488–95.
149 D. Denfield and M. Gordon, 'The sociology of mate swapping: or the family that swings together clings together', *The Journal of Sex Research*, 6:2 (1970), 85–100, quote at 91.
150 D. McDonald, 'Swinging: pushing the boundaries of monogamy?', in Barker and Langridge (eds), *Understanding Non-Monogamies*, ch. 7, quote at p. 72.
151 Walshok, 'Emergence of middle-class deviant subcultures', 495.
152 Denfield and Gordon, 'Sociology of mate swapping', 92.
153 Bogle, *Hooking Up*, ch. 3. See also Regnerus and Uecker, *Premarital Sex in America*, ch. 4.
154 E. L. Paul, B. McManus, and A. Hayes, '"Hookups": characteristics and correlates of college students' spontaneous and anonymous sexual experiences', *The Journal of Sex Research*, 37:1 (2000), 76–88.
155 T. V. Ven and J. Beck, 'Getting drunk and hooking up: an exploratory study of the relationship between alcohol intoxication and casual coupling in a university sample', *Sociological Spectrum*, 29:5 (2009), 626–48.
156 For oral sex as 'not sex', see S. A. Sanders and J. M. Reinisch, 'Would you say you "had sex" if . . .?', *JAMA: The Journal of the American Medical Association*, 281:3 (1999), 275–7; L. M. Bogart, H. Cecil, D. A. Wagstaff, S. D. Pinkerton, and P. R. Abramson, 'Is it "sex"?: college students' interpretations of sexual behavior terminology', *The Journal of Sex Research*, 37:2 (2000), 108–16.
157 Kuperberg and Padgett, 'Partner meeting contexts', 55; R. Allison and B. J. Risman, 'Marriage delay, time to play? Marital horizons and hooking up in college', *Sociological Inquiry*, 20:10 (2016), 1–29, quote at 3. Emphases mine.

158 M. A. Monto, 'A new standard of sexual behavior? Are claims associated with the "hookup culture" supported by general social survey data?', *The Journal of Sex Research*, 51:6 (2014), 605–15, figures from 609.
159 A. Kuperberg and J. E. Padgett, 'The role of culture in explaining college students' selection into hookups, dates, and long-term romantic relationships', *Journal of Social and Personal Relationships*, 33:8 (2016), 1070–96, figure at 1088.
160 Moffatt, *Coming of Age in New Jersey*, pp. 199–200.
161 Quoted in Bogle, *Hooking Up*, pp. 148–9.
162 Ibid., chs 6 and 8.
163 H. H. Kettrey, 'What's gender got to do with it? Sexual double standards and power in heterosexual college hookups', *The Journal of Sex Research*, 53:7 (2016), 754–65, quotes at 754.
164 W. D. Manning, P. C. Giordano, and M. A. Longmore, 'Hooking up: the relationship contexts of "nonrelationship" sex', *Journal of Adolescent Research*, 21:5 (2006), 459–83; Regnerus and Uecker, *Premarital Sex in America*, pp. 65–70. Thus the title of a College of New Jersey study referring to 'Spontaneous and anonymous' sex is something of an exaggeration: Paul, McManus, and Hayes, 'Hookups'.
165 Bogle, *Hooking Up*, chs 3–5.
166 M. Berntson, K. Hoffman, and T. Luff, 'College as context: influences on interpersonal sexual scripts', *Sexuality & Culture*, 18:1 (2014), 149–65, quote at 151; R. Allison, 'Gendered jocks or equal players? Athletic affiliation and hooking up among college students', *Sociological Spectrum*, 36:4 (2016), 255–70, quote at 258.
167 M. Epstein, J. P. Calzo, A. P. Smiler, and L. M. Ward, '"Anything from making out to having sex": men's negotiations of hooking up and friends with benefits scripts', *The Journal of Sex Research*, 46:5 (2009), 414–24, quote at 414.
168 For example, M. A. Bisson and T. R. Levine, 'Negotiating a friends with benefits relationship', *Archives of Sexual Behavior*, 38 (2009), 66–73.
169 Epstein et al., '"Anything from making out to having sex"', 422.
170 Kinsey, Pomeroy, and Martin, *Sexual Behavior in the Human Male*, p. 600.
171 Clement, *Love for Sale*, pp. 3–4, 241–2.
172 W. Waller, 'The rating and dating complex', *American Sociological Review*, 2:5 (1937), 727–34, quotes at 727, 728.
173 Ehrmann, *Premarital Dating Behavior*, p. 197.
174 E. Anderson, *Code of the Street: Decency, Violence, and the Moral Life of the Inner City* (New York, 2000), ch. 4. This is not to deny another culture ('decency') based on sexual respectability, which Anderson also discusses.
175 Ibid., pp. 150–1, 154.
176 Ibid., pp. 150, 177.
177 Ehrmann, *Premarital Dating Behavior*, pp. 154–6.
178 Anderson, *Code of the Street*, pp. 152, 173.

179 E. Anderson, *The Monogamy Gap: Men, Love, and the Reality of Cheating* (New York, 2012), p. 5.
180 Epstein et al., '"Anything from making out to having sex"', 421.
181 Bogle, *Hooking Up*, ch. 8, esp. p. 159.

5

A transgender story: the diaries of Louis Graydon Sullivan

Although it may be an exaggeration to claim a 'transgender turn' in recent times, it is certainly true that what is now termed 'trans*' has come to feature prominently in contemporary culture and cultural history.[1] The starting point for this history is contested. Some have maintained that convictions of gender dislocation have always been there: 'one indisputable fact remains: transsexualism exists and has always existed'.[2] For others, however, transsexuality was a late twentieth-century phenomenon, an example of the way in which the medicalisation of sex (in this case through new medical technology) has influenced or facilitated new sexual subjectivities. If it was not for advanced surgical techniques and endocrinology, they imply, there could have been no transsexuality and transgender.[3] Although Joanne Meyerowitz's influential book on the subject has charted individual and sporadic instances of surgery and experimental sex modifications in Europe and (even more rarely) in the US from the early twentieth century, she effectively begins her story with the intense publicity surrounding the 'sex change' of Christine Jorgensen in the 1950s: 'Ex-GI becomes Blonde Beauty'.[4] Transsexuality, a category that had once not existed, became a widely recognised term after it had been first named by D. O. Cauldwell in 1949 and then described in more detail in Harry Benjamin's *The Transsexual Phenomenon* (1966), Robert Stoller's *Sex and Gender* (1968), and Richard Green and John Money's edited collection *Transsexualism and Sex Reassignment* (1969).[5] Before that, those who experienced gender disjunction would invariably have explained those feelings in terms of homosexual or heterosexual transvestism.[6] Over the next ten years, the US national picture changed from one of no significant institutional support for transsexual endocrinology, therapy, and surgery to a situation where by 1975 about twenty major medical centres were offering treatment and some thousand transsexuals had been provided with surgery.[7] Though the early focus was on what are now termed trans women (then called male-to-female transsexuality, as with Jorgensen), research, discussion, and treatment increasingly included trans men, the female-to-male, with a 1974 study estimating a ratio of two to three trans women for every trans man and possibly even approaching parity.[8]

One of the fascinating aspects of trans history is the rapid shift in sexual configurations. The transgender community emerged in the 1980s and 1990s, more diverse than the older transsexual community (which it incorporated). Holly Devor's work on trans men during this period saw its point of departure from previous research in terms of a willingness to recognise sexual indeterminacies and uncertainties and shifting identities.[9] Transgender included people who wanted to create and/or retain characteristics of both genders and who saw themselves as neither or both male and female.[10] Genny Beemyn and Susan Rankin's large-scale survey discovered hundreds of different self-identity descriptions among those in the survey who classified themselves as 'other' or 'transgender', the more common self-descriptions including genderqueer, androgyne, and bi-gender.[11] In treatment too there has been a shift. As Walter Bockting has explained, 'there is no one way of being transgender . . . Feminizing and masculinizing hormones and genital-reconstructive surgery are no longer two steps of one linear process of sex reassignment . . . Clients no longer necessarily need surgery to live and be recognized in the desired gender role.'[12] The Internet has played a significant role in this recent history; Beemyn and Rankin's survey argued that it was crucial to transgender identity work among younger trans participants.[13]

Transgender has become so established in the American cultural psyche that it is difficult to imagine another time. We are concerned here with this earlier phase of trans history, from the 1960s to the 1980s, before the Internet, when sexual and gender definitions and categories were more fixed, and many experts, and many so-termed transvestites and transsexuals, thought that they knew exactly what transvestism and transsexuality were. Transvestites cross-dressed but did not want to be the sex of those whose clothing they wore. Cross-dressing in female garb was common: cross-dressing in male clothing was rare. Transsexuals, on the other hand, saw their bodies as a kind of dress and wanted to rearrange them to correspond to their true being: male-to-female transsexuals modified their bodies to reflect their essential femaleness; female-to-male transsexuals adapted to correspond to their masculinity. And trans men were less common than trans women. Sexual desire was believed to mirror gender in a similarly structured – and heteronormative – manner. The trans man, as a man, desired women. The trans woman was sexually attracted to men. There was little or no conceptual space for the gay trans man or the lesbian trans woman. Of course the situation was more complex and contentious than this simple formulation, but these were the essential ground rules for operating in a transgender world at that time.[14]

You will not find the story that follows anywhere else – at least not quite in the way recounted here. There are biographical accounts of Louis Graydon Sullivan, two books since the first draft of this chapter was written.[15] But my approach is different. Studies of Lou have either focused on the making of a trans activist, almost as if he were a local politician, rather than exploring the complications and convolutions of this making.[16] If aware of these intricacies, as Lani Rodemeyer undoubtedly is, given her selection of Sullivan's diary extracts and her theoretical discussion, there is insufficient interrogation of his journey: 'Sullivan identified himself as a man and saw himself as always having been male'; 'we see Sullivan struggling with his identity as a gay man'.[17] Or there is a tendency towards a master narrative. As another of these recent biographers writes, 'His unwitting quest to become a trans activist unfolded in quilt-like fashion with Lou's collecting seemingly disparate experiences and models of masculinity into a patchwork that would ultimately come together as the founder of the FTM (female-to-male) community.'[18] There is an inexorability about that story: the making of a 'female-to-male transsexual gay man' and transgender role model, encapsulated by the image of Sullivan on the cover of the 'Heroes' issue of a trans man magazine in 2013 (see Figure 37).[19]

It is true that Sullivan was active in FTM organisational and support groups and was involved with the San Francisco Gay and Lesbian Historical Society; we will see that he created the first information booklet for female-to-male transsexuals and wrote the historical work *From Female to Male*, published shortly before his death. And it is true that Lou was a pioneer in not only female-to-male transgender, less commonly recognised in those earlier years than male-to-female, but also as a trans man who wanted to have sex with men rather than women. The gay trans man was barely acknowledged when Sullivan was transitioning; now he is not at all unusual. But this story is more interesting, if untidier, than other accounts of Sullivan's life. In keeping with trans sensibilities I will be using the pronoun 'he' for Sullivan. But in a sense this distorts the original diaries, which clearly start as the diaries of a girl (an unusual girl) and then display much more uncertainty and ambiguity. Though not wishing to denigrate those who seek comfort in certainties, there was nothing inevitable about Sullivan's trans story; it could have taken a different trajectory almost at any point.

37 Lou Sullivan, 1988. An image used on the cover of *OP: Original Plumbing: Trans Male Quarterly*, The Hero Issue, 2013. GLBT Historical Society, San Francisco, Louis Sullivan Photographs (#1991-7), Courtesy of Gay, Lesbian, Bisexual, Transgender Historical Society.

Louis Graydon Sullivan was born Sheila Jean Sullivan in Milwaukee (Wisconsin) in 1951. When he was 10 years old, he was given a diary for Christmas, a pink one, but did not effectively become a diarist until 1964, in his early teens, when he started the journals that still survive.[20] They begin as a normal US girl's teenage diary, Sheila's diary, indeed records her first menstrual period in 1964: 'My second day of menstruation. I love it . . . I love being a girl. So delicate.' 'I'm growing up and I'm a real female. I love being a girl.'[21] Sullivan is obsessed with the pop group the Beatles, 'All the kids at school say I'm the most Beatled kid. Everyday they say, "Hey, Sheila, what's new with the Beatles?" I love it.'[22] He refers to dresses and flirtations with boys. But there are other elements. He muses about what a boy thinks when he looks at a girl. He dresses (Beatle-style) in a white shirt, tie, and black slacks for his guitar lessons. He recalls childhood games where the girls in the family played at being boys, with boys' names and acting like boys. And Sullivan wrote about vulnerable young delinquents. By 1965 there is a clear fascination with prison stories and descriptions of whippings and homosexuality – the tingling feeling that he experiences when 'I read about severe whippings'.[23] At the end of 1966 he confides in his diary that he is working on an idea for a story about male homosexuality and writes that he is obsessed with the subject and becomes aroused thinking about it. Sheila, as he was then known, is frank about sexual thoughts and temptations to masturbate: 'I have a horrible temptation for sex acts. I'd never do them with anyone, though I do play with myself, which is supposed to be wrong. But I can't see it's wrong.'[24] His priest says that it is immoral and advises prayer: 'Great help!' He had not been to confession for months. What was he supposed to say to the priest: 'I masturbated about 1,000 times'?[25]

In 1966 he refers to his admiration of boys' independence and his desire to be like Bob Dylan – 'But this is impossible since I'm a girl.'[26] He wants to 'roam & write'. It would be difficult, 'dangerous', 'But I'd dress like a guy.'[27] 'Sometimes I think I was intended to be a boy. I can feel a boy's feelings sooner than I can a girl's. I can understand a boy more than a girl. I'd rather *be* a boy than a girl. I don't like these two big (ha ha) things stickin out of my front.'[28] And Sullivan is attracted to boys not girls. We have a picture from that year of a long-haired figure, guitar in hand (see Figure 38).

By the late 1960s Sheila (for that is still his name) is attending hippie gatherings and hangs out with long-haired boys. In 1967 he goes to a Milwaukee coffee house called The Avant Garde, where folk music and blues were played, but complains of the poetry on free sex: 'all their poems were bout free sex, sex, open sex, public sex and nudity. I was really gettin sick.'[29] He seems conflicted: writing, on the one hand, of disgust at the commercialisation of sex and disapproval of sex before marriage, and, on the other hand, recording sexual attraction to an experimental band called the Velvet Whip (a name that hints at S/M) and to male homosexual sex ('REALLY turn me on. Just thinking about it.')[30]

In the early 1970s, now in his twenties and working as a secretary at the University of Wisconsin-Milwaukee, Sullivan's psychosexual imaginings acquire shape as he draws on the more alternative side of popular culture to make sense of his desires. He is drawn to sexual ambiguity. He reveres Andy Warhol and his circle. He quotes Terence Stamp's character in Federico Fellini's short film *Toby Dammit* (1968), who, in response to the

38 Lou Sullivan, 1966. GLBT Historical Society, San Francisco, Louis Sullivan Photographs (#1991-7), Courtesy of Gay, Lesbian, Bisexual, Transgender Historical Society.

question as to why he enjoyed equal success with men and women, replied that he was masculine enough to please men and feminine enough to please women. Lou empathises with the drag queens in John Rechy's hustler novel *City of Night* (1963) and reading Rechy prompts the observation: 'what can become of a girl who's [*sic*] real desire & passion is with male homosexuals. That *I want to be one*. That I fancy him to be one & pretend I'm a man when we make love.'[31] Then he sees Mick Jagger in the film *Performance* (1970):

> the role Jagger played turned me on so – I could *identify with a bisexual male*, that's how fucked up *I* am that I had possibly *the* most satisfying sex contact with Jim [Sullivan's boyfriend] that nite I've ever had. There's so much written about all kinds of sexually wierd [*sic*] people but a female who imagines herself a bi-sexual male is way beyond anything I have ever read.[32]

Though this cannot exactly be described as the moment when Sullivan decides that he wants to be, or is, a male homosexual – not just a male, but a male homosexual – it is certainly a formative psychological moment.

Nevertheless, Sheila had sex with males as a female. He and his boyfriend – in true sexual revolution style – had an open relationship and experimented in their own sexual and gender interactions: 'I'll be the woman & you can be the man', Jim, the boyfriend, tells Sullivan.[33] In 1973

Sheila begins to admire the Velvet Underground singer Lou Reed – whose name he adopts (hence the Lou) – and describes behaviour at a bar, wearing a leather jacket with a glove down his pants to simulate a bulge and acting all masculine with the women there. He records that he likes to fuck on all fours: 'I am the youth making love to this other lovely youth.'[34] He talks to his grandmother quite frankly but does not tell her that 'when I have sex I have to fantasize I'm a man making love to this other man before I can have an orgasm'.[35]

Sullivan and Jim moved on the margins of the gay community and attended meetings at the Gay People's Union – 'WE'RE COMING OUT!'[36] Again there are some incongruous juxtapositions in the diary entries: cruising or hustling (both terms are used) males at a bar one night, and then attending a lesbian discussion group the next, before blowing a guy in the early hours of the following morning. Sullivan was propositioned by a lesbian who told him that she would make him feel fantastic. He told her 'I don't even know if I'd want a lesbian experience . . . finally told her I consider myself a male homosexual . . . she was pretty grossed out about that.'[37]

Sullivan was fascinated by images of passing (the term used in the diary) and went to male drag shows. He heard stories of the drag artist who performed as a woman in straight venues and provided oral sex without any of the recipients realising that he was really a man; of the legal secretary who married a gay man who knew that she was male and adopted a son who was now studying to be a priest and did not know that his mother was a man. (We are a long way from current sensibilities about trans expression.) Sullivan starts to have sex with homosexual and bisexual men, sometimes as a male. He meets a lesbian at a bar and they have sex in the car park. 'Put my hands down her pants but didn't do anything. And I thought of gay men to have my orgasm.'[38] Several of the men that he had sex with were unsure whether he was male or female. When harassed by teenagers calling him 'queer' and 'fag', Sullivan was pleased that it implied his masculinity but upset by the harassment.[39] He moved to San Francisco in 1975 with his long-term boyfriend, who began to experiment in the gay male world.

Sullivan (still Sheila) keeps trying to make sense of his feelings. Here is the entry for 22 March 1976:

> I don't feel like a 'male trapped in a female's body' [one of the conventions of transsexuality] nor do I think I *could* be a man. It's the fantasy . . . if I had a mastectomy I'd have to beat off 24 hours a day because I'd be so turned on by myself. The whole scene for me is just a wonderful sexual fantasy.[40]

Yet he is contemplating more radical bodily reassignment and has clippings regarding sex-change surgery (another term used then and relayed in the diary). 'I'm really becoming uncomfortable in and tired of my ambiguity.' The 'fantasy' was giving way to 'intense desire' to act.[41] A friend, Elizabeth, a trans woman, was more cautious, 'Remember when we talked about (you) getting too involved in TSism instead of TVism . . . I'm scared for you Sheila because you enjoy playing at being a boy even though *your mind* and feelings are a *woman's*. Don't get carried away with the game.'[42] Was Sullivan a transvestite rather than transsexual? Elizabeth was sceptical about Sheila's (Elizabeth always referred to Lou by his female name) transsexuality. Hormones

> won't get rid of your fat ass . . . you are fucking up your whole mechanism . . . facial hair? Your pussy will dry up too . . . I know it isn't like getting the sex change just to take hormones, but! Remember when dressing as a man was just fun, now it seems like a necessity? *Do you want to BE a man? I don't think YOU ARE a man* . . . Are *you* a female or male, the 'you' that's reading this letter *not the you in a mirror* or the you that other people get to see – just the You inside that Fat Skull . . . Shit! You're heading into such a bummer, Sheila.[43]

Sullivan's archive contains a copy of his (unsuccessful) application to the Stanford University Gender Dysphoria Program in 1976. The answer to their question regarding 'her' preferred method of sexual contact was likely to have raised some concerns in what was, as we will see, an essentially cautious experiment: 'I want to be a gay male having sex with another gay male. All kinds of male–male sex acts. There will be no need for fantasy – we'll be there.' Nor would the responses to enquiries about earliest fantasies and sexual contacts with males and females have reassured therapists who, in respect of what they described as female-to-male transsexuals, were looking for masculine (heterosexual) attractions to women rather than (homosexual) longings for men. Sullivan's earliest fantasies, as declared in the application, were of 'boys-in-bondage and man-whipping boy type fantasies'. Sex with Jim, whom Sullivan was still with at that time, entailed picturing him as 'a "faggot" or imaging myself a man having sex with Jim'. As for sex with women, Sullivan referred to the brief encounter with a lesbian but thought of gay men to achieve orgasm. This was hardly the sort of profile that the Stanford team would have been seeking.[44]

It was no inexorable trans journey for Sullivan, who, to return to 1960s and 1970s terminology, oscillated between transvestism and transsexuality. He attended what were then called transvestite/transsexual group meetings but found that the small group consisted of trans women. There was a moment of personal legitimation when he read an interview with a San Francisco woman who said that she felt like 'a gay male trapped in a woman's body', exactly how Lou/Sheila had felt for some time, but such moments were rare.[45] He tried counselling, but the counsellor did not approve of Sullivan's 'anti-female sentiments'.[46] He became concerned by his inability to fit in anywhere. As he recorded, why would the gays accept him as a woman? Feminists did not accept his dress. Lesbians? 'I like men.' The straights? 'No way.' Transvestites? They were all male-to-female rather than female-to-male. He told his counsellor that he was past the 'crisis of wanting a sex change'.[47] On their advice, he bought a dress, joined a women's group to counter his perceived misogyny, and obtained a copy of the feminist text *Our Bodies Ourselves* (1973). Sullivan was soon reading female liberation books and had three dresses, writing to Elizabeth in 1977 that he was 'growing more & more comfortable with myself as Sheila – able to relax more as a female who digs sometimes passing/looking like a male. I'm giving myself permission to be a female transvestite.'[48]

But the homosexual longings continued. In early 1977 Sullivan picked up two men and had sex with them, though fantasised about them having sex together, something that the men themselves avoided. He worried that he was attracted to young men more by his desire to *be* them than his desire to *have* them. In 1978 he attended a TV/TS group in Berkeley, advertised as 'for women', and recorded his disappointment when he found that it was five male, middle-aged transvestites, 'all dressed and talking in their butch voices' – but then his later elation when he discovered someone like himself at the same group: 'I found someone like me!!! A heterosexual female transvestite.'[49] Then there was group conflict. Sullivan talked to the group president and suggested that they have serious discussions rather than just socialising. The president said that not all the members were as intelligent as 'her' and just wanted to cross-dress rather than talking about it. Sullivan's sex with men continued. There are graphic descriptions in 1979 of what he does to one of the members of what was to become a famous US punk band, and vice versa. Afterwards, the person whom the musician knew as Sheila told him 'I envision myself as a gay man.' The band member did not seem too disconcerted. When Sheila expressed a liking for making out with 'gay guys', he replied 'you've really set up a challenge for yourself'.[50]

Lou remains unclear about his identity. 'I don't believe I *am* a man, but I am certain I *want* to be one', he wrote to Mario Martino, the trans man autobiographer and gender counsellor, in September 1979; 'I don't know if I am a deluded transvestite or an overly-cautious transsexual.'[51] In letters to another female-to-male contact Sullivan claimed transvestism rather than transsexuality: that is, desiring men as a cross-dressed woman rather than as a male craving other males:

> get the guy on his stomach & put the back of your hand against your crotch & stick a finger out like a little cock & get on top of him, you can fuck him & its great. You can just go off into your own little fantasy that you're a guy fucking this other guy & its the greatest turn-on. I usually like to keep my undershirt on so I can pretend easier that my chest is a guy's. And dammit if all these male TVs and gay guys can be so out about what turns them on, then shit, we can be out about what WE like.

'We are heterosexual transvestites just like 80% of the male TVs', Sullivan continued. 'If they can crossdress & like women, we can crossdress & like men.' 'I get immense sexual gratification just by dressing & going to the mens' bars & cruising & pretending I'm like the other guys there. I've never yet picked up a guy from one of the bars where it turned out at all satisfactory, but that's not the main goal.' And he claimed that he had not followed through with the Stanford application because he had realised that he was not transsexual and could 'find a way to accept myself as a female who wanted to be a gay male. It sure isn't a terribly fulfilling life, but I'd rather be who I am than try to act a way I don't feel.'[52] Mark Brannigan, Sullivan's correspondent, likewise presented as a 'heterosexual female transvestite'.[53]

Yet a month later, towards the end of 1979, and after saying that he was not transsexual, Lou wrote, 'Well Mark I'm taking the big step, I'm going to begin taking male hormones & live fulltime as a guy . . . It came because I no longer want to live in a fantasy world . . . I'm tired of pretending.' His counsellor was encouraging:

> I told him I didn't feel like a 'man trapped in a woman's body' & he said nobody did, that was just some catchy phrase the medical profession made up. I told him that I didn't fit any of the stereotypes of a TS & he said that being a TS does not dictate anything about you other than the way you feel about yourself & that I have a perfect right to be a gay man if that's what I want.[54]

Sullivan was obviously in crisis once more. 'Now I find myself yearning for the total male look again.'[55] Someone who had had MTF surgery said that a reputable clinic would not do anything for Sullivan because he lacked 'the typical transsexual story they want to hear'. The friend talked about the possibility of being a 'cross-liver', taking hormones and living the desired gender role but not necessarily having surgery – actually a solution more in tune with current trans thinking but different to the pressure for total transformation that dominated in that earlier period.[56] However, Sheila decided to go through with the gender reconciliation contemplated several years before. One obstacle to support for that transition had been an admission to a lack of sexual interest in women. The heterosexual gatekeepers at the time preferred what they termed male-to-female transsexuals to desire men and female-to-male transsexuals to be sexually attracted to women. So Lou decided that when he filled out the application for sexual reassignment he would say that 'girls are looking a lot better to me'.[57]

There is another application to the Stanford Program, this one dated 17 October 1979, and Lou had indeed stated that 'the closer I get to cross-living as a man, the better women are looking to me'. However, the application still stressed a gay male sexuality:

> Prefer contact with gay or effeminate men. Enjoy any activity during which I can fantasize myself as a male. I like to be the aggressive partner. I sometimes imagine I am my male partner, thinking how he must feel having sex as a man, or fantasize I am another man and my male partner is loving me. Very much enjoy my recent sex partner, who takes the role of female, while I am the aggressive male. We engage in mild S & M (he as the passive partner), some crossdressing, anal and oral activities during which we exchange in being the passive or active member.[58]

Perhaps Lou thought that this declaration of sex with a female-acting man indicated that he was on the road to sex with women – to heterosexuality – but this was unlikely to have comforted the Stanford therapists. His application was turned down because the history it provided was 'not typical' of those who had been treated successfully. Lou replied that he had anticipated rejection because of his 'interest in men as sexual partners':

> I realize that this is an unusual 'twist' for the female-to-male. Yet it is very common for male-to-females to become lesbians after surgery. It is unfortunate that your Program cannot see the merit of each individual, regardless of their sexual orientation. The general human populace is made up of many sexual persuasions – it is incredible that your Program requires all transsexuals to be of one fabric.[59]

So Lou may have been trying to make a point in the first place.[60]

Sullivan's diaries provide a sense of the fluid sexual identities in San Francisco in the late 1970s and early 1980s. Sheila (as Sullivan was known to this lover) continued to have sex with the friend from the punk band and told him of an impending gender-confirming surgery. He was intrigued, seemed to relish the transformation – 'can we be buddies afterwards?' – and provided some dubious wisdom: 'that's the attractive thing about the gay world – the easy availability of sex . . . one problem with having sex with women is you've got to talk to them beforehand'. In anticipation of the gay male status perhaps, the musician lets Sullivan do exactly what he wants to him. Sheila lies on top of him and pretends to fuck him. He fucks Sheila in the arse.[61]

Sheila also went to a drag bar and groped and kissed a 'black queen'. A young man joined them and then became agitated when he discovered that the queen was male. He became even more disturbed when he was told that Sheila was female: he had thought that the female was male and the male female. Sheila writes in her diary that it would not have made any difference: it would have been a threesome. 'God, if he'd 've done a 3-way with a girl & a guy, why not after we turned out to be a girl & a guy anyway?'[62]

Sheila's driving licence was changed in 1980 after a letter from her consultant, none other than Wardell Pomeroy, formerly of the Kinsey Institute. Sheila was now Louis Graydon Sullivan. It was also in 1980 that Sullivan produced his pioneering *Information for the Female-to-Male Crossdresser and Transsexual*, into its third edition by 1990, and used playfully by Marjorie Garber in *Vested Interests* (1992), her famous academic study of cross-dressing – though she did not connect the book with Lou.[63] While Lou's trans man heirs might have strong reservations about being described as 'physically handicapped' men, postmodern men with vaginas may well approve of his recommendation that they make use of any erogenous zone, regardless of whether it conflicted with their bodily perceptions, for the pamphlet contained informed guidance on both transvestism and transsexuality.[64] Lou was not afraid to challenge conventional wisdom, including scepticism about the gender experts' claims for the rarity of female crossdressing for erotic ends. Lou was clear that female transvestites included those who used male clothing for masturbatory purposes.[65] 'Are gender specialists actually encouraging women to take the transsexual route by denying a possible existence as a "female transvestite"?'[66] There was advice on passing, based, as we have seen, on practical experience. 'The biggest problem when going female-to-male is that a 30-year-old female when crossdressed as a man, can end up looking like a 14-year-old boy. What can the female-to-male crossdresser do to look older?'[67] Sullivan's answers, including adapting a popular male dress guide's advice for making the smaller man more distinguished, ranged from coats and ties, watches and glasses, to the combing of eyebrows, cutting of sideburns, and even the encouragement of facial acne ('That pimply, pitted look is very masculine'). There was advice on posture, hands (a bit of a giveaway), clothing and shoe size (including a menswear conversion chart), breast-binding (a midriff bulge belt can be pushed up to contain the breasts of small-breasted women, for example, or a modified trainer bra can achieve the illusion of covered male pectorals), and 'the crotch' ('stuffed with two socks (*dress socks* . . . be realistic!)').[68] There were explanations of transsexuality generally, and female-to-male transsexuality in particular. Transsexuals modified their bodies to conform to how they felt in the inside, and that inner feeling was for a body other than theirs. 'To identify strongly with the stereotypical thoughts/feelings of the opposite sex can be a dichotomy, but to identify strongly with the physical attributes of the opposite sex is totally disorienting.'[69] As for sexuality, female-to-male transsexuality was different to lesbianism. The latter involved sexual contact between 'two female bodies': the former 'revolved around the contact of a man's body and a woman's body – with the transsexual participating in the man's body'.[70] Lou did not complicate his explanation with the possibility of the contact between a female-to-male transsexual and a man.

By 1981, having had both hormone treatment and a mastectomy, Lou had decided that he was transsexual rather than transvestite, writing to Virginia Prince, the well-known male-to-female transvestite, 'Maybe I never was a true TV. I never wanted to be a female, even a female dressed in men's clothing. I just wanted to be a gay man.'[71] Meanwhile, Lou participated in homosexual sex as a homosexual man, avoiding contact that would reveal any femaleness. He engaged in oral and masturbatory sex, even visiting gay porn theatres. In retrospect, writing for *The Advocate* in 1989, Lou observed that ignorance about the mere existence of the female-to-gay-male worked in his favour: 'No one could possibly imagine that the smooth-faced young person in the men's room of a gay bar was a female.'[72] Some men discovered Lou's female bodily attributes, but did not care, others did not seem to notice. The casual encounters could pass without too much interrogation – 'I just cannot believe all the fucking *action* I'm getting in the fucking Mission District.'[73] Longer-term relationships proved more awkward: 'But what ARE you? You're not a man & you're not a woman! . . . You have a pussy but you're still a man.'[74] Sullivan had a heterosexual boyfriend who had sex with women and vaginal sex with Lou, but tired of the arrangement: 'I really am bored with this heterosex we have constantly.'[75] He also had sex with a male-to-female transvestite: 'she says I'm the best man she's ever had . . . and she's had REAL ones. Too bad I can't get too excited about her.'[76] Although Lou did not know it at the time, the reader of his diary is aware that he was having unprotected sex on the eve of the early years of AIDS.

Sullivan had done research on transsex in the 1970s and 1980s while embarking on the various stages of his bodily modification, and the news had not been comforting. A female-to-male correspondent sent him a photograph of his own breast reduction surgery, asking Lou for reassurance that his reassigned nipples were not too close together, when, in truth, his chest was a terrible mess and his nipples were the least of his problems.[77] Another contact told him of a surgeon who performed breast surgery on a trans man and then offered to complete the remainder of the modification even though he had never carried out the procedure before (Lou advised against it).[78] Mario Martino sent him a picture of a phalloplasty from the University of Virginia. 'I am enclosing a picture of his phallus as it looks today – horrid. It was very painful from every aspect, but as he, you and I know this was very experimental.'[79] The famous Stanley Biber from Trinidad, Colorado, advised Lou against the creation of a neophallus through the unhooding of the clitoris, with testicular implants in the labia majora – metoidioplasty, the procedure that Lou eventually opted for – because it 'makes a very small penis'. Instead, for close to $15,000, he offered 'the formation of a hollow tube abdominal pedicle graft with insertion of testicular implants and breast removal . . . pan hysterectomy with partial vaginectomy and possibly appendectomy'.[80]

Experts from Oklahoma City explained that they could construct a penis that 'will function sexually with the insertion of a baculum or rod into the hollow central shaft of the penis'. Though penis urination was initially promised, 'It has become evident with time that a urinary tract hook-up should not be done as they have not been all that successful. The female urethra makes such an angulation as compared to the male urethra that it is very difficult to avoid break down, strictures, or fistula formation.' The illustrated penis in the information sheet certainly looked of an impressive size, but it was an organ without feeling and erectile tissue. The booklet continues:

> The clitoris, near the base of the neo-penis, serves as the climactic organ since the head of the neo-penis is usually without sensation. Hair must be shaved or removed by a depilatory crème from the head of the neo-penis as well as through the shaft. Urination, at this stage, is still through the female urethral opening and requires a sitting position.[81]

Sullivan's papers also include a 1988 summary of penis surgery possibilities offered by the Stanford Gender Dysphoria Program. The 'abdominal tube penis', the method used in Oklahoma, involved the formation of a penis on the abdominal wall using skin from the hip. It used a rod for erection, with the rod pressing on the clitoris and labia minora during intercourse – surely a female orgasm for a new male body. The claimed advantage was that the penis was 'natural or even large' and 'realistic' in appearance. The new organ's disadvantage was that it was without feeling or the ability to urinate. That required further operations that were in development, using the nerves from forearm and clitoris to give feeling to the penis and a urinary extension to enable urination through the penis. This outline of ongoing medical innovation was not entirely encouraging. Permanent penile implants were 'not without mechanical problems'. It was possible to enfold the labia minora and to utilise part of the removed vagina to carry urine into the penis but there was a substantial risk of obstruction and infection – all to achieve urinating while standing.[82]

Nonetheless, Lou progressed from testosterone treatment to breast surgery in 1980, and finally to genital reconstruction in 1986 after he convinced his doctors and counsellors both of his sexual attraction to women (more acceptable to therapists than same-sex attractions) and that he did not use his vagina during sex. The genital reconstruction was both painful and problematic; some disturbing diary pages described this process from a patient's point of view.

Then, in early 1987, Lou was diagnosed with HIV. His diary entry for 7 January reads:

> Well, diary, I didn't think I'd be writing the Last Chapter soon. My penmanship is pretty bad because I have an intravenous needle in my right wrist & I'm in the hospital. I have AIDS. How in the hell could this have happened? I, who have been a sexual recluse for so long, contract a disease associated with promiscuity . . . a fatal disease.[83]

Fully aware of the irony that, having struggled so hard to become a gay man, he was to die of AIDS, he wrote, 'My whole life I've wanted to be a gay man & it's kind of an honor to die from the gay man's disease.'[84]

The remaining diaries deal with the travails of AIDS: the impact of those first months, signing up for AZT, the use of alternative treatments as well as conventional medicine, medical errors or at least a mix-up of files at his AIDS clinic, and then later chronicles of pain and medical deterioration amid moments of hope, work on his book *From Female to Male: The Life of Jack Bee Garland*, published in 1990, and lucid interviews with the academic Ira Pauly (now available on YouTube).[85] There are descriptions of an attempted sex life: the issue of whether and/or when to tell a potential sexual partner that one has AIDS ('Do I have to tell him having sex with me could kill him?') and the subtle distinction between saying 'I have

AIDS' and 'I have the virus'.[86] There is an amusing visit to a rather thinly populated (safe-sex) jack-off club, an encounter with a naked man in a gay porn theatre, where Lou was the only patron and the prospective sexual contact was the ticket-taker, and depressing descriptions of disastrous meetings through Lou's contact with the 'Small Endowed Gay Men's Club'.[87] Sullivan reports several instances of men unconcerned about practising what was almost certainly risky behaviour, and contradictory messages from doctors and AIDS support groups about the safeness of safe sex: his doctor told him that

> no way is any kind of intercourse – oral, anal, vaginal – safe, not even with a condom, saying rubbers have never been reliable in preventing pregnancy and so are not reliable in preventing the spread of the virus . . . that 'masturbation and dildos' are some of the safe things I can do.[88]

Sullivan died of AIDS in 1991. He was only 39.

When trying to make sense of his feelings in 1973, Sullivan went to a lecture by Christine Jorgensen, the celebrated MTF transsexual, but recorded that it was difficult to attend because it was a public declaration of being interested in 'this male/female thing'.[89] He researched what was then commonly called transvestism, observing that Esther Newton's study of drag queens, *Mother Camp* (1972), had 'a beautiful picture of exactly what I want to be: it was of Desirée, a female impersonator who honestly looks exactly like a beautiful young woman, figure & all. In the picture he was naked except for a G–string & he looked like a beautiful boy-woman.'[90] As we have seen, Sullivan experimented with transgender: a panty girdle over the breasts to flatten them and a stuffed sock or glove in the crotch. Sullivan said that drag was liberating because it made a person feel that masculinity and femininity were not natural, 'that it's *not* in anyone's *nature* to be masculine or feminine'.[91] The diaries record an oscillation between feelings of transvestism and transsexuality; it was certainly no easy narrative of a man trapped inside the body of a woman, the plot that trans men were encouraged to adopt during that period. Sullivan worried that phalloplasty (the construction of a penis) would affect the ability to orgasm. He oscillated between discomfort with ambiguity and fear of giving in to what he thought, and feared, was fantasy.

The story of Lou Sullivan is compelling because it threatens the very categorisation that his biographical sketch posthumously forced him into. The notable thing about Sullivan, as revealed in the diaries, is that he moved in a world of gender and sexual indecision and flexibility. Lou knew a trans man, Christiaan D'Arcy, who had lived with a trans woman for thirteen years, when, for much of that time, 'she was he and I [D'Arcy] was she. We had heterosexual sex for 7 years.' D'Arcy was interested in having sex with women but was also attracted to 'Male to females . . . Women with penises'. Lou was puzzled by this irresolution:

> You stated 'I try to think what it would be like to be gay as I never had sex with a genetic female.' But, Christiaan, if you feel like a man and have only had sex with men, wouldn't that make you a gay man?? I'm confused. You love women but have never had sex with them? Is it that you feel like a man, and just WANT to have sex with a female that makes you heterosexual??? Help me understand what you mean.[92]

Sullivan's trans woman friend Elizabeth Marshall oscillated between maleness and femaleness and the names – Elizabeth, Eliot, Dale – that proclaimed their identity. She sought and then decided against surgery (admittedly when it was refused by Cook County Hospital), stopped taking hormones, went back to them again, and then stopped. Marshall threw out her women's clothes. She cut her hair short. 'I'm really back? (forward!) to being MALE.' Lou had a photograph of her on a Florida beach, an image of an attractive, bare-breasted, tanned woman. Sullivan and Marshall discussed their inability to fit categories. 'We're further [a]head than any of those TV–TSs. To be able to incorporate your ambiguity is far more revolutionary & futuristic than trying to resolve it along some obscure conventional lines.' They talked of living 'in the middle', being neither male nor female.[93]

Lou corresponded with a lesbian who was attracted to trans men, with a trans man who had sex with bisexual men but who also 'turned tricks' as a 'gay male', and with a trans man who had had another trans man as a lover – 'Do you use your vagina during sex? (I mean during male/male sex).'[94] He heard of a woman who had once been attracted to gay men (her husband had a male lover) but then decided that she was probably lesbian.[95] In response to a personal advertisement in the magazine *Coming Up* (1984–85), he was contacted by a trans woman who was 'strongly lesbian identified' and liked to be sexually dominated: Lou replied, 'we really are coming from opposite directions'.[96]

Those with whom Lou/Sheila had sex, as both/either Lou/Sheila, are as interesting in their flexibility as our main protagonist. In 1980, when he was undergoing hormone treatment, Sullivan went to a bar and picked up a drag queen. Sullivan paid for their drinks: 'She sat down & I was the man, she was the loose woman.' They went back to Lou's place for sex. The drag queen said to Lou that he looked a little effeminate (she told him later that she had thought that he was a hermaphrodite). The drag queen had anal sex with Lou and told him that he was 'going to make a really great gay boy'![97] The diaries, then, record a woman, Sheila, who wanted to be, and then decided that he was, a man – a homosexual man. Sheila/Lou wanted, enjoyed, sex with men, but as a gay man. As the famous punk band member told his occasional girlfriend Sheila, 'she' had indeed set up a challenge for 'herself'.

Notes

1 S. Stryker and P. Currah, 'Introduction', *TSQ*, 1:1–2 (2014), 1–18, quote at 3. See also A. Tompkins, 'Asterisk', *TSQ*, 1:1–2 (2014), 26–7.

2 M. L. Brown and C. A. Rounsley, *True Selves: Understanding Transsexualism – For Families, Friends, Coworkers, and Helping Professionals* (San Francisco, 1996), p. 25.

3 B. L. Hausman, 'Demanding subjectivity: transsexualism, medicine, and the technologies of gender', *Journal of the History of Sexuality*, 3:2 (1992), 270–302.

4 J. Meyerowitz, *How Sex Changed: A History of Transsexuality in the United States* (Cambridge, MA, 2002), p. 1.

5 D. O. Cauldwell, 'Psychopathia transexualis', *Sexology: Sex Science Magazine* (December 1949), 274–80; H. Benjamin, *The Transsexual Phenomenon* (New York, 1966); R. J. Stoller, *Sex and Gender: On the Development of Masculinity and Femininity* (New York, 1968); R. Green and J. Money (eds), *Transsexualism and Sex Reassignment* (Baltimore, MD, 1969).

6 For a useful recent survey, see K. Sutton, 'From sexual inversion to trans*: transgender history and historiography', in F. Mildenberger et al. (eds), *Was ist Homosexualität?* (Hamburg, 2014), pp. 181–203.

7 Meyerowitz, *How Sex Changed*, pp. 217–22.

8 I. B. Pauly, 'Female transsexualism: part I', *Archives of Sexual Behavior*, 3:6 (1974), 487–507; I. B. Pauly, 'Female transsexualism: part II', *Archives of Sexual Behavior*, 3:6 (1974), 509–26.

9 H. Devor, 'Sexual orientation identities, attractions, and practices of female-to-male transsexuals', *The Journal of Sex Research*, 30:4 (1993), pp. 303–15.

10 A. Bolin, 'Transcending and transgendering: male-to-female transsexuals, dichotomy and diversity', in G. Herdt (ed.), *Third Sex, Third Gender* (New York, 1996), ch. 10.

11 G. Beemyn and S. Rankin, *The Lives of Transgender People* (New York, 2011), pp. 23–6.

12 W. O. Bockting, 'Psychotherapy and the real-life experience: from gender dichotomy to gender diversity', *Sexologies*, 17:4 (2008), 211–24, quote at 214.

13 R. Ekins and D. King, 'The emergence of new transgendering identities in the age of the internet', in S. Hines and T. Sanger (eds), *Transgender Identities:*

Towards a Social Analysis of Gender Diversity (New York, 2010), ch. 1; Beemyn and Rankin, *Lives of Transgender People*, pp. 44–5, 54, 57–9, 75, 121, 140–1.

14 I have looked at the complexities and conflicts of the period in B. Reay, 'The transsexual phenomenon: a counter-history', *Journal of Social History: Societies & Cultures*, 47:4 (2014), 1042–70.

15 L. M. Rodemeyer, *Lou Sullivan Diaries (1970–1980) and Theories of Sexual Embodiment: Making Sense of Sensing* (New York, 2017); B. D. Smith, *Lou Sullivan: Daring To Be a Man Among Men* (Oakland, CA, 2017), Ebook.

16 For a good account of Sullivan's activism, see S. Stryker, 'Portrait of a transfag drag hag as a young man: the activist career of Louis G. Sullivan', in K. More and S. Whittle (eds), *Reclaiming Genders: Transsexual Grammars at the Fin de Siècle* (New York, 1999), ch. 3.

17 Rodemeyer, *Lou Sullivan Diaries*, pp. xi, n. 1, xii.

18 Smith, *Lou Sullivan*, Ebook, loc. 327.

19 I am referring to the cover of *OP: Original Plumbing: Trans Male Quarterly*, The Hero Issue, 2013.

20 Most of what follows, unless indicated otherwise, comes from San Francisco History Center, San Francisco Public Library, Louis Graydon Sullivan Papers (hereafter Sullivan Papers), Box 1, Folders 4–20: Sheila/Louis Sullivan Diaries and Journals (hereafter, Sullivan Diaries), 1961–91. Rodemeyer has published selections of the 1970–80 diaries as chapters 1, 3, and 5 of her book *Lou Sullivan Diaries* (see note 15 above), but my account draws on the diaries over a much longer period and makes use of Sullivan's correspondence too.

21 Sullivan Diaries, 3 March and 30 May 1964.

22 Ibid., 3 December 1964.

23 Ibid., 24 March 1965.

24 Ibid., 12 January 1966.

25 Ibid., 7 August and 4 September 1966.

26 Ibid., 14 February 1966.

27 Ibid., 10 April 1966.

28 Ibid., 21 April 1966.

29 Ibid., 28 June 1967.

30 Ibid., 2 May 1968.

31 Ibid., 22 November 1970. Emphasis in the original.

32 Ibid., 13 January 1971. Emphasis in the original.

33 Ibid., 7 January 1973.

34 Ibid., 17 March 1973.

35 Ibid., 7 July 1973.

36 Ibid, 26 February 1973.

37 Ibid., 23 June 1973.

38 Ibid., 21 April 1975.

39 Ibid., 16 June 1975.

40 Ibid., 22 March 1976. Emphasis in original.

41 Ibid., 5 and 21 August 1976.
42 Sullivan Papers, Box 2, Folder 110: Letter from Elizabeth Marshall, 7 October 1975. Emphasis in the original.
43 Ibid., Letter from Elizabeth Marshall, 14 March 1976. Emphasis in the original.
44 Ibid., Box 1, Folder 1: Application to Stanford Gender Dysphoria Program, October 1976.
45 Sullivan Diaries, 23 September 1976.
46 Ibid., 6 September 1976.
47 Ibid., 26 November 1976.
48 Sullivan Papers, Box 2, Folder 110: Letter to Elizabeth Marshall, 15 August 1977.
49 Sullivan Diaries, 14 and 26 May 1978.
50 Ibid., 21 January 1979.
51 Sullivan Papers, Folder 44: Letter to Mario Martino [Angelo Tornabene], 12 September 1979. Emphasis in the original.
52 Ibid., Folder 49B: Letter to Mark Brannigan, 4 September 1979.
53 Ibid., a copy of *The TV–TS Tapestry*, 3 September 1979, a New Hampshire newsletter. Brannigan contributes to the Forum section, with a picture, and is described as 'a heterosexual female transvestite'.
54 Ibid., Letter to Mark Brannigan, 2 October 1979.
55 Sullivan Diaries, 9 October 1979.
56 Ibid.
57 Ibid., 5 October 1979.
58 Sullivan Papers, Folder 45: Application to Stanford Gender Dysphoria Program, October 1979.
59 Ibid., Letters from and to Judy Van Maasdam, 12 and 22 March 1980.
60 For the rejection and Lou's response, see Stryker, 'Portrait of a transfag drag hag'.
61 Sullivan Diaries, 9 October 1979.
62 Ibid., 1 February 1980.
63 L. Sullivan, *Information for the Female-to-Male Crossdresser and Transsexual* (San Francisco, 1985 [1980]); M. Garber, *Vested Interests: Cross-Dressing and Cultural Anxiety* (New York, 1997), pp. 41–51.
64 Sullivan, *Information*, p. 40.
65 Ibid., pp. 5–10.
66 Ibid., p. 7.
67 Ibid., p. 22.
68 Ibid., pp. 22–7. Emphasis in the original.
69 Ibid., p. 14.
70 Ibid., p. 15.
71 Sullivan Papers, Box 2, Folder 115: Letter to Virginia Prince, 7 February 1981.
72 L. Sullivan, 'Sullivan's Travels', *The Advocate*, 6 June 1989.
73 Sullivan Diaries, 7 September 1981. Emphasis in the original.
74 Ibid., 22 August 1981. Emphasis in the original.

75 Ibid., 15 January 1984.
76 Ibid., 4 March 1984. Emphasis in the original.
77 Sullivan Papers, Box 2, Folder 76: Letter from Steven Royce, 12 October 1983.
78 Ibid., Folder 79: Letters from and to Karl Vieau, 29 April and 21 May 1980.
79 Ibid., Folder 44: Letter from Mario Martino [Angelo Tornabene], 3 October 1980.
80 Ibid., Folder 39: Letters from Stanley Biber, 3 February and 31 March 1986.
81 Ibid., Folder 41: Letters from Charles Reynolds, Urology Center, Inc., Oklahoma City, 29 June 1978; and David William Foerster, July 1981 and 9 October 1984.
82 Ibid., Folder 45: Correspondence with Stanford Gender Dysphoria Program, 1976–89.
83 Sullivan Diaries, 7 January 1987. Ellipsis in the original.
84 Ibid.
85 L. Sullivan, *From Female to Male: The Life of Jack Bee Garland* (Boston, MA, 1990); http://youtube.com/watch?v=DbK5Ye7aSIY (last accessed 26 April 2018).
86 Sullivan Diaries, 9 December 1987.
87 Ibid., 17 and 28 September and 2 November 1987.
88 Ibid., 9 December 1987.
89 Ibid., 23 March 1973.
90 Ibid., 7 July 1973.
91 Ibid., 13 July 1973. Emphasis in the original.
92 Sullivan Papers, Box 2, Folder 52: Correspondence with Christiaan D'Arcy, 1987. D'Arcy was murdered in 1993: http://articles.courant.com/1993-02-15/news/0000105921_1_cabbie-union-station-beauty-school (last accessed 26 April 2018).
93 Ibid., Folder 110: Transcripts of letters to and from 'Liz' [Elizabeth Marshall], 1975–78; Folder 109: Letters from Elliot/Dale [Elizabeth] Marshall, 1980–81.
94 Ibid., Folder 110: Letter to Elizabeth Marshall, 9 March 1976; Folder 59: Letters from Gene Gilson, 26 April, 2 June, and 23 July 1981; Folder 67: Letter to David Liebman, 18 September 1984.
95 Ibid., Folder 110: Letter to Elizabeth Marshall, 9 March 1976.
96 Ibid., Folder 127: Replies to personal advertisement in the magazine *Coming Up!* 1984–85.
97 Sullivan Diaries, 14 January 1980.

6

Sex in the archives: David Louis Bowie's New York diaries, 1978–93

There are some very queer diaries in the not always queer archives of the Manuscripts and Archives Division in the Humanities and Social Sciences Library of the New York Public Library. They are embargoed until 2068, but I was granted special permission to consult them. I have trouble recalling what initially piqued my interest but it must have been the catalogue entry: 'David Louis Bowie Diaries 1978–1993 . . . Illustrated diaries of the daily activities and sexual encounters of a Queens resident who died of AIDS-related causes. (Restrictions apply.)' This brief description by no means prepares the reader for the contents of these remarkable documents.[1]

Bowie – not to be confused with his more famous namesake – worked in the transport service industry, first as a passenger service supervisor for Pan American Airways and then for a firm that specialised in shipping expensive artworks. The diaries cover the years from 1978 until 1993 when Bowie died of AIDS. But they are the remnants of a larger archive, for we learn from the entries themselves that Bowie was burgled in 1986 and that the vanished safe contained his diaries from 1964 to 1977 as well as the one for 1983. 'Every day of my entire life during those years is in those diaries. The most passionate, emotional, erotic, jet-set crazy years . . . On top of that, I had done the most exotic and erotic graphic art I ever created in those books along with photographs.'[2] So what we have is only a little over a half of the diaries that might have been. The 1960s and early 1970s, clearly of interest in US sexual history, are lost. There are also tantalising references to photograph albums and slides and Polaroids of trysts but this separate visual archive seems not to have survived.[3] Bowie was an amateur artist, and the Leslie–Lohman Museum of Gay and Lesbian Art in New York has one of his paintings and a file of slides of his art, including *A Green Nocturnal Dream* (1966), a Salvador Dali-like painting of a tree of penises, a theme with a relevance that will soon become apparent.[4]

The diary format appears relatively uncomplicated. Volumes start with colour photographs of 'My Boy of the Year' (in 1978, of a young Hispanic male 'Miguel'), tabulation of sexual contacts, month by month, and for the year (the totals include multiple contacts) – 273 in 1978 – and then the diary text. They usually conclude in the same manner, with comments on the previous twelve months – 'this era of gay liberation had allowed me to enjoy the excesses of permissiveness like I never experienced before', he noted of 1978 – and copies of his handmade Christmas cards in two versions for 'straight' and non-straight friends respectively. The alternatives for Christmas 1982 were photographs of a flying seagull and an ejaculating penis (in flight too, in a sense). His 'erotic' card for 1981 was an image of a man fisting himself, above the festive ('fistive') caption 'joy to the world' (see Figure 39).[5]

The diaries contain references to day-to-day living (watering the house plants, mowing the lawn) and work-related activities, but they are principally chronicles of sexual encounters:

> Raul, Mario and I fisted each other into the night. Then Raul made Demitasse while I took a shower . . . later I dropped Mario off at his place in 'The Village' and I continued on to 'The Ramrod' . . . Then Dewey and I went on to 'The Mine Shaft' where I carried on with two humpy guys in two different sex sessions. Dewey and I got home . . . at 0640. After a hot, spermy sex-session on the living room floor, Dewey and I settled down for some much needed sleep at 0725.[6]

Then, interspersed with the text, are the drawings: mainly of the penises of Bowie's sexual partners. Take the illustrated example of combined text and drawing for the pages of 2 and 3 January 1978, where it is as if the penis is draped over the open diary – a potentially embarrassing archival moment for the reader if observed by fellow researchers. These texts are graphic in both senses of the term (see Figure 40).

These are not philosophical or romantic reminiscences but sex diaries. They contain sexual accounts, sexual histories, yet they are also sexual exhibits. This chapter deals both with a described sexual world and the source that represents it.

The diaries provide details of New York sex in the periods before and after AIDS, what their author called a 'Daily Diary of an American Gay Experience'.[7] They provide an extended glimpse of a sexual milieu that, as Andrew Holleran once observed, can now seem 'as exotic as ancient Egypt'.[8] As well as casual sex and organised fisting, more of which later,

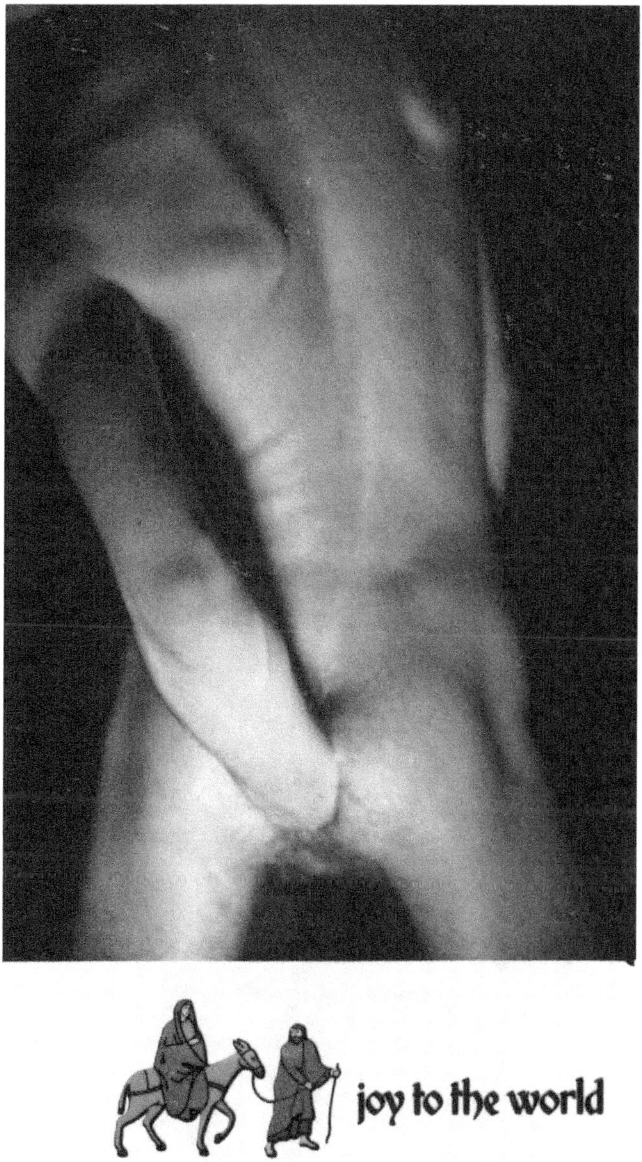

39 Bowie Diaries, 1981 [the photograph was taken in 1975]. Manuscripts and Archives Division, The New York Public Library, Astor, Lenox and Tilden Foundations.

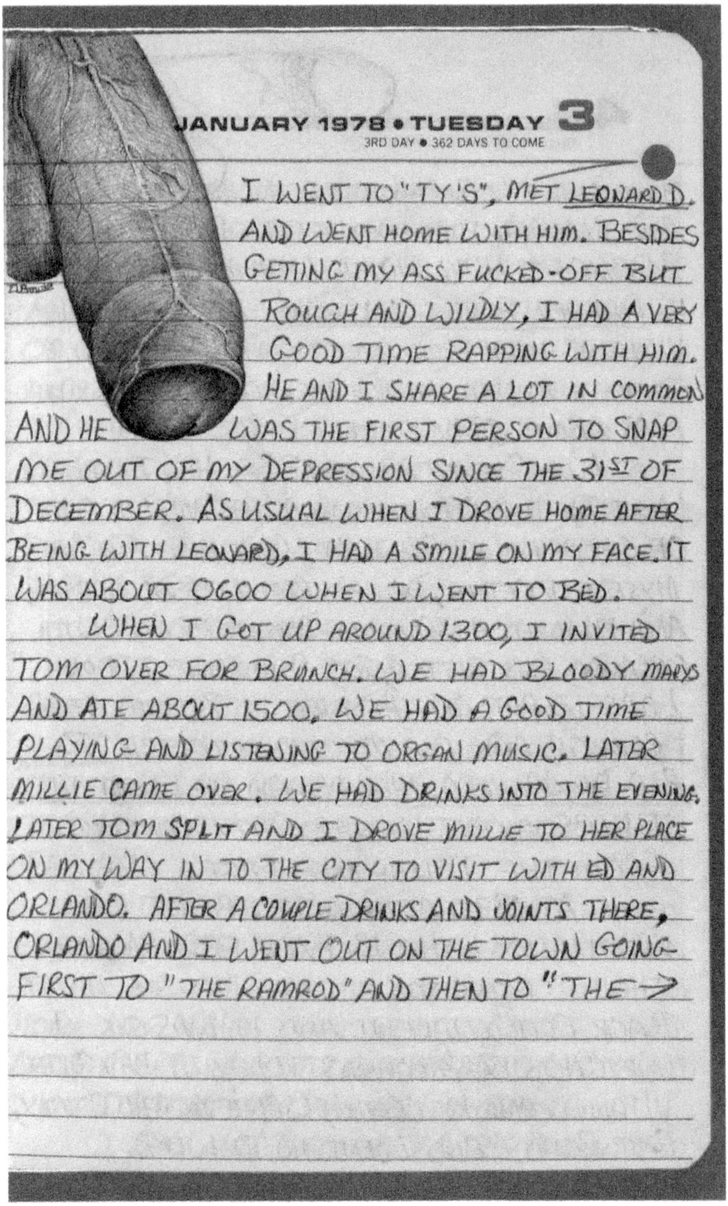

JANUARY 1978 • TUESDAY 3
3RD DAY • 362 DAYS TO COME

I WENT TO "TY'S", MET LEONARD D. AND WENT HOME WITH HIM. BESIDES GETTING MY ASS FUCKED-OFF BUT ROUGH AND WILDLY, I HAD A VERY GOOD TIME RAPPING WITH HIM. HE AND I SHARE A LOT IN COMMON AND HE WAS THE FIRST PERSON TO SNAP ME OUT OF MY DEPRESSION SINCE THE 31ST OF DECEMBER. AS USUAL WHEN I DROVE HOME AFTER BEING WITH LEONARD, I HAD A SMILE ON MY FACE. IT WAS ABOUT 0600 WHEN I WENT TO BED.

WHEN I GOT UP AROUND 1300, I INVITED TOM OVER FOR BRUNCH. WE HAD BLOODY MARYS AND ATE ABOUT 1500. WE HAD A GOOD TIME PLAYING AND LISTENING TO ORGAN MUSIC. LATER MILLIE CAME OVER. WE HAD DRINKS INTO THE EVENING. LATER TOM SPLIT AND I DROVE MILLIE TO HER PLACE ON MY WAY IN TO THE CITY TO VISIT WITH ED AND ORLANDO. AFTER A COUPLE DRINKS AND JOINTS THERE, ORLANDO AND I WENT OUT ON THE TOWN GOING FIRST TO "THE RAMROD" AND THEN TO "THE →

40 Bowie Diaries, 1978. Manuscripts and Archives Division, The New York Public Library, Astor, Lenox and Tilden Foundations.

Bowie engaged in solitary masturbation using dildos and other sex aids, all dutifully recorded. He took drugs to enhance his sexual experiences: cannabis (marijuana, hash, THC, and Purple Haze), LSD (acid), the amphetamine Eskatrol, angel dust (PCP), cocaine (nasally and anally), mescaline, crystal meth (nasally and anally), the psychedelic MDA, and amyl nitrite. He frequented New York's numerous clubs: The Mineshaft, The Ramrod, Badlands, The Cockring, Kellers, The Candlelight, Chaps, The Strap, Billy the Kid, The Spike (where he met the famous photographer Robert Mapplethorpe in 1982), J's, Ass Trick, The Eagle, Alex in Wonderland, Rawhide, and The Anvil. The evocatively named Alex in Wonderland 'has something for everyone . . . three levels of decadence from the fist-fuck bar on the cellar level to the pumping disco on the main level to the pool room, coat check and orgy room on the third level'.[9] He visited the Hell Fire Club in 1982,

> one of the most decadent dens of iniquity in N.Y.C. All types of people go there. Guys and girls, straights and gays, cops, nurses, secretaries, pimps, hustlers, hookers, executives, leather types, and just anyone who can cough up the pretty stiff door fee to join in the madness. A bathtub with one or two fornicating in it in piss up to their necks was the only toilet. The screaming, beating, fucking, and sucking went on through thick smoke and dim red and black light bulbs sparsely situated. The smell of booze, piss and sex reeked about the joint.[10]

One of the more fascinating aspects of the diaries is their material relating to the New York fisting scene, an organised sexual culture in which Bowie was heavily involved. He also participated in the more public venues of the clubs – there are references to the orgy rooms of The Mineshaft and Ass Trick – but most such activity occurred in apartments and other private residences with small networks of aficionados, 'the underground, private world of "fist-fucking"',[11] the venues that Gayle Rubin found central to San Francisco S/M.[12] 'Unless one has experienced it', Bowie wrote, 'there is no way to understand the experience . . . [it] puts your mind into the glorious state only approached by the most exotic, pure drugs which used to be available.'[13] Apart from his attempt to evoke the intensity of the performance, something also stressed in Rubin's accounts, he described rather than analysed such activity, with references to Crisco, poppers, slings, music (what Rubin called 'Music to Fuck By'),[14] and a suggestion that the whole experience was greater than the force of its sex.

> Mario lives in a simple, clean, light apartment. A person's environment says so much about the individual and I thoroughly enjoyed this first visit to Mario's

> place. We had wild, fist-fucking, sperm sessions while listening to his great 'Quad' sound system. Later I took a shower and had some of his homemade cheesecake. What a pleasure this evening was with Mario.[15]

It is true that Bowie hinted at fisting's democratic possibilities: 'The orgy contained the broadest spectrum of guys one could imagine such as a doctor, a minister and an ex prisoner with his parol[e] officer plus white, black and yellow races. It was one hell of a blast!'[16] But generally his descriptions lack philosophising.

It is unfortunate that the 1983 diary is missing for it must have covered the early days of AIDS. Bowie returned to The Mineshaft in 1984: 'I couldn't get over how packed the place was . . . I was amazed by so many guys all "doing-it". Hasen't [*sic*] anyone heard of A.I.D.S.?'[17] (This entry is followed by an account he provides of having oral sex with an anonymous Italian youth.) By 1986 he was noting the effects of the virus on the world of more extreme sex (at least one of his fisting partners had succumbed and another would a few years later), yet he still participated in such activity, as demonstrated by his account of attending a sex party: 'some precautions were taken such as the use of rubber gloves, avoiding swapping of sperm and frequent washing of hands. But the party was reminiscent of the promiscuity enjoyed during the peak years of gay liberation.'[18] Indeed Bowie's described experience varies from Rubin's claims for the inhibiting impact of AIDS on San Francisco practices.[19] He was still fisting while in the final stages of the deadly syndrome. He appears to have thought (mistakenly) that sex was safer if confined to those he knew: 'I did lots of cruising . . . but not enough to take the risk . . . of bringing home a stranger . . . [because of] the A.I.D.S. risk of going to bed with someone you don't know.'[20] He refers to invitations to 'safe sex' orgies but does not elaborate on what that safe sex might have entailed.

There is certainly a great deal of described casual sex – between two and three hundred 'sex episodes' or 'sexperiences' in many of the yearly tabulations, or between twenty and thirty a month – with partners only identified by their first names ('a guy named Jim', 'a sexy, lean, black youth named Robbie', 'a little Italian guy from Long Island named Carlo'), or merely by physical or other characteristics ('a very young Hispanic with a perfect body', 'a sexy, horny black youth', 'street tuffy', 'big, black youth', 'hungry mouth', 'guy with a moustache'), or what he labelled 'many others where names didn't enter the encounter'.[21] There were so many that it was easy to lose track: 'I got home to bed at 0400 with a guy named Richard. My notes don't indicate if this was a new encounter or not.'[22] However, there are named contacts and recurring partners, though the depicted sex was without commitment. His identified interactions included a renowned ballet dancer, a designer, a sculptor, a musician, a future male companion of a well-known New York socialite, and the model of a celebrated photographer.[23]

We should situate Bowie's behaviour in its historical context, for his gay experience was not out of place in the urban US of the 1970s and 1980s, the milieu touched on in Chapter 4 of this book.[24] It is also worth comparing the descriptive frugality of Bowie's journals with far more literary accounts of The Mineshaft and its associated sexual practices. The writer Edmund White's evocation begins before he even enters the club:

> The Mine Shaft is located on a dark corner in the West Village meatpacking district. In the morning this area is noisy with hissing air brakes and quick with butchers in bloody white aprons guiding dead animals out of refrigerated trucks into cold storage. Travelling hooks swing sides of beef across sidewalks. On cold days metal oil drums blaze with fire and the men warm their hands over the flames. At night the streets are deserted, the pavement slick with blood. Everything smells of lanolin.[25]

White's Mineshaft is far more than a dark space with slings for fucking or being fucked. It represents a wider cultural moment where sex has become everything: 'our sole mode of transcendence and our only touchstone of authenticity'.[26] Or there is the casual sex of Samuel Delany's trucks, involving up to a hundred strangers, a 'libidinal saturation' that had to be experienced to be truly comprehended, not the predictable abandonment of pornographic representation but rather

> hugely ordered, highly social, attentive, silent, and grounded in a certain care, if not community. At those times, within those van-walled alleys, now between the trucks, now in the back of the open loaders, cock passed from mouth to mouth to hand to ass to mouth without ever breaking contact with other flesh for more than seconds.[27]

There was little such reflection – or describing of the indescribable – in Bowie's recording of his acts.

We might also consider *Tricks* (1981), Renaud Camus's recounting of homosexual sex in Greenwich Village at much the same time and doubtless in the same venues as those charted by Bowie.[28] Here too there were encounters without words, based merely on a smile and glance, male same-sex acts recalled in graphic detail without any theorising about their significance, where, as we saw in Chapter 4, the physical intensity and closeness of contact contrasts with the lack of intimacy of verbal interaction. (Joel Brodsky said of The Mineshaft that it was a place 'where cultural inhibitions were displaced, rather than discussed . . . an arena of critical practice, rather than critical discourse'.)[29] Camus exhibited the ennui of excess and was remarkably indifferent to some of his casual sex. But Bowie never seemed world-weary.

The 1970s classic *The Joy of Gay Sex* warned that one of the risks of one-night stands was compulsivity: 'Everything about your sex life, including you, becomes routinized.'[30] Indeed there was nothing especially random – little that was casual – about the rituals of cruising, the chosen bars, and the private arrangements for the rites of fisting. Bowie always knew the names of those involved in fisting, apart perhaps from the spontaneous encounters in The Mineshaft. (Rubin has explained that because of the intensity and intimacy of fisting, 'even casual encounters could lead to deep affection and lasting friendships'.)[31] Moreover, contact was neither strictly anonymous nor arbitrary, given that many of Bowie's (and Camus's) tricks were known by sight or by name (we will see that there were many Michaels). Bowie also had long-standing arrangements for no-strings, sexual contact friendships that lasted for years. One such connection was married with children: 'I've known Lenny since . . . he was only 16 . . . Since then he got married, worked . . . as a Corrections Officer at Reikers [*sic*] Island . . . Our relationship has its ups and downs but it still goes on.'[32] He described others as 'friend, roommate, fuck-buddy, companion, lover, brother and confidant', or 'boy-friend/sex-buddy'.[33] A 'pig-mate', he explained, was someone that you would have sex with when no one else was available.[34]

Although analysis of homosexual sex has tended to focus on public sites – bars, clubs, movie theatres, porn stores, restrooms, the trucks, piers, baths, and the 'meat racks' found at certain beaches and parks – the Bowie diaries remind us of the importance of the private room, apartment, or house in this activity. The fisting sessions were usually in homes and apartments. His house in Queens, where contacts visited or came back with him after a night in the clubs and bars, was known as 'cock castle'.[35] Bowie constructed his personal space to reflect his sexual longings: his massive bed, pictures, paintings, pornographic collection, and sex toys (there was a rush to remove incriminating material when the police were called after his burglary). The paving of his garden with cobblestones taken at night from the streets of Chelsea, near the clubs and piers, symbolised this symbiosis between public and private.

Most of Bowie's sexual contacts were with males. But there are descriptions of heterosexual sex: one-to-one ('I may be gay but I'm straight enough to enjoy a nice hot pussy occasionally', he wrote next to his drawing of a vagina) and group (he referred to one such woman as 'a sexy party pussy').[36] Moreover, some of Bowie's sexual interactions were with men who also engaged in sex with women and whose willingness to participate in homosexual sex was much like the heterosexual homosexuality described in my book *New York Hustlers* (2010), though I knew nothing of Bowie when I wrote it. These were working-class men – white, Puerto Rican, and African American (Bowie was attracted by the lure of cross-class and cross-race sexual contact) – for whom sex was just sex regardless of the gender of their partner, and who might trade their bodies occasionally. Strictly speaking, a hustler is a male prostitute, nearly always to men, who makes his body available in exchange for cash, but many men who traded on their looks or physical attributes did so for food, drink, clothing, or a room – as well as, of course, for pleasure's sake, without any monetary barter, though if there was also profit so much the better. As I have argued elsewhere, a wide range of young, working-class, heterosexual men in America's past were homosexually available, and hustling and trade should be seen in economic as well as sexual terms as a way of getting a living. *Some* of the young men who spent time with Bowie, enjoying his food and accommodation as well as sex, may have occasionally robbed him. He rarely called such men hustlers, indeed stated in his diaries that he avoided the dangers of hustler sex, but that is what a few seem to have been. The boundaries were more blurred than Bowie recognised.[37]

Bowie's promiscuity included interracial promiscuity. Race was a strong ingredient in Bowie's cross-class encounters. His diaries recount sex holidays to Rio de Janeiro, three trips in 1978 alone. Clearly he eroticised these men of colour, both in his sexual tourism and back in New York. There are repeated references to 'little brown animals', 'foreskinned, aromatic, Puerto Rican prick', 'hot, Puerto Rican, male animals', even to a dildo called José ('it looked like so many of my friends'), as well as to 'big, black, uncircumcised cock', 'a beautiful black beast', and what he termed his 'black period'.[38] Bowie was obsessed with foreskins, as is clear from the hundreds of drawings of uncircumcised penises, and his race and foreskin fetishes were closely linked.[39] This racial othering heightened his sexual contacts, yet we should guard against endowing these fancies with the power of more serious dehumanisation.[40] They were fantasies: 'My life is so blessed with Puerto Ricans and it is amazing the triangular and circular love affairs I get into with them.'[41]

Bowie claimed that his diary was a record of gay life, but it was no direct account. Some entries were written soon after encounters, when memories were vivid and their writing was virtually a ritualistic part of the sex represented, as in this description of a visit to The Mineshaft in 1979, which is practically post-coital:

> My first encounter was with an athletic looking, black youth who I fucked a load into. Then along came a very young, dark haired youth named Chuck who licked my still erect, oozing prick clean. I had a beer and then fucked another lean youth wearing leather pants, got my dick sucked some more by another guy with big nipples, sucked off a child with a perfect body, and finished up my morning with a very hot, moustached, lean youth who I fucked a load into. Whew!
>
> I drove home feeling just great. I got in at 0530, *wrote in this diary* [my emphasis], had a bite to eat and went to bed at 0635.[42]

However, other entries occurred months after the described events: 'I am writing this page on Saturday 17 January 1979 (almost 10 months after the date) so the information is quite sketchy . . . according to my sex calendar, I carried on with two guys on this date. Probably in The Mine Shaft.'[43] 'Since I have no notes for this date, most of the details have to be omitted . . . But my social sexual calendar indicates that I carried-on with Michael on this date. Although I researched 17 Michaels from my past I could not place the one I was looking for.'[44] He refers to taking notes for his journals that would be worked up years later. 'My notes were sketchy . . . and considering how I partied during this era and the fact that I'm making this entry into this diary nearly ten years later, it is a wonder that I had as many details as I had here.'[45]

Moreover, the care taken with his drawing, the constant drafting, the working and reworking, went on for years. (As has been hinted, the crafting was artistic rather than literary: he focused on his drawings rather than his prose. His 1978 diary, for example, 'like finishing a canvas', was not completed until 1988.)[46] The diaries have a fetishistic quality. They are sexual objects, Bowie's own sexual archive. He was aroused both by the memories they stored and his textual and visual renderings, and refers to masturbating to his drawings – even while executing them – as in this entry for 1988: 'While writing and drawing about my encounter with Heribaldo in my 1978 diary, I "whacked off". That was a torrid, memorable day in my life.'[47] There was also a fetish within the fetish: Bowie's fixation on foreskins, referred to earlier. This is an archive imbricated in its chronicled sexual history in many intriguing ways.

Finally, the journals were a memorial to those friends he lost to AIDS, nearly fifty by the time of his own death. AIDS was, he reflected in 1987, 'The thorn in the side of the pleasure of life . . . For me it has become a psychological burden on my sexual activity, social and daily life.'[48] He described the indignities of dental work: 'A young guy went to work on my teeth. He was very well garbed, gloved and shielded to protect him from me . . . he looked more like he was going to work with radioactive particles than another human being.'[49] This was the limit to his deliberation. Bowie's AIDS reporting is very different to Eric Michaels's late 1980s *Unbecoming*, a deeply reflective work. The visual effects of AIDS written on Michaels's body (the sarcoma) prompted the script on the page as he assessed his life and his dying, his unbecoming, his social death before his actual physical departure –

> I watched these spots on my legs announce themselves over a period of weeks, taking them as some sort of morphemes, arising out of the strange uncertainties of the past few years to declare, finally, a scenario. As if these quite harmless-looking cancers might, when strung together, form sentences which would give a narrative trajectory.[50]

Moreover, Michaels was aware that what he wrote might be published. With Bowie, however, AIDS was an unwelcome postscript to diaries long begun rather than an occasion for deep contemplation or savage observation. He had no expectation of publication. Bowie was a chronicler rather than a diarist. Yet there is a quiet power in the account of his own travails, with its unembellished referencing of chronic diarrhoea, gastritis, vomiting, pancreatitis (caused by anti-viral medication), hepatitis, bleeding toes, thrush and gingivitis, and transfusions to combat acute anaemia.

The visual divergences between Michaels and Bowie are striking too. *Unbecoming* begins with a photograph of its defiant author, revealing the disfigurement of his lesions. In contrast, Bowie's friends are remembered as healthy bodies. While his photographic commemorations, a steady stream from 1984 onwards, are no different to the (beefcake) imagery of his Boys of the Year, this eroticisation heightens rather than undermines their impact. The haunting image of 'Chipmunk' rises from the sand and gazes across another image of himself (at another time) directly into the eyes of the viewer. It is a brilliantly poignant tribute (see Figure 41).

We have Bowie's diaries because of the death of their creator. The volume for 1993 finishes with an entry for 23 January. After that, the pages are blank. The chronicling stops; there are no more meticulous drawings. While it is tempting to read this whiteness as Bowie's own stark memorial,

41 Bowie Diaries, 1986. Manuscripts and Archives Division, The New York Public Library, Astor, Lenox and Tilden Foundations.

he should be remembered rather for the exuberant text that precedes this representational caesura: as the recorder of a lost culture in pursuit of sexual pleasure and creator of a wondrous example of sex in the archives.

Notes

1 The New York Public Library, Humanities and Social Sciences Library, Manuscripts and Archives Division, MSS Col 353, David Louie Bowie Diaries 1978–93 (hereafter Bowie Diaries). The library closed the collection for seventy-five years when it was donated in 1993 because people were named in the diaries (Letter from Mary B. Bowling, Curator of Manuscripts, to Richard Schaneman, 18 June 1993). However, one of the archivists provided me with the donor's contact details and I approached him for special permission to consult them, which was granted without reservation ('As a matter of fact, this is exactly the reason I made the effort to get them into the possession of the New York Public Library': email from R. Schaneman to B. Reay, 8 June 2010). I have, of course, preserved the anonymity of those mentioned in the diaries. I am most grateful to Richard Schaneman, the executor of Bowie's estate and the trustee of the diaries, for permission to consult them and to reproduce the images that appear here. I would also like to thank Tal Nadan, Reference Archivist in the Manuscripts and Archives Division, for her help and encouragement during the preparation of this chapter. The images are reproduced by permission of Manuscripts and Archives Division, New York Public Library, Astor, Lenox and Tilden Foundations.

2 Bowie Diaries, 12 January 1986.

3 Richard Schaneman, Bowie's former Queens' neighbour, does not recall seeing any albums when Bowie's house was cleared after his death (personal phone conversation, 12 April 2013).

4 The painting, *Cream of Mushrooms* (1991), features dripping penises in a mushroom patch: Leslie–Lohman Museum of Gay and Lesbian Art, New York. I am grateful to Wayne Snellen, Deputy Director for Collections, for locating the Bowie file.

5 Bowie played with the words festive and 'fistive' on more than one occasion. An entry for 1 January 1979 describing fisting writes 'What a "fistive" way to arrive into this New Year!' His homoerotic humour here is reminiscent of Carl Van Vechten's scrapbooks: see J. Weinberg, '"Boy crazy": Carl Van Vechten's queer collection', *Yale Journal of Criticism*, 7:2 (1994), 25–49.

6 Bowie Diaries, 25 January 1978.

7 Ibid., 23 December 1985.

8 A.Holleran, *Chronicle of a Plague Revisited: AIDS and its Aftermath* (New York, 2008), p. 2.

9 Bowie Diaries, 12 June 1982.

10 Ibid., 6 June 1982.

11 Ibid., 30 April 1988.
12 G. S. Rubin, 'The catacombs: a temple of the butthole', in her *Deviations: A Gayle Rubin Reader* (Durham, NC, 2011), ch. 9. The essay was first published in 1991.
13 Bowie Diaries, 19 March 1984.
14 Rubin, 'The catacombs', p. 231 (for music to fuck by).
15 Bowie Diaries, 14 February 1978.
16 Ibid., 8 March 1986.
17 Ibid., 6 October 1984.
18 Ibid., 8 March 1986.
19 Rubin, 'The catacombs', p. 236.
20 Bowie Diaries, 8 February 1986.
21 For example, ibid., 31 October 1978; 24 September, 7 October, and 30 December 1979; 13, 17, 19, and 30 August 1980. For an example of monthly totals, see the volume for 1980: J20 F26 M22 A22 M24 J20 J19 A16 S29 O29 N23 D20.
22 Ibid., 29 April 1979.
23 For the privacy reasons discussed earlier I cannot name these people.
24 The best discussion of this is by S. Seidman, *Romantic Longings: Love in America, 1830–1980* (New York, 1991), pp. 176–91. See also B. Gove, *Cruising Culture: Promiscuity, Desire and American Gay Literature* (Edinburgh, 2000).
25 E. White, *States of Desire* (New York, 1980), p. 282.
26 Ibid.
27 S. R. Delany, *The Motion of Light in Water: Sex and Science Fiction Writing in the East Village* (Minneapolis, MN, 2004 [1988]), pp. 225–6.
28 R. Camus, *Tricks: 25 Encounters*, trans. R. Howard, with preface by R. Barthes (New York, 1981).
29 J. I. Brodsky, 'The Mineshaft: a retrospective ethnography', *Journal of Homosexuality*, 24:3–4 (1993), 233–52, quote at 248.
30 C. Silverstein and E. White, *The Joy of Gay Sex: An Intimate Guide for Gay Men to the Pleasures of a Gay Lifestyle* (New York, 1977), p. 141.
31 Rubin, 'The catacombs', p. 236.
32 Bowie Diaries, 29 June 1984.
33 Ibid., 13 November 1981; 17 May 1980.
34 Ibid., 9 April 1982.
35 Ibid., 31 October 1980.
36 Ibid., 17 June 1978; 22 April 1987.
37 See B. Reay, *New York Hustlers: Masculinity and Sex in Modern America* (Manchester, 2010).
38 In order of quotes: Bowie Diaries, 16 July 1978; 1 January, 4 June 1980; 4 July 1987; 9 February 1980; 1 January 1988; 22 October 1980.
39 For foreskin fetishes, especially in the land of the circumcised, see H. Kalha, 'Fantasy uncut: foreskin fetishism and the morphology of desire', in T. Dean, S. Ruszczycky, and D. Squires (eds), *Porn Archives* (Durham, NC, 2014), ch. 19.

40 I have benefited here, and elsewhere, from reading T. Dean, *Unlimited Intimacy: Reflections on the Subculture of Barebacking* (Chicago, 2009), esp. ch. 3.
41 Bowie Diaries, 3 May 1979.
42 Ibid., 4 March 1979.
43 Ibid., 26 April 1978.
44 Ibid., 24 May 1978.
45 Ibid., 19 August 1980.
46 Ibid., 13 February 1988.
47 Ibid., 30 January 1988.
48 Ibid., notes at end of 1987 volume.
49 Ibid., 24 October 1991.
50 E. Michaels, *Unbecoming* (Durham, NC, 1997 [1990]), p. 3. For a thoughtful analysis of this and other AIDS diaries, see R. Chambers, *Facing It: AIDS Diaries and the Death of the Author* (Ann Arbor, MI, 1998).

7

ANONYMOUS and Badboy Books: a 1990s moment in the history of pornography

with Nina Attwood

In Manhattan in the early 1990s a diverse group of female and male former college students from the City University of New York (CUNY), drawn together by their love of the role-playing fantasy game Dungeons & Dragons, started to write gay pornography. The organising force behind the venture was a young Hispanic man from the Lower East Side, soon to be known either as ANONYMOUS or Julian Anthony Guerra, his other nom de plume. Remarkably, this (by his own admission) 'confused kid from the projects' would rewrite famous erotic classics for sale into the mass market and produce and edit collections of modern gay pornographic fiction. ANONYMOUS said that he (we are willing to disclose his gender) wrote this gay material based on his (then) limited sexual interactions with women and his rich fantasy life, changing females to males in his stories. He had taught himself to write in his teens to express and record his persistent urges and fantasies (involving men as well as women), and nurtured his creativity through role-playing games and the consumption of both pornography in the form of the Times Square chapbooks (more of which later) and the horror and action films showing in 42nd Street movie houses. Though he would revise Victorian, Edwardian, and interwar classics, adding extensions and working from photocopies of the originals that his publisher had procured from bookseller and collector contacts, he did so without any period research. Astonishingly, he was a novice.

In the space of only five years (1992–96), ANONYMOUS and his amateur collaborators produced some dozen books. Their work, for the publisher Richard Kasak and his ventures Masquerade and Badboy Books, included ANONYMOUS's reworking of the classics *Sins of the Cities of the Plain*, *Memoirs of a Voluptuary* [republished as *A Secret Life* and *Youthful*

Days], *Imre: A Memoir*, and *The Scarlet Pansy*, all revised, cut, and extended for modern tastes, as well as Guerra's edited anthologies of gay pornography. The titles of the collections, *Men at Work*, *Slow Burn*, *Badboy Fantasies*, *Badboy War Stories*, and *Come Quickly*, provide clues to their contents. 'The one thing I asked all of them', Guerra wrote of his contributors to *Come Quickly*, 'was to use as few words as possible to turn me on as fast as they could. Well, let me tell you something: I gave each of those stories a test drive, and boy am I sore!'[1]

The first of the anthologies, *Men at Work* (1992), was written with Guerra's Dungeons & Dragons friends. Although each chapter appears under a male name, most were by women who were writing as gay men. Steven Isenstyne was a 'straight guy'. But Len Hecht was a woman. Michael Chelsea, Chris Morris, Randy O'Brian, and Andrew Edwards were also female. It was a pattern repeated in the later anthologies. ANONYMOUS/Guerra, who described himself as 'a kid raised in a chaotic environment who became a sexually confused young adult', recalled that out of all the short story collections, only one author was a gay male and only one was a lesbian. Most were straight and many were female.[2]

ANONYMOUS took two weeks a book, producing a staggering nine in 1992 alone. He was in at the beginning of Badboy's brief history from 1992 to 1998. According to the figures on the Open Library website, Badboy's yearly output was 12 editions in 1992, 21 in 1993, 16 in 1994, 19 in 1995, 54 in 1996, 3 in 1997, and 7 in 1998.[3] Effectively, then, ANONYMOUS/Guerra *was* Badboy in 1992, producing most of their output for that opening year. He was paid $500 each for *Sins* and *Secret Life*, and $750 for *Scarlet Pansy* (the early extended classics). He got $1500 each for editing the collections, and paid contributors $100–$150 a story. Sales, mainly through gay bookshops, but also through some mainstream outlets (Borders and Barnes & Noble), were around 20,000 to 25,000 per title, so at $4.95 each, gross takings per title could be almost $124,000.

His publisher Kasak was producing serious pornography: Pat Califia, Samuel Delany, Lars Eighner, John Preston, Larry Townsend, Aaron Travis (Steven Saylor), and Alexander Trocchi (posthumously) were on his list, some of them featuring in the collection *The Best of the Badboys*, issued almost as soon as the imprint started.[4] They included the 'Häagen Dazs' writers in what Kasak likened to a grocery business: 'You know you need a certain number of eggs every day, and a certain number of milk bottles. But sometimes you also think: Maybe today I'll buy some Häagen Dazs, just to dress up the store. And we do that.'[5] While honest about the profit motive – 'When you say "great", I assume you mean What will make money?' – Kasak was proud of his imprint Richard Kasak Books and used sales in Badboy, Masquerade, and Rosebud (lesbian erotica) to subsidise what he considered to be worthwhile works that would not necessarily sell. He clearly saw himself as a champion of erotic literature, particularly consensual sado-masochism and gay and lesbian sex. Kasak said in an interview in 1996 that he had done for queer sex what Barney Rosset and Grove Press had done for heterosexual sex: 'in a little way, I have become very important for getting gay and lesbian erotica into the mainstream'.[6]

The rules for writing for Badboy were few. ANONYMOUS listed no extreme torture, under 18s, or bestiality.[7] Kasak said that he would not publish 'anything that's demeaning to any religion or race. I try to steer away – in the S&M books – from having a man or a woman just destroyed in an act of sexuality.'[8] Alice Joanou, one of his authors, recalled that the guidelines were 'You couldn't do scat. You could do enemas, but no shit. No pedophilia. No bestiality.'[9] Apart from these minor restrictions, the experience of ANONYMOUS and his fellow authors suggests a spirit of enterprise where the possibilities seemed limitless. Our focus here is on those CUNY amateur pornographers, nearly all of whom, including ANONYMOUS, moved on to other things. Only one or two became professional writers like Joanou. It is a fascinating moment in the history of pornography.

The pulps of the 1990s have been overshadowed by the emergence and competition of another medium, the moving image. 'As hardcore gay porn won a triumph of the visual in the 1970s', writes Whitney Strub, 'pulp resided in the shadows, held down by an occasionally expressed baggage of "past"-ness that made it seem a relic in the face of the proud gay bodies onscreen.'[10] But even within the parameters of their own medium they have been rather taken for granted. They are too late for the golden age of pulp from the 1930s to the 1960s, charted so successfully in Paula Rabinowitz's *American Pulp*.[11] They fall outside gay fiction's own claimed golden age from the late 1940s to the 1970s.[12] They are too crude to be included in gay literary anthologies and are barely supplemental to the history of the gay literary elite of the so-termed Violet Quill.[13] The most that the 1990s books have managed, as far as we can ascertain, is a couple of pages on Badboy and Masquerade in Ian Young's pictorial history of gay pulps.[14] However, their mention in passing by respected gay writers and academics suggests some familiarity, perhaps one-handed rather than literary. 'Anyone who's been in a gay bookstore lately', wrote Felice Picano in the early 1990s, 'has seen those inexpensive paperbacks with their black-and-white cover photos of hot young men: a new line called Badboy Books.'[15] Apart from reference to Samuel Delany's *The Mad Man* (1994),

Badboy and Masquerade do not appear in *The Cambridge Companion to Gay and Lesbian Writing*.[16] They are not mentioned at all in *The Cambridge Companion to Popular Fiction*.[17]

When the books that we will be dealing with have been discussed, the outcome has not been flattering. Paul Hallam described the Masquerade/ Badboy version of *Sins of the Cities of the Plain* as 'a graceless addition', 'modern porn masquerading as "a classic"'.[18] Wolfram Setz has referred to 'disgraceful additions', and, 'even worse', a 'continuous distortion of the situations and details, and a linguistic "modernization" in the sense of political correctness'.[19] James Gifford has dismissed ANONYMOUS's *Imre* as 'highly altered and scurrilous'.[20]

Our aim in this chapter is to take Badboy and ANONYMOUS more seriously. This episode in the history of pornography is intriguing on a number of levels and raises some productive questions. How common was it to use amateurs in this industry? Was it normal (perhaps not quite the right word) for non-homosexuals to produce homosexual erotica, and for women, lesbians even, to write gay male pornography? We have made contact with ANONYMOUS and obtained access to his files of extensions and rewriting so we can discuss in some depth the recasting of erotic fiction from one era to fit the perceived tastes of another. In other words, we are able to consider issues of authorship, content, and method that are seldom available in discussions of pornographic literature. In the interests of confidentiality – and tantalisation – ANONYMOUS will remain anonymous, apart from the fact that he is male.

At first we were rather taken by the role of women in the Badboy project, much in the way that David Bergman was when Larry Townsend told him that some of the authors of 1960s gay pulp fiction were women.[21] But we should not have been surprised. Women writing as men and writing (or consuming) male homoerotic literature – what Carola Bauer has dubbed cross-voyeurism – is not at all unusual.[22] The creators of same-sex relationships in fan writing about male characters or actors in film or television or popular literature were often straight women, as was their audience.[23] Although what was termed slash's origins seem to have been in the fanzine literature around *Star Trek*'s Kirk and Spock in the 1960s and 1970s, one of its earlier forms was the group-circulated letter or APA (based on science fiction fandom) that flourished in the early 1990s at the time of the Badboy collections. ANONYMOUS told the authors that he was indeed aware of the genre and 'collected APAs based on Star Trek, comics, horror, and weird fiction from the mid-70s through to the late-80s'. Importantly, he also said that for him 'the sensibility that women could effectively write "male" fiction came from the APAs'.[24]

The appeal, for women, of homoerotic imagery and fantasy was explained at that time by fans: identification with a main rather than supporting character, but identification that was amplified by its cross-gender nature. Some said that it did not involve identification at all but rather a longing that came from distance: 'a pleasure in exerting . . . authorial control over sexy male bodies'.[25] One slash participant wrote in 1993 that it was the very difference of male–male sexual scenarios that held the appeal: 'Writing (and reading) about things we can't experience directly, we can fantasise that these relations can be beyond the best sex WE may have ever had.'[26] There were many themes in terms of the respective roles of heterosexuality, homosexuality, and gender in slash fiction, what Henry Jenkins summarised as female pornography, androgynous romance, fantasy identification, and homosocial desire.[27] But for the slash writer M. Fae Glasgow it was all about the sex: 'It's the sex! . . . as long as we had at least two men buggering each other into next week.' 'We like it because it makes us hot and wet!'[28] There was no huge step from those readers and writers to female authorship of gay male pornography.

A study of lexical frequency in lesbian erotica of the late 1980s and early 1990s found many more 'cunts' and 'clits' than 'cocks' and 'dicks' in the short fiction of those years.[29] However, lesbian pornography involving male subjects was being produced in the 1980s by the San Francisco-based magazine *On Our Backs* and by the writer Pat Califia in her collection of erotic fiction *Macho Sluts*.[30] And these were but two of many lesbian BDSM-themed erotic publications in what Wendy Chapkis called 'an explosion of feminist-created sexual culture'.[31] *Macho Sluts* contained stories featuring men, male–male and male–female sex, including one, 'The Surprise Party', where a leatherdyke has (ostensibly) coerced sex with three male police officers.[32] 'Hasn't anybody but me wondered', Califia wrote, 'why porn produced for lesbian consumption has to be about women only?'[33]

So, content-wise, pornography penned by women at the time that ANONYMOUS was active included gay male themes and may well have reflected those influences on the sexual culture of lesbianism from the 1980s onwards.[34] Califia's work also entailed what she termed identity sedition. 'I've adopted many personas as an author of sexually-explicit fiction', she (then Pat, later Patrick) wrote in 1997. 'For more than ten years, I wrote an advice column for *The Advocate*'s classified section, which many readers assumed was penned by a gay man, and I also wrote "The Sexpert" advice column for *Advocate Men*.'[35]

In short, the concept of women creating male homosexual pornography was not exactly alien by the 1990s. Indeed, Cleis Press published a 1996 anthology called *Switch Hitters: Lesbians Write Gay Male Erotica and Gay Men Write Lesbian Erotica* that dealt with that very theme, 'a kind of literary drag'.[36] Its contributors included newcomers as well as women already operating in the male pornographic writing scene. Cecilia Tan had published two collections of gay male erotica.[37] Wickie Stamps briefly edited the gay leather magazine *Drummer* in the mid 1990s.[38] Laura Antoniou, as Christopher Morgan, wrote the novel *Muscle Bound* (1992) and the collection of stories *Steam Gauge* (1996), both published by none other than Badboy Books, their names indicative of their brand of eroticised (and ventriloquised) S/M masculinity.[39] Morgan wrote in 'his' introduction to a republished volume that he 'was honored' when *Muscle Bound* was 'mentioned in a scholarly book on how gay men can find mythic stories that reflect their lives. Gee, and I thought I was just writing a dirty little tale about hot guys at a gym.'[40] When, as Antoniou, she edited a collection in honour of John Preston (more of whom shortly), she noted that all the 'hypermasculine leather-sex', 'every SM-tinged piece of porn' in the anthology, was written by women.[41] It was something of an understatement, then, on David Bergman's part when he observed that 'gay men were not always the authors of gay pulp fiction'.[42]

An author's sexual identity or orientation, therefore, could be just as unknown as their sex or gender. V. K. McCarty wrote as a woman (under the name Mam'selle Victoire) and as a gay man (Victor King). She wrote on 'the straight female side' in the 1970s, and 'did most of my gay writing in the early 1980s'.[43] McCarty identified herself 'as a heterosexual woman, even though I am in a primary relationship with a woman. Then, next to that, very quickly after that, I identify as male, as a gay man. And I am most comfortable with that identity.'[44] Antoniou wrote as Christopher Morgan but also as Sara Adamson (for Masquerade). In 1995 she described herself as lesbian but her sexual orientation 'primarily' as a sadomasochist – 'It's the filter I see the world through.'[45] She had a long-standing relationship with a male leather daddy who was bisexual and related to him 'as though I were a young gay man'.[46] Caro Soles wrote 'SM sci-fi porn' as Kyle Stone, which Michael Rowe, journalist and anthologist of gay porn and erotica (and gay himself), described as 'some of the hottest porn I had ever read'.[47] Not only was Soles a woman but also 'a suburban wife and mother with an impeccable patrician WASP background . . . writing lustily (and with disconcerting authority) about – among other things – sadomasochism, dildos, and sex in outer space'.[48] Despite being married (to a man), Soles did not define herself as heterosexual, nor as bisexual, gay, or part of the BDSM community.[49] John Preston was the only gay male pornographic author that she had read before writing her erotic novel, *The Initiation of PB 500*, published by Masquerade in 1994, and she had not written any pornography before that point.[50] Writing under a male pseudonym and from the perspective of a gay male character was not so much empowering but more about making her feel 'free to pursue things in a different way than I could otherwise'.[51] She also told Rowe that her S/M representation came from a purely psychological understanding of it – in contrast to Antoniou, Califia, and McCarty whose writing was informed by their experiences. Rowe found it difficult to understand how Soles could write so convincingly without any direct involvement in the world that she was representing – 'It comes through with an authenticity that's a little disconcerting.'[52]

Writing erotic fiction under an assumed name was not new either. Most of the writers of gay pulps in the 1960s and 1970s used pseudonyms.[53] William Maltese, also known as William J. Lambert III, Chad Stuart, and Lambert Wilhelm, wrote well over a hundred pulps, both gay and straight pornography, under multiple pseudonyms. He read a friend's book, thought that he could write to a perceived formula, and did so for the money; 'I continued completely ignorant that I had become part of a major gay revolution in pulp fiction.' Maltese recalled that he wrote *Trucker Sucker* (1975) and *Bugger Boy* (1975) while on a Pacific cruise with a wealthy older woman. 'I still wasn't aware of the ongoing revolution in gay pulp fiction, even though I was by now a major participant in it . . . What sex I was having was decidedly straight, my imagination providing the homosexual antics of the gay characters.'[54] It was not that he had no gay experience (he said that he was bisexual), but just that at that time he was having heterosexual sex.[55]

The lesbian pulp novels of the 1950s and 1960s were notoriously pseudonymous. Many, most, were written by men for men (what have been termed 'virile adventures'), but even those classified by experts as genuinely lesbian ('pro-lesbian'), by women for women, with female characters as central rather than ancillary, were usually under pen names. Indeed the use of female pseudonyms has confused commentators. How satisfactory is Yvonne Keller's distinction between the straight-male, lesbian pulps and their pro-lesbian alternative when part of her definition is that the former has a 'male author or, rather, an author with a male pseudonym' while the latter's writers 'often are female or at least use female pseudonyms'?[56] Susan Stryker thought that Kay Addams, author of *Queer Patterns* (1959), was a lesbian pulp writer who also assumed the male name Orrie Hitt to produce 'semipornographic sleaze novels for a predominantly male audience'.[57] The opposite was the case. Orrie Edwin Hitt, creator of those immortal words 'Her nipples could stay hard longer than a bear could hibernate', wrote 150 (perhaps more) pulps under his own name and a variety of others, including Kay Addams.[58] Paul Little was said to have written 500 sleaze and lesbian pulps using the name Sylvia Sharon.[59]

Let us start with the Badboy editions of the famous gay classics. Again this was not as novel as one might think, for the revival of Victorian and Edwardian erotica was not unknown in the US publishing world. Barney Rosset's Grove Press published *My Secret Life* (not Badboy's *My Secret Life*) and many other pornographic classics in the 1960s, a project billed on the jacket of one such book as the uncovering of 'an entire body of underground Victorian and Edwardian literature'.[60] Although Grove's *My Secret Life* was also published in an abridged Black Cat version (which sold nearly 750,000 copies), the marketing of this material was in terms of its authenticity, making available texts that hitherto had been limited to collectors and select scholars with access to the relevant archives.[61] The covers employed artwork in keeping with the texts' origins. Masquerade/Badboy Books, in contrast, changed the original texts and modernised the cover illustrations to appeal to their perceived market. There was no academic pretence (see Figures 42–3). The cover images include work by famous erotic photographers. Trevor Watson became known for his photographs of BDSM and heterosexual imagery. Charles Hovland took photographs for many gay porn magazines (as well as being a member of the AIDS advocacy group ACT UP).[62]

Masquerade/Badboy's choice of classics, presumably determined by Kasak from the copies and typescripts procured for him by his book trade contacts, is intriguing. They come from very different eras and have disparate agendas and varying sensibilities. *Sins of the Cities of the Plain* (1881) was a product of a Victorian sexual landscape described by Morris Kaplan as 'diffuse' and 'ambiguous', with desires 'beyond the grasp of our own sexual imaginary'.[63] It represented a sexual regime where categories that would later be called heterosexual and homosexual were indistinct.

Edward Irenaeus Prime-Stevenson's novel *Imre* (1906), written under the pseudonym Xavier Mayne, privileged a manly homosexuality: 'Are we not the extreme of the male? its supreme phase, its outermost phalanx? – its climax of the aristocratic, the All-Man?'[64] *Imre* also contains a sustained criss-crossing between friendship and love: 'the Friendship which is Love, the Love which is Friendship'.[65] The book's author went on to write *The*

42 Anonymous, *Sins of the Cities of the Plain* (New York, 1992). Cover photograph by Trevor Watson. Collection of Barry Reay.

43 Anonymous, *The Scarlet Pansy* (New York, 1992). Cover photograph by Charles Hovland. Collection of Barry Reay.

Intersexes, which provided a glimpse at the possibilities of homosexual awareness as experienced by an intelligent, well-read, informed, and obviously experienced member of the elite at the beginning of the twentieth century.[66] *Imre* was a serious work by a serious writer.

Robert Scully's *A Scarlet Pansy* (1932), the most recently dated of the novels adapted by ANONYMOUS, embodies the sexual configurations of yet another time.[67] This was the world of the fairy (or the pansy) in the sexual culture of early twentieth-century America, represented by the gender-ambiguous illustration adjoining the original book's title page of the beautiful, fine-faced young man with the swept-back hair, sculpted eyebrows, and full lips. It was a time when male homosexuality was conceived in terms of effeminacy, where a man might seek sex from a fairy as much as from a woman, and when such a choice was not considered especially significant.[68]

The original *Scarlet Pansy*, the fairy version, probably pseudonymous, and which Jay Gertzman later claimed as an important modernist work, had been printed as a sex pulp by the well-known New York publisher Samuel Roth.[69] But there was another imprint, Royal Publishers' abridged, 1952 version, which cut, at a rough count, about 24 per cent of the original.[70] It was a cleaner version. Fay's promiscuity is more emphatic in the original: 'Morally, from then on, she was to go down, down, down. Not till he had completely defiled her and sated his lust did she come back to her normal self'; 'Fay Etrange had become a oncer – that is, she was through with a man after one experience.'[71] The 1952 edition sheds the cruder 1932 references: Kuntzville is Huntsville, Theodore Cocke becomes Cooke, and Miss Kitty Fuchs is simply Miss Kitty.[72] The role of the knowingly named Miss Fish is reduced.[73] The equally suggestive Miss Browning becomes Miss Billie, and Mrs Morrison Godown is Goway.[74] No one is 'nicknamed "Clittie" for obvious reasons'.[75]

By the time ANONYMOUS got his hands on it, then, the book already had a past in terms of disguised identity, pulp links, and editorial intervention. There are, in effect, three versions of *The Scarlet Pansy*: the 1930s fairy version; the 1950s effeminate/gay version; and the 1990s hybrid of hypermasculinity and effeminacy. Ironically, because he used the first edition, ANONYMOUS is closer to the spirit of the original – albeit in bricolage – than the 1950s expurgated edition.

Such were the raw ingredients for ANONYMOUS's project: queer sex (before queer sex) in a Victorian classic; early twentieth-century musings about manly love and homoerotic friendship, hailed as a 'landmark' work of American gay fiction;[76] and an interwar *roman à clef* about male effeminacy

– most unpromising material, one might think, in terms of the hypermasculine, BDSM tropes of 1990s gay pornography.

A textual study of gay erotic anthologies from the 1980s which contained material from the pornography and skin magazines – the sort of material that would have been consumed by the young ANONYMOUS before he turned his hand to writing for Badboy – relentlessly charted references to body parts and erogenous zones, with the penis and anus the most mentioned and semen the most frequently cited bodily fluid. There were 50 different terms for the penis (cock and dick were the most common) and several pages of individual descriptions of said penises, 33 words for semen (with 'cum' and 'load' at the top of the list), and 76 described 'actions of semen'.[77] *Straight to Hell*, one of the chapbooks read by the young ANONYMOUS, blurred the reader–writer distinction with its first-person accounts of sexual encounters either provided by its consumers or invented by its editor – what John Heywood has termed 'a pornography of truth'.[78] The chapbook's obsession with 'straight' men having 'gay' sex, its valorisation of masculinity, and proud perversity (it was not subtitled *The Manhattan Review of Unnatural Acts* for nothing) was excellent preparation for a short career in pornography. ANONYMOUS had a substantial, if sometimes repetitious, repertoire to draw on.

It was the language of the new version of *Sins of the Cities* that exercised its critics, the 'disgraceful additions' bemoaned above by Setz and Hallam – nearly 30 per cent more text than the original on a rough count from ANONYMOUS's files. Sexual scenes and descriptions that had been circumspect were rendered explicit and elaborate. New scenarios were invented. While both texts note that the book's narrator, Jack Saul, 'was favoured by nature by a very extraordinary development of the male appendage', the Badboy edition renders it so extraordinary that 'it appeared as if a tremendous length of sausage had been stuffed down along the thigh of his right leg, setting in relief an hypnotic tube from which my eyes were hard-pressed to leave. By the sizeable accompaniment of bulges through the pleats, I should say his balls were gigantic as well.'[79] In another of Badboy's inserts, Saul finds that 'Before long I was riding his great, teenaged Italian sausage, my legs splayed to either side of his muscular hips and my hungry arsehole shimmying up and down his leaning tower.'[80] Needless to say, there are no sausages in the original 1881 text, though 'sausage' was listed among the terms for the penis in the earlier-mentioned study of 1980s printed gay pornography.[81]

Whereas ANONYMOUS upped the ante on the already explicit sex in *Sins of the Cities*, he added blatant sex where there was none in *Imre*. Gifford noted in the introduction to his modern (post-Badboy) edition of the original gay classic that 'In spite of its reputation as the first overtly gay American novel, there are no scenes of physical intimacy'; it was 'a tale almost exclusively of the mind'.[82] However, ANONYMOUS inserted a multitude of lengthy passages musing on what Oswald wanted to do to/with Lieutenant Imre in a much more bodily sense. The 'current of immediate mutuality which sped back and forth between us', in the original, is excised in favour of a more animated elaboration of male same-sex sexual desire:

> my desire for his friendship was abetted and ignited by a yet more forceful fire – that of the fire in my loins . . . I feared the sharp need to possess him . . . I would take Imre, lay him down there in the lonely, twilit out-of-doors, and I would worship the tortured soul locked within the flesh and muscle and sinew of his firm and heated body. Running my fingers over the hard ridges of his torso's grand musculature – the hints of which I had seen impressed through the soft, crisp officer's shirt he'd worn that afternoon – I would taste the tanned skin of his belly, and slowly pull his undergarments to unveil his beautiful and prominent cock, itself standing and pulsing at full attention, fattened and fortified with passion.[83]

Such lengthy and explicit additions could not be further from the original text. The Badboy edition circumvented the radical change that more physical encounters would have effected on the nature of the original by rendering most of them dreams. But there are 'real' physical sexual episodes in the Badboy book. The original scene where Oswald and Imre's feelings for each other are finally expressed – 'I *love* thee, as can love only the Uranian' – ended with the men getting back on their tram to return to their respective accommodations.[84] The Badboy edition kept most of this confessional conversation, but concluded with Imre leaning in with a kiss that turns into a five-page, explicit encounter:

> The simple touch of his most sacrosanct anatomy [not, of course, the above-mentioned lips], offered to me thus, moved my heart and passion farther than any fantasy I had yet dared to dream. Unable to wait any longer, I introduced my member to the edge of that blessed abyss and then, without pause, I plunged my dagger into its rightful sheath.[85]

No wonder Gifford was so horrified (see Figure 44).

The Badboy edition of *The Scarlet Pansy* shares the explicit and detailed descriptions – both imagined and narratively realised – of sexual acts that the original version had merely intimated. The first imagined encounter has Randall Etrange, 'the precocious child', being both praised and reprimanded by 'the dignified and fatherly' Mr Fisher, who demanded that Randall 'drop his drawers for a good spanking'; 'Randall groaned with pleasure at his

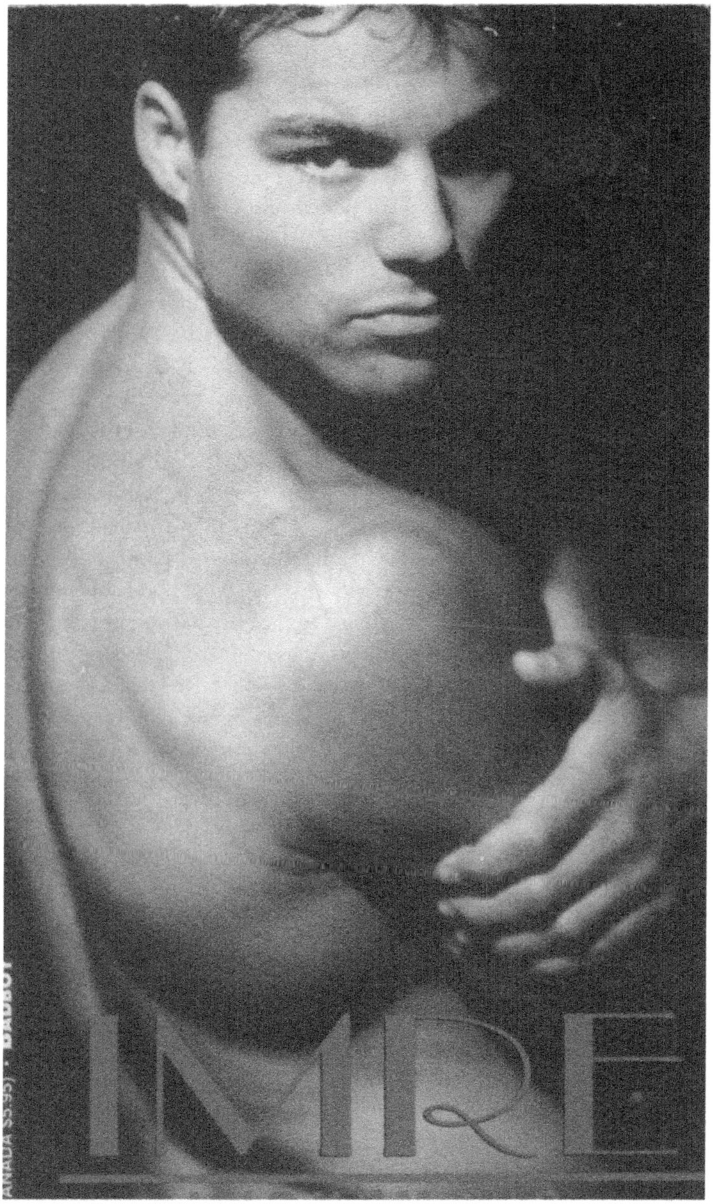

44 Anonymous, *Imre* (New York, 1992). Cover photograph by Trevor Watson. Collection of Barry Reay.

revelry', and 'the rapid growth of his thick and reddening cock' during these 'romantic dreams' both worried him and foretold events to come.[86] He dreamed about Lieutenant Frank: 'How Randall wanted to simply devour him, gaze upon his cock and eat it up, push that red and mushroom-headed member deep into the hole of his buttocks and ride him to bliss.'[87] Call a cock a cock was Lars Eighner's advice in his how-to guide for writing gay erotica, *Elements of Arousal* (1994), a Richard Kasak book: 'Yes, sometimes it should be "fuckpole". "One-eyed-snake" never was erotic.'[88]

Randall's 'real' sexual encounters involve even more lengthy and graphic retellings. Early in the (Badboy) novel, he 'came face to face with the enraged priapus of his night's date', the abovementioned Mr Fisher. What appears to be Randall's first encounter with oral sex ends with Fisher's 'stifled shout as blobs of white semen rose from his balls to be deposited in Randall's eager mouth'.[89] A week later Randall 'was upon Fisher's cock as a starving dog to a bone'.[90] The reader is regaled with descriptions of Randall's anal deflowering, voyeurism, and group sex.[91] Penises are not merely present in the 1990s version, they are 'thick-headed', 'engorged', 'throbbing', 'tremendous', and 'gigantic', none more so than that of a policeman who 'discharged his meaty gun deep within his [Randall's] bowels'.[92] (Eighner would probably not have approved of meaty guns.) 'Balls were filled to the brim with oceans of sperm', ejaculations came in 'pints', are 'great jets', and sometimes occur 'fully into Randall's face'.[93] Randall comes 'volcanically' and receives a 'pearlescent arc' of a sexual partner's ejaculant over his back and buttocks.[94] Randall 'sixty-nines', his penis 'an overlarge pacifier' in Karl's 'pouting mouth'.[95]

It was not just more explicit sex that was added to these texts. While it cannot be said that ANONYMOUS made *Sins of the Cities* more violent – birching was, after all, a staple feature of Victorian pornography – he did add S/M of a more modern kind to Saul's repertoire. In one new Badboy segment, Saul was 'overcome by a sudden, sadistic desire to wipe that grin . . . from his [guest's] beautiful face':

> Glancing about for a proper instrument of punishment, I seized one of the great candles still burning at the far end of the table, and its molten wax spilt o'er him as I brought it to my lips that I might extinguish it before setting it to its sinister work. How he shrieked as the droplets of steaming wax struck his bare flesh; the scream had a chilling yet appealing effect on me, and, holding my breath, I reached the still-lit beacon o'er his seething torso once more and tilted it yet again. . . . Blowing out the candle, I then brought it low, turning it 'round so that it's heavy end could be pressed against the rosy bud of my trembling houseguest's arsehole. The heat of that gorgeous anal sphincter would be adequate to soften the hard edges of this thick and weighty tool,

> but it would prove to be no barrier to my onslaught, and I soon managed to plunge this unusual device deeply into that orifice.[96]

One of the more explicit insertions in the Badboy version of *Imre* was an S/M encounter – another of Oswald's fantasies/dreams. He imagines Imre is being dominated and disciplined by his army superior, and ordered to 'lower his fatigue trousers at once to receive corporal punishment'. The captain pulls Imre on to his lap and gives him

> a swift and brutal spanking . . . Lieutenant Imre's member had grown long and thick and stiff as it had been pushed violently, repeatedly, between the Captain's thighs . . . Brief moments later he did indeed gasp under the voluptuous waves of pain and pleasure that were the height of his ecstasy; and Imre flooded the fork of Clement's trousers . . . with volcanic jets of sperm-loaded semen.[97]

This theme was not one replicated again in Badboy's *Imre*, in Oswald's dreams or otherwise. BDSM was not the brand of homosexuality on display in either version of the text, evidence that ANONYMOUS could be mindful of the original spirit of the work.

A noticeable way in which ANONYMOUS's version of *Sins of the Cities* differs from the nineteenth-century original is in the ages of the participants, which have been raised to bring them in line with 1990s cultural and legal strictures about underage sex, one of the few Badboy rules for writers. (The issue was less pressing for *Imre*, given that the story involved two adult males.) Hence the original text has Saul ejaculating for the first time and performing (and receiving) anal sex when he is aged just 10, and his fellow boarders drawing lots to see who will penetrate him – 'who will have my bottom first'.[98] In the original, the winner of the draw was 'about fourteen'. Our author changes this to 'seventeen' in his final draft, but it is 'eighteen' by the time the Badboy edition is published (to conform to the 18-and-over rule, no doubt).[99] Such changes to age occur throughout the text. One of the more significant occurs in a story that one of Saul's cohort tells him:

> I can always earn a poney [*sic*] [twenty-five pounds] if I take a little girl of about fifteen to a certain house in Paris; in fact, they will give me an extra fiver for every year she is under that age . . . now and then I get them a boy for a change, as they are in great demand for the rich visitors to Paris, especially for the Americans, who are nearly all sodomites.[100]

In the Badboy edition, the 15-year-old girl becomes an 18-year-old boy.[101] The procurement of young female virgins may well have been a common trope in Victorian pornography, but not so much for an envisaged 1990s gay male readership.

Hallam has claimed that '[e]xplicit and almost exclusively gay content was rare in Victorian erotica' and that *Sins of the Cities* was a notable exception in this regard.[102] But surely he has underestimated the degree of sexual fluidity in the original text, where the sexual encounters involve men with women, men with men, and sometimes men, dressed as women, with men – or with women. The Badboy edition largely opts for uncomplicated homosexuality. Sex with Saul's cousin Jenny becomes masturbation with his cousin Jerry. Sex with a female housekeeper is sex with a manservant. Schoolboy sex with female school cooks is sex with male cooks. True, a certain amount of gender play remains. Saul has sex with Boulton while both are dressed as women and using female names (Boulton/Laura and Saul/Eveline). But whereas, in the original, Boulton (dressed as Laura) has sex with a Miss Bruce after convincing her that his penis is a 'malformation' (and that he is something of an hermaphrodite), ANONYMOUS substitutes Mr for Miss in his version. It is a similar plot line – Mr Bruce thinks that he is having sex with a woman – but this time the 'straight' sex is really 'gay'.[103]

While there are definitely passages that valorise sex with men over sex with women in *Sins of the Cities*, and the sexual descriptions are undoubtedly explicit, it is the multiplicity of sexual couplings that is so striking in the original. It was ANONYMOUS and the Badboy edition of 1992 that laboured to make *Sins of the Cities* 'almost exclusively' gay (to use Hallam's phraseology). While Saul tells the narrator in the original edition that his penis is 'my only fortune . . . it provides for all I want, and often introduces me to the best of society, ladies as well as gentlemen', the Badboy edition removes the 'ladies' in favour of 'discerning gentlemen'.[104] Whereas 'the sight of the many handsome girls and young fellows had a perfectly maddening effect upon me' in the original, Badboy limits the impact to that of 'handsome young fellows'.[105] It did not take huge adjustments to make the required changes, for the language and descriptions are remarkably similar. Just as a pronoun could be switched from 'she' to 'he', so could a 'cunt' become a 'mancunt' and the 'folds of her cunt' be 'the cheeks of his arse'. Jenny's 'crack of love' turned into Jerry's 'shaft of love'. The 'throbbing lips of that heavenly cunt' became the 'throbbing hole of that heavenly mancunt'.[106] The result is decidedly more conventionally gay; in fact ANONYMOUS recalled that he 'would have preferred a more pansexual approach, but my instructions were explicit regarding gender: be considerate of the purpose of the book for its gay male audience'. As Kaplan noted, the publishers appeared 'to find the Victorian novel just too queer for today's market in gay pornography. The original is an epic of polymorphous pansexuality and gender fuck.'[107]

Something comparable happens with *The Scarlet Pansy*. Fay Etrange, the fairy protagonist, is referred to as 'she' and 'her' from the opening lines of the book in both 1932 and 1952. The unwary reader could be forgiven for thinking that it is the story of a woman; indeed we know that some early Chicago readers were unable to fix on the sex of the main character.[108] In the original novel, Fay was a fairy, an effeminate male homosexual. As Byrne Fone has noted, Fay Etrange translates, 'in whimsical French', to 'strange fairy'.[109] She inhabits a world of trade, cruising, drag, pansies, fairies, queens, and camp – all terms used in the novel. Fay found that 'the more virile the man, the more readily he succumbed to her open advances'.[110] She went to a Greenwich Village restaurant, where the 'aunties' went with their good-looking clerks and the fairies sat with 'their sailors or marines or rough trade' and exchanged crude banter: 'Sailor boy, if you don't take back those indecent words, I'll bring my longshoreman over here and he'll almost choke you to death. He's big enough. He's done it to me several times. At first I thought I'd never get over it.'[111]

However, Fay becomes Randall in the Badboy edition. Both Fay and Randall are (biologically) male, but whereas Fay is consistently described with feminine pronouns in the original, Randall is almost exclusively referred to as male ('him', 'he', 'his'). Badboy's Randall Etrange is from a different era. He is a gay man rather than a fairy, who dresses as a man for the most part, is referred to as a man with same-sex desires, but who camps up and plays with effeminacy: Badboy's cover blurb refers to *The Scarlet Pansy* as 'A white-hot gay camp classic.' Where Fay dressed and looked feminine throughout the original, Randall is masculine or feminine, depending on the circumstances. His gender is more performative.

When Fay/Randall has sex with a policeman – rendered explicitly in the Badboy edition but not described in any detail in the original – it is made obvious that Randall's masculinity is not of the same degree as the policeman's. Sexual encounters with Fay need never mention that she took the feminine role, yet the situation was explicit with Randall: 'It stood to reason that Randall should have to play the woman's role to such a he-man. No police officer would get caught dead giving up such an intimate area, either in public or private.'[112] Playing the 'women's role' gets taken to a new level in Randall's encounter with a cowboy who

> treated him as his 'lady' and kissed and caressed him with all the passion and romance of a courting gunslinger. He squeezed and sucked Randall's nipples as if they were 'perfect little titties', and he called Randall's twitching anal sphincter his 'hot little pussy chute', or 'daddy's little squeeze box'.[113]

Such passages have no comparison in the original, as no sex is ever described explicitly, merely hinted at, as in the earlier reference to choking. But Fay does seem to be perceived differently than Randall in these encounters – even while both play the cowboy's 'lady'. Further sexual encounters with the cowboy in the Badboy version involve buttock slapping and the cowboy's ejaculation over Randall's 'tapered, muscular back'; 'Randall adored being manhandled' and 'tossed about like a rag doll'. 'Gripping the horn and the rear of the saddle for support, Cowboy began to fuck Randall's fanny with the type of gusto for which his kind is known.'[114]

The problem was that the perceived readership for the 1990s version was attracted to the hard masculinity of the men to whom the original Fay was drawn, not to the effeminacy of Fay herself. This white-hot, gay camp classic could not be too camp! While it cannot be said that 'gender fucking' was ever Badboy's *modus operandi* in their reissuing of 'classic' gay texts, 'fucking' most definitely was.

There were deletions as well as insertions. Unsurprisingly, large tracts of sexological discussion were removed from *Imre* – ANONYMOUS says that they were already excised in the working copy provided by the publisher.[115] The slow and 'cerebral' pace of the original was ill suited to a 1990s one-handed reader; education came second to more fully realised sex. Both *Imre* and Prime-Stevenson's *Intersexes* were aimed at challenging sexology's conceptualisation of same-sex desire as femininity.[116] As Gifford has noted, 'Unlike the enervated, languid, "neurasthenic" subjects of earlier case studies, Imre and Oswald are direct, aggressive men who seek partners with similar strength of character.'[117] Imre's 'features were delicate enough, but without womanishness. Imre was not a pretty man; but a beautiful man.'[118] Oswald and Imre 'always are, always will be, too much *men*! So super-male, so utterly unreceptive of what is not manly, so aloof from any feminine essences, that we cannot tolerate women at all as a sexual factor! Are we not the extreme of the male?'[119] Prime-Stevenson's elevation of an ideal manliness – what Oswald calls 'true similisexual masculinity' – came with lengthy diatribes against effeminate homosexuals: 'Ah, those patently depraved, noxious, flaccid, gross, womanish beings, perverted and imperfect in moral nature and in even their bodily tissues!'[120] This passage, and others like it, were deleted from the Badboy edition.

However, 'similisexual masculinity' was something of a preference for Badboy too, if the early anthologies are anything to go by. *Men at Work*, *Slow Burn*, and *Badboy Fantasies* were all published in 1992, within five months of each other. They are anthologies consisting of short stories by (on the face of it) different authors. As noted above, many of these authors were women writing under male names, and most of them were straight. Guerra/ANONYMOUS contributed to two anthologies and edited all three. He confirmed that there were more listed authors than there were actual authors, that individuals wrote more than one chapter using different names.

The preface to *Men at Work* claims to cater for a variety of sexual tastes: 'there's something of a treat for almost everyone in these pages'.[121] Yet there are more similarities than differences in the stories and anthologies. Hypermasculinity rules; fit and sculpted bodies trump the unfit and unshaped. Most involve consensual sex, even when it initially appears forced (reminiscent of the *Macho Sluts* story cited earlier). The women who appear are there mainly to validate the heterosexual masculinity of objects of gay male desire: 'Alejandro's twenty-three and cool. The females in the hood are schemin' on him twenty-four seven, man. They want him bad because he's got the look.'[122] Women facilitate descriptions of male–male sex: Louise found Hank, the narrator, 'bent over on the couch with Steve's cock pumping deep up my ass, and I was loving every minute of it'.[123] In the story 'Strip twister', watching a homemade video of described heterosexual sex provides the occasion for a more painstakingly depicted male–male encounter.[124] Or women are stand-ins for the real thing: 'I don't normally go for dames, especially married ones . . . but sometimes you gotta take what you can get in this world.'[125]

Casual sex predominates; the characters are having sex with men they have just encountered or have known for hours rather than months. The intended focus is, of course, on the sex, and the third anthology, *Badboy Fantasies*, achieves this more quickly by altering the format, injecting more BDSM, providing twice the number of stories (fifteen rather than seven or eight) but at half the page length. This brings them more in line with Eighner's recommendation for come shots that count: 'Potent as the reader is, one comeshot per story or chapter is about all he can handle.'[126]

The description of penises and their ejaculations follow the template used in Badboy's vintage revisions discussed above. In most stories penis size is specific and important. In Guerra's 'Demolition man' there is an 'eight-inch tubesteak' and 'monstrous 10-inch cock'.[127] In Chris Morris's 'The dough boys' there is an 'eight-and-a-half-inch monster' and a 'nine-inch python'.[128] In Isenstyne's BDSM cop story 'Blue magnets' one penis is 'all ten thick-bottled inches of cut meat, with a gleam of pre-cum shining in its wicked little red eye'.[129] The ejaculations are just as spectacular. They are copious – like a 'geyser' or 'as if an entire lake had been unleashed from my nuts' – and often 'at shotgun force' or 'squirting up like a gushing fire hose left unmanned and out of control'.[130] As already noted, the men are usually ultra-masculine. *Men at Work* contains policemen, firemen, demolition men, and farmhands, and *Slow Burn* connects all its stories to a gym called the 'Body Shoppe'. Guerra's preface to *Slow Burn* describes it as a collection of 'tales of masculine muscle-sex': 'Watching the male body, pumping, grinding, forcing itself forward, growing in size and shape – there's the rub!'[131]

The men on the covers of the Badboy anthologies reflected the themes conveyed within the pages. *Men at Work* has a muscular, bare-chested construction worker staring intently and directly out at the reader: he means business. Badboy's covers are essential to their message. Black-and-white photographs of attractive, muscular men who more often than not stare straight out at the camera/reader, intentionally grabbed the attention of the potential buyer, almost asking them 'Do you like what you see?' Sol Immerman, art director at Pocket Books for almost thirty years, claimed that 'Each book [by means of its cover] must be its own salesman, advertisement, and direct contact with the buying public.'[132] David Earle has stressed the importance of what he terms the visual material character of the cheap paperback: 'If we consider the outward aspects of a text, such as cover, font, price paid, and venue as integral to a book's overall "aura", then the marketing of a book is an important text in its own right.'[133] Ann Bannon, the best known of the lesbian pulp authors, told Amy Villarejo that editors had control over cover art and photography – 'they clearly had learned to calibrate the level of desired sleaze as precisely as a Swiss horologist' (see Figure 45).[134]

Rabinowitz has argued that golden age pulp provided a modernist combination of image (cover art), text (contents), and material form (cheap paperback).[135] While this is certainly true of our 1990s books with the beefcake artwork on supposed classics, racy text, and low purchase price, they were postmodernist rather than modernist, supplementing and subverting the original message, juxtaposing jarringly modern imagery on premodern text, playing with identity and gender in authorial attribution, consciously trashy in terms of creation, contents, and disposal, and reflective, perhaps constitutive, of the beginnings of what has come to be termed the pornification of media and society. If the golden age pulps repackaged highbrow fiction for a popular readership, 1990s pulp made available its version of gay classics. The hinted sex of the golden age covers and text was made explicit in Masquerade and Badboy books. The rather restrained sexuality

45 J. A. Guerra (ed.), *Men at Work* (New York, 1992). Cover photographer unknown. Collection of Barry Reay.

of the 1950s and 1960s lesbian pulp – aimed variously at both straight men and lesbian women – contrasts with the explicit gay male pornography produced by Badboy's (straight and lesbian) female writers.

Were the books that we have been discussing merely what in an earlier era would have been dismissed as 'fuck books' or 'fuck and suck books', demanded by 'one-handed readers' unconcerned with literary merit?[136] The anthologies such as *Come Quickly* undoubtedly were; as we saw at the start of this chapter, they were unabashed in this proclaimed aim. The revised classics certainly added this missing ingredient, but they were hybrids that skilfully maintained much of the craft and disposition of the original. ANONYMOUS and Badboy Books represent a mere episode in the history of pornography and gay erotica. But it is a significant moment. When Masquerade produced their anthology *A Century of Gay Erotica* in 1998, five of the chapters were the work of ANONYMOUS, six if we include another piece that he had helped to shape. He is there alongside Andros, Califia, Delany, Preston, Townsend, Travis, and the author of the famous classic *Teleny* (by a different 'Anonymous'). He had more entries than any other writer.[137]

John Preston wrote in 1992, at the birth of Badboy, that 'For myself and other gay men, pornographic writings were how we learned the parameters of our sexual life. We could have more than a simple ejaculation with a nameless partner. Pornography was how we developed our fantasies, both sexual and emotional.'[138] We have seen that the content of these texts was what we have labelled an uncomplicated homosexuality, where the rewritten classics reshaped an original polymorphous perversity into a more monolithic gay sexuality, against ANONYMOUS's preference but in keeping with the anticipated market – paradoxically at the very moment that queer theory was emerging.[139] It is intriguing that amateurs and lesbian and straight women, as well as straight and not-quite-straight men, were so involved in this Badboy history. If we focus on these authors rather than just their messages, it may have been a victory for gender fuck after all.

Notes

1 J. A. Guerra (ed.), *Come Quickly: For Boys On the Go* (New York, 1996), p. 9.
2 Conversations with ANONYMOUS, 2014 and 2015.
3 Open Library, Publisher: Badboy, https://openlibrary.org/publishers/Badboy (last accessed 16 October 2014).
4 M. Lowenthal (ed.), *The Best of the Badboys* (New York, 1995).

5 D. Garner, 'Pulp friction: a conversation with the 90s prince of porn paperbacks', *Salon*, 30 July 1996, http://salon.com/1996/07/29/kasak/ (last accessed 26 April 2018).
6 Ibid.
7 Conversations with ANONYMOUS, 2014 and 2015.
8 Garner, 'Pulp friction'.
9 R. Gathman, 'Dirty words: investigating the collective gestalt of erotica', *Austin Chronicle*, 11 August 2000.
10 W. Strub, 'Historicizing pulp: gay male pulp and the narrativization of queer cultural history', in D. Gunn and J. Harker (eds), *1960s Gay Pulp Fiction* (Amherst, MA, 2013), pp. 43–77, quote on p. 45.
11 P. Rabinowitz, *American Pulp: How Paperbacks Brought Modernism to Main Street* (Princeton, NJ, 2014).
12 D. W. Gunn (ed.), *The Golden Age of Gay Fiction* (Albion, NY, 2009).
13 D. Bergman, *The Violet Hour: The Violet Quill and the Making of Gay Culture* (New York, 2004).
14 I. Young, *Out in Paperback: A Visual History of Gay Pulps* (Toronto, 2007), pp. 69–71.
15 F. Picano, 'Interview with John Preston', in L. Antoniou (ed.), *Looking For Mr. Preston* (New York, 1995), pp. 27–39, quote on p. 27.
16 T. Dean, 'The erotics of transgression', in H. Stevens (ed.), *The Cambridge Companion to Gay and Lesbian Writing* (Cambridge, 2011), ch. 4; R. Canning, 'The literature of AIDS', in Stevens (ed.), *Cambridge Companion to Gay and Lesbian Writing*, ch. 8.
17 D. Glover and S. McCracken (eds), *The Cambridge Companion to Popular Fiction* (Cambridge, 2012).
18 P. Hallam, *The Book of Sodom* (London, 1993), pp. 19, 20.
19 W. Setz, 'Introduction', in Anonymous, *The Sins of the Cities of the Plain*, ed. W. Setz (Richmond, VA, 2014), pp. vii–xxv, quote at p. xxiii.
20 J. J. Gifford, 'A note on the text', in E. Prime-Stevenson, *Imre: A Memorandum*, ed. J. J. Gifford (Peterborough, ON, 2003 [1906]), p. 30.
21 D. Bergman, 'The cultural work of sixties gay male pulp fiction', in P. J. Smith (ed.), *The Queer Sixties* (New York, 1999), ch. 2, quote at p. 27.
22 C. K. Bauer, *Naughty Girls and Gay Male Romance/Porn: Slash Fiction, Boys' Love Manga, and Other Works by Female 'Cross-Voyeurs' in the U. S. Academic Discourses* (Hamburg, 2012).
23 K. Hellekson and K. Busse (eds), *The Fan Fiction Studies Reader* (Iowa City, IA, 2014).
24 Email from ANONYMOUS, 2015.
25 S. Green, C. Jenkins, and H. Jenkins, '"Normal female interest in men bonking": selections from *The Terra Nostra Underground* and *Strange Bedfellows*', in H. Jenkins (ed.), *Fans, Bloggers, and Gamers: Exploring Participatory Culture* (New York, 2006), p. 69.

26 Ibid., p. 70.
27 H. Jenkins, *Textual Poachers: Television Fans & Participatory Culture* (New York, 1992), ch. 6.
28 Green, Jenkins, and Jenkins, 'Normal female interest', p. 82; http://fanlore.org/wiki/M._Fae_Glasgow (last accessed 26 April 2018).
29 L. Morrish and H. Sauntson, 'Discourse and identity in a corpus of lesbian erotica', *Journal of Lesbian Studies*, 15:1 (2011), 122–39.
30 P. Califia, *Macho Sluts* (Vancouver, 2009); L. Henderson, 'Lesbian pornography: cultural transgression and sexual demystification', in S. Munt (ed.), *New Lesbian Criticism: Literary and Cultural Readings* (New York, 1992), ch. 10.
31 W. Chapkis, 'Introduction', in Califia, *Macho Sluts*, pp. 35–45, quote at p. 37.
32 P. Califia et al., *Forbidden Passages: Writings Banned in Canada* (San Francisco, 1995), p. 117.
33 Califia, *Macho Sluts*, p. 59.
34 A. Ziv, 'Shameful fantasies: cross-gender queer sex in lesbian erotic fiction', in D. M. Halperin and V. Traub (eds), *Gay Shame* (Chicago, 2009), pp. 165–75; V. Koller, 'No ordinary boy: language, masculinities, and queer pornography', in T. M. Milani (ed.), *Language and Masculinities: Performances, Intersections, Dislocations* (New York, 2015), ch. 8.
35 P. Califia, 'Identity sedition and pornography', in C. Queen and L. Schimel (eds), *PoMoSexuals: Challenging Assumptions About Gender and Sexuality* (San Francisco, 1997), pp. 87–106, quote at p. 87.
36 C. Queen and L. Schimel, 'Introduction', in C. Queen and L. Schimel (eds), *Switch Hitters: Lesbians Write Gay Male Erotica and Gay Men Write Lesbian Erotica* (San Francisco, 1996), Ebook, loc. 45.
37 Ibid., loc. 1837.
38 Ibid., loc. 2034.
39 C. Morgan, *Muscle Bound* (New York, 1992); C. Morgan, *Steam Gauge and Other Stories* (New York, 1996).
40 C. Morgan, *Muscle-Bound and Other Stories* (Los Angeles, 2002), p. xi.
41 L. Antoniou, 'Introduction', in Antoniou (ed.), *Looking For Mr. Preston*, pp. 1–9, quote at p. 8.
42 Bergman, 'Cultural work of sixties gay male pulp fiction', p. 27.
43 M. Rowe, *Writing Below the Belt: Conversations with Erotic Authors* (New York, 1995), p. 204.
44 Ibid., pp. 204, 212.
45 Ibid., pp. 48, 52.
46 Ibid., p. 45.
47 Ibid., p. 299.
48 Ibid., p. 300.
49 Ibid., p. 301.
50 Ibid., p. 318.
51 Ibid., p. 303.

52 Ibid., pp. 316–17.
53 Gunn and Harker (eds), *1960s Gay Pulp Fiction*, pp. 313–18.
54 W. Maltese, 'On being there . . . but not', in Gunn (ed.), *The Golden Age of Gay Fiction*, pp. 127–33, quotes at pp. 130, 131.
55 W. Maltese, 'Introduction', in W. Maltese, *Draqualian Silk: A Collector's and Bibliographic Guide to the Books of William Maltese 1969–2010*, ed. R. Reginald (Rockville, MD, 2010), pp. 10–33.
56 Y. Keller, '"Was it right to love her brother's wife so passionately?" Lesbian pulp novels and U. S. lesbian identity, 1950–1965', *American Quarterly*, 53:2 (2005), 385–410, quote at 400.
57 S. Stryker, *Queer Pulp: Perverted Passions From the Golden Age of the Paperback* (San Francisco, 2001), pp. 60, 61, 66.
58 B. Ritt, 'The sleazy side of the street', 29 May 2009: http://jamesreasoner.blogspot.co.nz/2009/05/sleazy-side-of-street-guest-blog-by.html (last accessed 26 April 2018).
59 V. Taylor, 'For my granddaughters . . .', in R. B. Ridinger (ed.), *Speaking For Our Lives: Historic Speeches and Rhetoric For Gay and Lesbian Rights (1892–2000)* (New York, 2014), pp. 233–40, quote at p. 237.
60 L. Glass, *Counter-Culture Colophon: Grove Press, The Evergreen Review, and the Incorporation of the Avante-Garde* (Stanford, CA, 2013), pp. 138–42, quote at p. 141.
61 Ibid.
62 Hovland contributed to the ACT UP Oral History Project: www.actuporalhistory.org/interviews/images/hovland.pdf (last accessed 26 April 2018); Watson's publications include *Exposed!* (Zurich, 2002), and *Kink!* (London, 2003).
63 M. B. Kaplan, *Sodom on the Thames: Sex, Love, and Scandal in Wilde Times* (New York, 2005), pp. 6, 269, 270.
64 Prime-Stevenson, *Imre*, p. 86.
65 Ibid., p. 103.
66 X. Mayne, *The Intersexes: A History of Similisexualism as a Problem in Social Life* (New York, 1975 [1908]).
67 R. Scully, *A Scarlet Pansy* (New York, 1932).
68 G. Chauncey, *Gay New York: Gender, Urban Culture, and the Making of the Gale Male World, 1890–1940* (New York, 1994), ch. 11; C. Heap, *Slumming: Sexual and Racial Encounters in American Nightlife, 1885–1940* (Chicago, 2009), ch. 6; B. Reay, *New York Hustlers: Masculinity and Sex in Modern America* (Manchester, 2010), ch. 5.
69 J. A. Gertzman, 'A scarlet pansy goes to war: subversion, schlock, and an early gay classic', *The Journal of American Culture*, 33:3 (2010), 230–9.
70 R. Scully, *The Scarlet Pansy* (New York, 1952).
71 Scully, *Scarlet Pansy* (1932), pp. 39, 145.
72 Ibid., pp. 10, 77, 253.

73 Ibid., pp. 189–92.
74 Ibid., pp. 254–5.
75 Ibid., p. 335.
76 R. Austen, *Playing the Game: The Homosexual Novel in America* (Indianapolis, IN, 1977), p. 26.
77 R. Bolton, 'Sex talk: bodies and behaviors in gay erotica', in W. L. Leap (ed.), *Beyond the Lavender Lexicon: Authenticity, Imagination, and Appropriation in Lesbian and Gay Languages* (Luxembourg, 1995), ch. 9.
78 J. Heywood, '"The object of desire is the object of contempt": representations of masculinity in *Straight to Hell* magazine', in S. Johnson and U. H. Meinhof (eds), *Language and Masculinity* (Oxford, 1997), ch. 11, quote at p. 190.
79 *Sins of the Cities of the Plain or The Recollections of a Mary-Ann, With Short Essays on Sodomy and Tribadism, In Two Volumes* (London, 1881), vol. 1, p. 8; Anonymous, *Sins of the Cities of the Plain* (New York, 1992), pp. 7–8.
80 Anonymous, *Sins of the Cities*, p. 126.
81 Bolton, 'Sex talk', p. 191.
82 J. J. Gifford, 'Introduction', in Prime-Stevenson, *Imre*, pp. 13–26, quotes at pp. 13, 21.
83 Prime-Stevenson, *Imre*, p. 44; Anonymous, *Imre* (New York, 1992), pp. 27–30.
84 Prime-Stevenson, *Imre*, p. 103.
85 Anonymous, *Imre*, pp. 132–3.
86 Anonymous, *The Scarlet Pansy* (New York, 1992), pp. 25–6.
87 Ibid., p. 312.
88 L. Eighner, *Elements of Arousal: How to Write and Sell Gay Men's Erotica* (New York, 1994), p. 55.
89 Anonymous, *Scarlet Pansy*, pp. 31–2.
90 Ibid., p. 36.
91 Ibid., pp. 79, 114–15, 150.
92 Ibid., pp. 67, 68, 175, 199, 122.
93 Ibid., pp. 199, 200, 68.
94 Ibid., pp. 106, 150.
95 Ibid., p. 270.
96 Anonymous, *Sins of the Cities*, pp. 21–2.
97 Anonymous, *Imre*, pp. 78–80.
98 *Sins of the Cities of the Plain*, vol. 1, p. 36.
99 Ibid.; Anonymous, *Sins of the Cities*, p. 42.
100 *Sins of the Cities of the Plain*, vol. 2, pp. 70–1.
101 Anonymous, *Sins of the Cities*, p. 147.
102 Hallam, *Book of Sodom*, p. 18.
103 *Sins of the Cities of the Plain*, vol. 2, pp. 14–16; Anonymous, *Sins of the Cities*, pp. 97–8.
104 *Sins of the Cities of the Plain*, vol. 1, p. 13; Anonymous, *Sins of the Cities*, p. 12.
105 *Sins of the Cities of the Plain*, vol. 1, p. 65; Anonymous, *Sins of the Cities*, p. 67.

106 *Sins of the Cities of the Plain*, vol. 1, pp. 31, 53, 74; Anonymous, *Sins of the Cities*, pp. 34, 55, 71.
107 Kaplan, *Sodom on the Thames*, p. 223.
108 Reay, *New York Hustlers*, p. 149.
109 B. R. S. Fone, *A Road to Stonewall: Male Homosexuality and Homophobia in English and American Literature, 1750–1969* (New York, 1994), p. 227.
110 Scully, *Scarlet Pansy* (1932), p. 144; Scully, *Scarlet Pansy* (1952), p. 95.
111 Scully, *Scarlet Pansy* (1932), pp. 147–8; Scully, *Scarlet Pansy* (1952), pp. 97–8.
112 Anonymous, *Scarlet Pansy*, p. 122.
113 Ibid., p. 147.
114 Ibid., pp. 149–50.
115 Prime-Stevenson, *Imre*, pp. 90–2, 96, 118–19; email from ANONYMOUS, 2015.
116 Gifford, 'Introduction', p. 21.
117 Ibid., p. 17.
118 Prime-Stevenson, *Imre*, p. 52.
119 Ibid., p. 86.
120 Ibid., pp. 101, 86.
121 J. A. Guerra (ed.), *Men at Work* (New York, 1992), p. 9.
122 R. J. Ortiz, 'Honor among thieves', in Guerra (ed.), *Men at Work*, pp. 67–88, quote at p. 69.
123 A. Edwards, 'Silent harvest', in Guerra (ed.), *Men at Work*, pp. 157–91, quote at p. 186.
124 G. Firestone, 'Strip twister', in J. A. Guerra (ed.), *Badboy Fantasies* (New York, 1992), pp. 141–52.
125 L. Hecht, 'A night in suburbia', in Guerra (ed.), *Badboy Fantasies*, pp. 105–16, quote at p. 107.
126 Eighner, *Elements of Arousal*, p. 131.
127 J. A. Guerra, 'Demolition man', in Guerra (ed.), *Men at Work*, pp. 31–46, quotes at pp. 35, 43.
128 C. Morris, 'The dough boys', in Guerra (ed.), *Men at Work*, pp. 89–112, quotes at pp. 107, 109.
129 S. Isenstyne, 'Blue magnets', in Guerra (ed.), *Men at Work*, pp. 113–36, quote at p. 117.
130 M. St. Augustine, 'A long hard road', in J. A. Guerra (ed.), *Slow Burn* (New York, 1992), pp. 111–34, quote at p. 133; J. Romero, 'Speed iron', in Guerra (ed.), *Slow Burn*, pp. 55–74, quote at p. 73; Guerra, 'Demolition man', p. 45; R. O'Brian, 'Trashfire', in Guerra (ed.), *Men at Work*, pp. 137–56, quote at p. 156.
131 Guerra (ed.), *Slow Burn*, pp. 7–8.
132 T. L. Bonn, *Undercover: An Illustrated History of American Mass Market Paperbacks* (New York, 1982), p. 84.
133 D. M. Earle, *Re-Covering Modernism: Pulps, Paperbacks, and the Prejudice of Form* (Farnham, 2009), p. 6.

134 A. Villarejo, *Lesbian Rule: Cultural Criticism and the Value of Desire* (Durham, NC, 2003), p. 167.
135 Rabinowitz, *American Pulp*.
136 D. Dean, 'Fuck books or gay literature', *Vector*, May 1973, 16–17.
137 P. Andros, S. R. Delany, J. Preston, L. Townsend, and A. Travis, *A Century of Gay Erotica* (New York, 1998).
138 J. Preston, 'Introduction: my life with pornography', in J. Preston (ed.), *Flesh and the Word: An Anthology of Erotic Writing* (New York, 1992), pp. 1–13, quote at p. 9.
139 D. E. Hall and A. Jagose (eds), *The Routledge Queer Studies Reader* (New York, 2013).

8

The body as amusement park: a quick history of masturbation

There are so many ways in which one could begin this chapter: with a joke, a masturbatory image, a philosophical conundrum, or perhaps the description of a performance piece – all will occur later in the chapter. However, let us begin with auto(erotic)ethnography. 'Auto(erotic)ethnography' is the title of Kristen Blinne's experiment, a hybrid of erotic story telling and auto-ethnography, where the focus, and possible outcome, is masturbatory.[1] Playing with, as she puts it, 'heightened sensual energy as a tool to cultivate a continuous state of arousal', Blinne attempts 'tantric writing-doing'.[2]

> Before I continue, I must confess:
> *I masturbate.*
> *I think you might masturbate, too.*
> *I enjoy masturbating. I want you to enjoy masturbating, too.*
> *I want to invite you – to feel me – to feel yourself*[3]

She toys with her readers: '*Are you as aroused by this topic as I?*'[4]

I start with this example not to discuss how erotic Blinne's writing might be, nor to assess her comparison between autoeroticism and the writing process, nor even to comment on her valorisation of self-love. 'Auto(erotic) ethnography' is significant because it exists. How have we reached the stage where an academic journal, albeit one called *Sexualities*, can contain such material?

There is a historical narrative that identifies modernity with an increased acceptance of sexual self-pleasuring, a history that moves from the practice's relative marginality, through societal obsession and repulsion, back to what Alan Hunt once dubbed an 'uneasy silence', and then to qualified Western cultural acceptance – from 'obscure vice' to 'sexual superstar' as Thomas Laqueur has expressed it.[5] When the sociologist Anthony Giddens charted contemporary sexuality at the end of the twentieth century, separating the strands of what made modern sex modern, one of the characteristics that he identified (along with changing attitudes to same-sex desires) was acceptance of masturbation, what he termed its 'coming out'.[6] Masturbation was 'widely recommended as a major source of sexual pleasure, and actively encouraged as a mode of improving sexual responsiveness on the part of both sexes'.[7] It had indeed come to signify gay freedom in the 1960s and 1970s, and then safe sex in an age of AIDS. Lucas Hilderbrand has shown that a branch of the Mattachine Society (an early gay rights organisation with a somewhat conservative reputation) was screening pornography in the 1970s in what became the Circle J [circle jerk] Cinema in San Francisco. One of the organisation's leaders recalled, 'We had anywhere up to fifty, sixty, seventy-five people a day visiting, and most of them jacking off . . . I believed in gay sex, and we were trying to achieve the freedom to have it.'[8] Autoeroticism represented female sexual freedom, with Betty Dodson's *Liberating Masturbation* (1974), which has sold over a million copies, and her Bodysex Workshops with their all-women masturbation circles.[9] 'It is my feeling that when a woman masturbates', she wrote in *Ms.* magazine in 1974, 'she learns to like her own body, to enjoy sex and orgasm and to become proficient and independent about sex. Our society does not really approve of sexually proficient and independent women' (see Figure 46).[10] Masturbation was a feminist issue. The Boston Women's Health Collective's classic feminist text, *Our Bodies Ourselves* (1973), included a section called

46 Betty Dodson at a sexuality conference, 1973. Schlesinger Library, Radcliffe Institute, Harvard University. Permission the Estate of Bettye Lane.

'Learning to Masturbate'.[11] A series of female masturbation films in the 1970s added to the instructional repertoire.[12]

As Greg Tuck has observed, 'We are a profoundly self-pleasuring society at both a metaphorical and material level; without self-pleasure, much of our contemporary sexual culture would not exist.'[13] Google's Ngram gives a visual sense of the increased usage of the term in English in the printed book (see Figure 47). The Internet is even more revealing. Type masturbation into your Google search engine and see how many million hits you get: 374,000,000 results at my last attempt.[14] There are politically conscious masturbation websites: the posters on masturbateforpeace.com are particularly amusing (see Figures 48–9). There is the 'Masturbation Hall of Fame' (sponsored by the sex toys franchise Good Vibrations).[15] Then there is *The Big Book of Masturbation* (2003) and the hundreds of (pun intended) self-help books, *Masturbation for Weight Loss, a Woman's Guide* (2015) only among the latest (and more opportunistic). There are masturbationathons, and jack-off-clubs and masturbation parties have, so to speak, come and gone since the impact of AIDS in the early 1980s, though they are collective rather than solitary endeavours.[16] There are some very amusing online comedy, parodic posts (see Figures 50–1).

Then there are Annie Sprinkle's famed public performances of masturbation in the 1990s.

> When the time is right, I press the vibrator (on high) to my trusty clitoris, stimulate my Goddess spot (g-spot) with my magic dildo, and gradually lift off into another dimension. I am not in Kansas any more—or at Show World Center doing strip speak. It's no fantasy. It's a very real, intense, wild ride, a close encounter of the fourth kind. A bizarre, interactive art/life/sex experiment.[17]

In her stage show 'Herstory of Porn' she masturbated to herself masturbating in a huge projected image from the film *Deep Inside Annie Sprinkle* (1982).[18] There was certainly no secrecy or shame in these performances that merged pornography and art (see Figure 52).[19] In fact, the music that accompanied her act, the Hafler Trio's electronic *Masturbatorium*, was released as a compact disc in 1991. Sprinkle, in her own words, took 'something that's usually done alone in the dark, putting it under a microscope, and shining beautiful theatrical light on it so we could all look at it together'.[20] In Berlin in 1991 Sprinkle passed her vibrator around the audience before she used it onstage.[21] A living archive of the history of sex – from sex work to sex addiction (she is a critic) and ecosexuality – Sprinkle's humour has always provided a self-reflexive, critical edge to all her commentary.[22] Her workshop, performance and video work included

47 Usage of words 'masturbation' and 'onanism' in the printed book from Google Ngram. Google and the Google logo are registered trademarks of Google Inc., used with permission.

48 All We Are Saying Is Give Peace A Hand. Poster from MasturbateForPeace.com: http://masturbateforpeace.com/posters.html

a female version of the famed male, pornographic money shot, the come shot, with an orgasm that lasted six minutes and visible female ejaculation (the sprinkle in Sprinkle).[23] When asked about experiments that did not work, she revisited her public masturbation performances:

49 War Can Wait, Masturbate! Poster from MasturbateForPeace.com: http://masturbateforpeace.com/posters.html.

50 The Clitoris is the Devil's Doorbell: Christians Against Drugs, 2015: Facebook: www.facebook.com/christiansagainstdrugsofficial/?hc_ref=ARSczm414oxe1R4QfhSUufBQcW2lFU_SZDvkzqTdt3nywWcBfvW8XkBaaUooVeBtyvA&fref=nf.

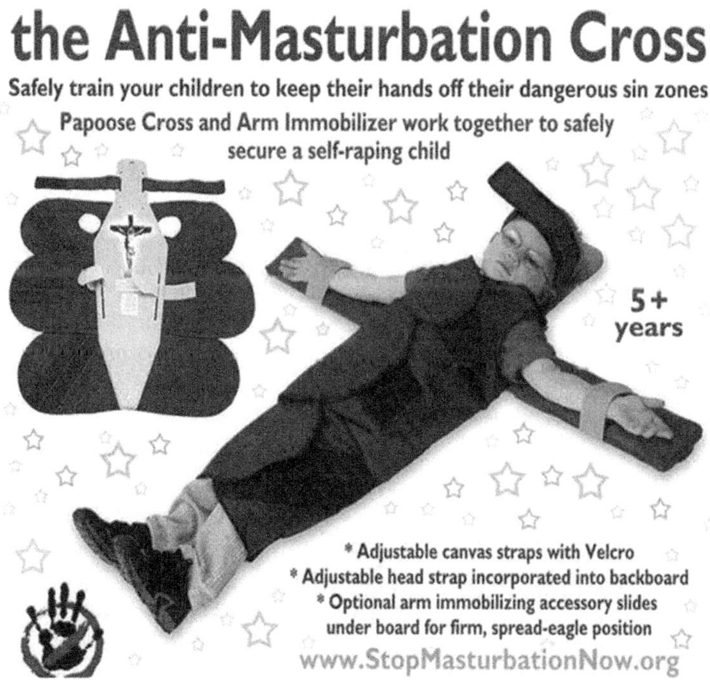

51 The Anti-Masturbation Cross, 2014: http://knowyourmeme.com/memes/anti-masturbation-cross.

52 Still from *Deep Inside Annie Sprinkle* (1981). Permission of Annie Sprinkle and Steven Morowitz (VIDEO-X-PIX).

> I tried whipping myself to get my skin to wake up. Must have looked pretty weird . . . I also tried blindfolding myself . . . but it alienated me from the audience. Also, while in Australia I did too many of those masturbation rituals, 30 in 5 weeks, and I burnt myself.[24]

Self-pleasuring has been a recurring theme throughout this book. Percy Grainger's 'self-help' and 'naughtiness' was discussed in the Prologue; the composer was an enthusiast. '[W]hat bliss self-help is, for man or woman!' he wrote in 1945, recalling his life at the start of the century. 'What unique ecstasies! What liberation! What protection from dangerous and exasperating diseases! What independence from women and marriage!'[25] He told his lover Karen Holten in 1908 that it was better to do it oneself, to be in control, than to have another do it, employing the musical simile that it was 'the difference between a good & a bad conductor'.[26] We considered photography that aided masturbation: Henry Faulkner's photographs in Chapter 1; Edward Melcarth, Thomas Painter, and Samuel Steward's in Chapters 2 and 3. In Chapter 5, we encountered Lou Sullivan's teenage masturbation and his patronage of adult jack-off clubs. His archive contains printed ephemera relating to the San Francisco Jack and Jill masturbation clubs of the 1980 and 1990s, including advertised events, one in 1989 with Betty Dodson as the guest of honour.[27]

David Louis Bowie's gay masturbatory journals of Chapter 6 describe him masturbating repeatedly: to recent memories of orgies, while drawing a picture of a partner's penis; to pictures in black erotic magazines; to his own diary entries; to pictures on his bathroom walls; to photographs of his Puerto Rican lovers and an erotic magazine called *Puerto Ricans*; to slides that he had taken of interracial heterosexual sex; and even to a 'straight dream' that he had about a topless dancer.[28] And masturbation is the *raison d'être* for the 'one-handed', *Come Quickly*, pornographic literature in Chapter 7. 'As the heart of a work of stroke fiction . . . is the erotic scene, the heart of the erotic scene is the comeshot', explained one of the experts of the genre. 'While I encourage the highest literary values in gay literature', he continued, 'I do not try to kid myself or anyone else what [the] stroke story is for.'[29]

Though the records of Bowie, Painter, and Steward are essentially masturbatory, and the Kinsey Institute has those films of the activity that are not accessible to researchers, masturbation seldom generates its own archive. Perhaps one rare example is Gerald Foos's 'Voyeur's Journal', which, for nearly thirty years from 1965 onwards, chronicled the sexual liaisons of his motel guests observed from an observation platform in the motel loft.[30] Although the journal's compiler saw himself (Kinsey-like) as a sex researcher, the impulse behind his 'research' was substantially masturbatory. One of Gay Talese's extracts from the journals relates Foos masturbating while watching one of his unsuspecting female guests self-pleasuring, 'a routine of teasing masturbation'. In a quaint piece of simultaneity, 'The Voyeur masturbated to orgasm along with her.'[31] But the point about this masturbatory archive is its singularity. Unlike other chapters that focus on specific archives, either institutional or counter-institutional, this chapter, somewhat like Ann Cvetkovich's *An Archive of Feelings* (2003), necessarily creates its own dossier. Based on evidentiary fragments from US sex surveys, masturbation forums, feminist texts, films, performance art, accounts of sex therapy, self-help books, philosophical discussion, and the body itself (in the form of the circumcised US penis), it becomes an archive of feelings with a different focus.

The aim of this chapter is to explore masturbation's recent history. How accurate is the picture of the valorisation of solitary sex? Has masturbation (to adopt a terrible pun) made something of a comeback? And, if autoeroticism is now culturally mainstream, does that indicate its total acceptance?

Of course, the claim for the modern acceptance of masturbation is normally contrasted with earlier periods of relative disregard. In ancient Greece and Rome, as Laqueur has shown, masturbation was either not much mentioned or treated as something a little vulgar, not in good taste, a bad habit, a joke: 'Ponticus, do you think it's nothing that you only fuck with your left hand as a handmaiden and make it the girlfriend of your lusts?'[32] In the middle ages and for much of the early modern period, too, masturbation, while sinful and unnatural, was not invested with huge significance. Jen Stengers and Anne Van Neck have reasoned from the evidence of historical silence that the subject was not high on the list of that period's social and cultural priorities.[33]

Modern tolerance is also compared to the high anxiety of the eighteenth and nineteenth centuries when everything changed after the publication of what became the best-selling pamphlets *Onania* (1716) and Samuel Auguste Tissot's *L'onanisme* (1760), when the practice of onanism, as masturbation was then called, became viewed with utter horror. 'Sin, vice, and self-destruction', to quote Stengers and Van Neck, were the 'trinity of ideas' that would dominate from the eighteenth into the nineteenth century.[34] Religion and medicine combined powerfully in this new and hostile discourse. Masturbation was a sin that caused medical disorder.[35] Michael Stolberg has argued that notions that the soul was present in semen merged with new scientific thinking about the importance of the retention of that vital fluid, which rendered its spilling both immoral and dangerous (the reader should be reminded that for much of that period medicine also believed in female semen).[36] Tissot wrote that the loss of an ounce of semen 'would weaken more than forty ounces of blood'.[37]

Any subtleties of the intellectual origins of this sexual shift seem hidden in the crude force of that transformation. The 'shameful vice', the 'solitary act of pleasure', was something too terrible to be described. Articulating the wickedness might lead to its practice; the very first page of *Onania* anticipates those 'who are of the opinion, that, notwithstanding the frequency of this sin, it never ought to be spoken of, or hinted at, because the bare mentioning of it may be dangerous to some, who without it would, probably, never have thought of it'.[38] However, there was little reticence in cataloguing its purported consequences, what Michel Foucault characterised as 'a sort of polymorphous, absolute illness without remission that accumulates every symptom of every possible illness'.[39] In *Onania* these included gonorrhoea, fits, epilepsy, consumption, impotence, and general bodily deterioration in men; and, in women, deflowering (loss of 'that valuable badge of their chastity and innocence'), disease of the womb, hysteria, and infertility.[40] Each edition of the pamphlet (I have been quoting from the 21st edition of 1776) incorporated letters from its readers (perhaps fabricated) who suffered from 'that abominable practice', and thus the list of ailments grew. Headaches, weakness of intellect, backache, pimples, blisters, glandular swelling, trembling, dizziness, heart palpitations, urinary discharge, wandering pains, incontinence, and enlargement of the clitoris were all attributed to onanism.[41]

Tissot was critical of *Onania*, 'a real chaos . . . all the author's reflections are nothing but theological and moral puerilities'; but he nevertheless listed 'the ills of which the English patients complain'.[42] He was likewise fixated on 'the physical disorders produced by masturbation', and provided a case study of a watchmaker who had self-pleasured himself into 'insensibility' on a daily basis, sometimes three times a day; 'I found a being that less resembled a living creature than a corpse, lying upon straw, meagre, pale, and filthy, casting forth an infectious stench; almost incapable of motion.'[43]

The reader could be forgiven for thinking that the fear was confined to men, but this was not the case. The full title of *Onania* was *Onania: Or the Heinous Sin of Self-Pollution, and all its Frightful Consequences (in both Sexes)*. Its author was aware that the sin of Onan referred to the spilling of male seed (and divine retribution for the act) but reiterated that he treated 'of this crime in relation to women as well as men, whilst the offence is Self-Pollution in both, I could not think of any other word which would so well put the reader in mind both of the sin and its punishment at once, as this'.[44] Tissot also stressed that women pursued 'the same career in these infamous practices' and consequently exposed themselves to 'the same dangers'; in fact he posited that 'the disorder seems even to make greater progress with women than with men'.[45] Still, it remains true that while the literature of this medical and moral terror included both sexes, and was aimed at both male and female readers and listeners, the bracketing in *Onania*'s title was accurate; the burden of discussion and weight of examples did indeed favour the male.

The anxiety extended into the nineteenth century. The Parisian publication *Le Livre Sans Titre* (1830), 'The book without a name', charted, in colour, the rapid decline of a rosy-cheeked youth through self-corruption: 'At the age of 17, he expires, and in horrible torment' (see Figure 53).[46] There were interesting national variations, for it took until the middle of the nineteenth century for the dread of masturbation to take hold in America. April Haynes has highlighted the role of the American female moral campaign societies and popular reform physiology lecturers in spreading the condemnation of masturbation in the 1830s and 1840s. It was not in the name of hostility to sex, Haynes stresses, for these women knew all about female sexual passion, and reform physiology was concerned with advice on healthy sexuality. Rather, their campaign against masturbation

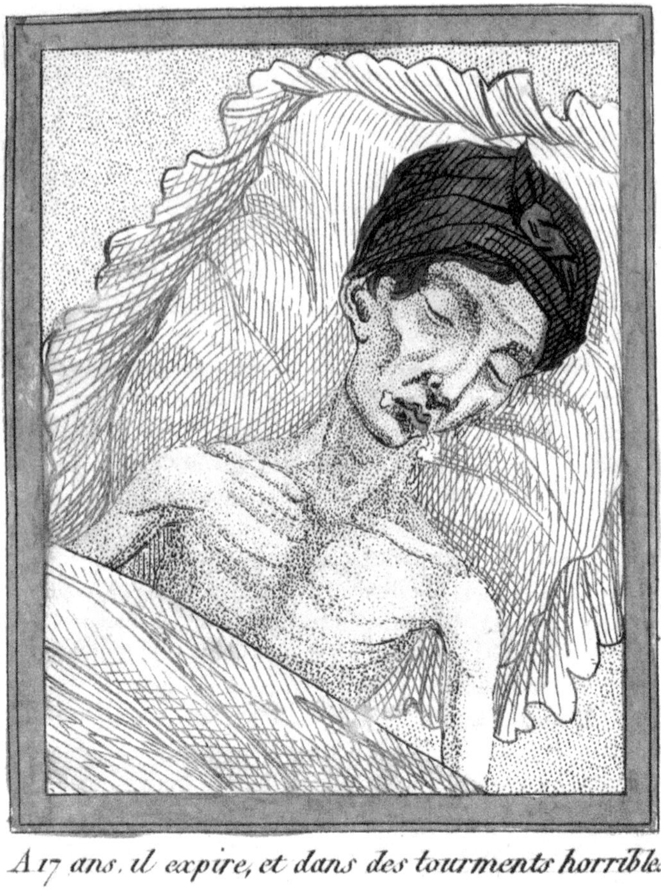

53 'At the age of 17, he expires, and in horrible torment': the fatal effects of masturbation. Illustration in *Le Livre Sans Titre* (Paris, 1830). Dittrick Medical History Center, Case Western Reserve University.

was motivated by encouragement of female self-control and what we would now term greater sexual agency – 'virtuous restraint' as she puts it. 'Renouncing solitary vice could be almost as pleasurable – and solipsistic – as masturbation itself.'[47]

This association of the campaign against masturbation with sexual citizenship and women's rights (both claimed by Haynes) certainly adds complexity to what is normally glossed over in terms of phobic stereotypes. Yet it is difficult to escape the intensity of the tropes of the great fear. Nicholas

Francis Cooke's 1871 description of the physical characteristics of the masturbating female ('Alas, that such a term is possible!') was really no different to that of Tissot in 1760.[48] The phrenologist James Barker, whose target was the male, was convinced that he knew the signs of the 'vile practice', writing in 1888 of 'cadaverous outlines of face and form; his skin sallow, blotched, and close drawn, his flesh clammy, flabby, and flaccid; the eyes resembling those of that interesting object generally known as a stale cod fish'. 'I have looked sometimes at bloated, flaunting, jerking, raven-like specimens of the masculine genus', he continued, 'as they perambulate along . . . with hands daintily poised breast high, or deep thrust into suspicious pockets, as if in sympathy with the excited, and inflamed organs that are always craving for the friction that they have been so well acquainted with since their first abnormal disturbance'.[49]

Some of the late nineteenth-century transatlantic anti-masturbation material examined by Hunt, which focused on male boarding school life, was vague about exactly what it was that was being condemned. 'Vice', 'the evil', 'temptation', 'sin', 'wickedness', 'the danger': Edward Lyttelton's social purity tract of 1883 used all those terms before eventually alighting on 'solitary vice'.[50] But his indeterminacy also hinted at more dizzying sins; reference to 'those younger ones whose attractiveness of manner or appearance exposes them to danger' suggested mutual as well as solitary masturbation – and perhaps even something more, what Hunt astutely describes as occupying 'a problematic location between heterosexuality and homosexuality'.[51]

J. H. Kellogg's *Plain Facts for Old and Young* (1877, 1891), which drew on the doctrine of reform physiology, contained both exaggerated horror stories and grand claims: 'neither the plague, nor war, nor small-pox, nor similar diseases, have produced results so disastrous to humanity as the pernicious habit of Onanism, it is the destroying element of civilized societies'.[52] The list of signs and effects was endless, including exhaustion, insomnia, mental confusion, bad posture, pimples, bitten fingernails, cold hands, and, more seriously, impotence and sterility, consumption, heart ailments, uterine and breast disease, epilepsy, and insanity. Kellogg suggested remedies for the scourge: exercise, strict bathing and sleeping regimes, compresses, douching, enemas, electrical treatment, and circumcision. Diet was vital.[53] This anti-masturbator, as the famous psychologist John Money pointed out, was the co-inventor of the breakfast cereal that still bears his name. 'Few of today's eaters of Kellogg's Corn Flakes know that he invented them, almost literally, as anti-masturbation food.'[54]

The traces are still with us, then, and not just in our breakfast bowls. Robert Darby has shown that the influential Anglo-American medical practice of male circumcision originated in part with the nineteenth-century obsession with the role of the foreskin in encouraging masturbatory practices.[55] Consciously or not, many American males are faced with this bodily reminder . . . well . . . every time they masturbate.

To return to modernity, there is much evidence for what Jane Juffer originally termed the 'mainstreaming of masturbation'.[56] Alfred Kinsey and his team are mainly remembered for the sex surveys that publicised the pervasiveness of American same-sex desires and experiences, but they also recognised the prevalence and normality of masturbation. Paul Robinson has called Kinsey one of 'the foremost modern defenders of autoeroticism'.[57] It was, for both men and women, one of the nation's main sexual outlets and involved most of the population: up to 97 per cent of males and 62 per cent of females in the Kinsey reports said that they had masturbated at some stage in their lives.[58] While heterosexual petting was the principal form of reported sex before marriage for women, and sexual intercourse the main form of women's married sex, masturbation 'is the one in which the second largest numbers of females engage both before and after marriage'.[59] And the rub (sorry) was that it was the sexual activity most likely to produce orgasm: women who masturbated reached orgasm in '95 per cent or more' of their masturbation.[60] Solitary sex for women was a sure way to satisfaction. Married sex, with at most 53 per cent of women reporting climaxing (depending on educational level/class and length of time married), was far less reliable.[61] Interestingly, in the light of the warnings in the preceding pages, some of the women in the Kinsey survey said that they had first learned about masturbation from the literature designed to discourage the practice.[62] Among single men, the Kinsey team found that those with the highest rates of masturbation were those with college-level education. Working-class and uneducated unmarried men were more likely to be fucking than engaging in solitary gratification like their middle-class counterparts.[63] Kinsey argued that the harm in masturbation was the psychic harm caused by those who condemned it, but that the activity itself had only beneficial effects for both men and women.[64]

Robinson saw the work of William Masters and Virginia Johnson in the 1950s and 1960s as another endorsing moment in the history of attitudes to masturbation, a completion of the 'autoerotic revolution'.[65] Not only did they celebrate the intensity of what they termed automanipulation, measurably higher than during coitus, but advocated its numerous benefits: from the relief of menstrual pain to improved methods of lovemaking.[66] *Human Sexual Response* (1966) included detailed discussion of 'how to stimulate the clitoris', which the authors considered lacking in other studies:

> The human female frequently is not content with one orgasmic experience during episodes of automanipulation involving the clitoral body. If there is no psychosocial distraction to repress sexual tensions, many well-adjusted women enjoy a minimum of three or four orgasmic experiences before they reach apparent satiation. Masturbating women concentrating only on their own sexual demands, without the psychic distractions of a coital partner, may enjoy sequential orgasmic experiences without allowing their sexual tensions to resolve below plateau-phase levels [the phase before orgasm in their schema]. Usually physical exhaustion alone terminates such an active masturbatory session.[67]

The highest percentages of performance *failure* in this laboratory sex resulted from intercourse rather than self-pleasuring. Of the overall minimal failures of 'orgasmic return' (only 3 per cent), 95 per cent involved coital activity and only 5 per cent masturbation.[68] When they ranked female orgasmic intensity, automanipulation came first, partner manipulation second, and coitus third.[69] Masturbation trumped sexual intercourse, although this was a message explicit in their findings rather than editorialised by the researchers themselves.[70] Masters and Johnson also employed self-stimulation in sexual research. (We saw in a previous chapter that Kinsey and his team filmed male ejaculation and women at the point of orgasm.)[71] Masters and Johnson recorded, measured, and filmed the physiological response during sexual arousal, using new technology, including a miniature camera inside a plastic phallus. Their book *Human Sexual Response* (1966) was based on data from over 10,000 orgasms from nearly 700 volunteers (around 400 women and 300 men), laboratory research involving sexual intercourse, stimulation, and masturbation by hand and with a transparent phallus.[72] Intriguingly, given the subject of masturbation, one of the main reported motivations of their participants (apart from payment) was release of 'sexual tension'.[73] Although the films seem no longer to exist, we have a rather vivid description by a psychoanalyst who watched one: 'The movie opens quite abruptly with a middle-distance shot of a naked woman standing . . . it is immediately apparent she is caressing, rather than covering, her parts.' The observer, Leslie Farber, referred to intercut close-ups of various bodies, of the skin rash and nipple hardening indicating heightening sexual pleasure, and then, when the woman was horizontal, internal shots of vaginal secretions and the final contractions of orgasm.[74]

Later sexual surveys have indicated the ubiquity of reported solitary sex. *The Hite Report on Female Sexuality* (1976) found that 82 per cent of women said they masturbated, and almost all (95 per cent) to orgasm; 'Many women used the term "masturbation" synonymously with orgasm.'[75] In a US National Survey (2009–10), 94 per cent of men aged 25–29 and 85 per cent of women in the same age group said that they had masturbated alone in the course of their lifetime; 69 per cent and 52 per cent respectively had engaged in the activity in the month before the survey.[76] (All surveys indicate lower *reported* rates for women.) In the more recently published results of the 2012 National Survey of Sexual Health and Behavior in the US, 92 per cent of straight men and 100 per cent of gay men recorded lifetime masturbation.[77] Some surveys have focused on quality rather than quantity. A recent University of Michigan study of 73 queer and heterosexual self-identified women concerning their sole and partnered sex found clearly identified pleasures associated with solitary sex: autonomy, freedom for fantasy and sexual exploration, intensity of experience, and opportunity for self-discovery. There were satisfactions in partnered sex that need not detain us, but masturbation had an integral role in these women's 'sexual well-being'. The researchers and the women themselves described the relationship between solo and partnered sex as supplemental or complementary, but it does not quite capture the overlaps and separations of the described desires. The crucial point was the pleasure of solitary sex.[78]

Masturbation has been used as a means of combating unwanted gender and sexual behaviour, notoriously in 1960s Anglo-American behavioural therapy. In aversion therapy it was combined with nausea-inducing injections and/or electric shock treatment to combat the desires of homosexual and transgender patients and to reinforce heterosexual fantasies.[79] In one anti-homosexual procedure, for example, the shocks were administered while the patient masturbated to images of naked men, or, alternatively, the man was permitted to masturbate into tissues to his own fantasies, but, at the moment of signalled ejaculation, a picture of a partially clad woman was illuminated until the patient indicated that he had 'finished'.[80] In a process called fading, the patient was encouraged to focus on their favourite masturbatory fantasy, and then, at the height of their arousal, heterosexual images were introduced.[81] The problem in such orgasmic reconditioning (when the masturbating patient used a disapproved image or memory to arrive at the point of orgasm and then shifted to the approved stimulus as they ejaculated) is that there was no guarantee that they had not invoked the original, more arousing, fantasy.[82]

Masturbation has been used more positively in sexual therapy – 'as a means of achieving sexual health', as an article by Eli Coleman, the director of the Program in Human Sexuality at the University of Minnesota Medical School, put it.[83] The University of Oregon Psychology Clinic treated inorgasmic women and sexually dysfunctional men in the 1970s, drawing both on the findings of Kinsey and Masters and Johnson relating to masturbation and the behavioural therapy discussed above. For sexually dysfunctional men who were not attracted to their partners, the client was encouraged while masturbating to first focus on erotic stimuli that they found particularly arousing and then, on the point of orgasm, switch to 'fantasies of sexual activity with his partner' (much as with the orgasmic reconditioning just discussed).[84] Inorgasmic women were treated in an elaborate nine-step process, from genital self-examination, through self-pleasuring by hand or vibrator to the point of orgasm, to partner intercourse accompanied by genital stimulation. Therapists were encouraged to normalise masturbatory activity by 'unashamedly discussing their own enjoyment of sexual activity'.[85] Other clinicians provided variants on this programme. The University Medical Center in San Francisco provided group treatment for what they preferred to term 'preorgasmic' women, excluding male partners from the immediate therapy ('partners can be a distracting element'), using a modified version of the Oregon format, and assigning readings from *Our Bodies Ourselves*.[86] Over 90 per cent of the participants were 'orgasmic with masturbation' by the end of the programme.[87] Another published study, this time in the *Journal of Consulting and Clinical Psychology* in 1977, outlined therapist-supervised female masturbation (with dildo, vibrator, and 'organic vegetables') as a way of encouraging vaginal orgasm.[88]

It is interesting, when as Kinsey or Masters and Johnson would have pointed out much of the problem lay with the men, that there was so much focus on women and privileging of sexual intercourse. During the 1980s therapists were distinguishing between 'primary' female 'orgasmic dysfunction' where women never achieved orgasm, and 'secondary inorgasmia' or 'secondary orgasmic dysfunction', which included women who experienced orgasm in masturbation but not in sexual intercourse. Masturbation was still advocated as therapy for the former; couples and group therapy and sexual technique coaching were preferred for the latter, given that the women involved were already able to masturbate to orgasm.[89]

Alternatively, self-help therapies had become more of a focus in masturbation-based therapy by the 2000s – self-help for self-help. Rather than performing homework exercises away from the clinic and reporting back to the therapist, a traditional method, the client moved towards self-administering, minimising direct contact with the specialist, though not dispensing with it entirely, by employing bibliotherapy (instructional reading), video viewing (again with practical advice), or Internet therapy (from email contact to more sophisticated online interactions).[90] Computer-assisted therapy has not always delivered (ironic given that online pornography must produce billions of orgasms every year). Sexpert, a programmed, predictive, interactive, online tutoring system, which promised so much in the late 1980s and early 1990s – 'Ellen . . . Approximately what percentage of the time does orgasm currently occur during masturbation?' – seems to have faded into obscurity.[91]

The rise of sexual pharmacology must have impacted on more traditional approaches, but masturbation still figures in current sex therapy, either in terms of the details of masturbatory practices elicited from clients during the early interviews, or in the treatment itself.[92] Although older dysfunctions have been recategorised in the *Diagnostic and Statistical Manual of Mental Disorders* (DSM–5) (2013), masturbation exercises, directed masturbation, and masturbatory retraining are still used for female sexual interest/arousal disorder (FDIAD), female orgasmic disorder (FOD), and an ever-increasing range of (purported) male ejaculatory problems. Modified masturbatory techniques are used too in the treatment of LGBTQ patients.[93]

There has certainly been no discursive silence on the topic of auto-eroticism. Doctors have written up studies of the failed experiments of unfortunate patients: 'Masturbation injury resulting from intraurethral introduction of spaghetti' (1986); 'Penile incarceration secondary to masturbation with a steel pipe', with illustrations (2013).[94] A somewhat self-referential 1977 study of sexual arousal to films of masturbation asked psychology students at the University of Connecticut to report their 'genital sensations' while watching those films. Erection? Ejaculation? Breast sensations? Vaginal lubrication? Orgasm?[95] A Danish study in the 1980s, published in the US, observed female student nurses masturbating in the laboratory, measuring the duration of their orgasms (the mean was about 26 seconds) and comparing the results to the subjects' own estimates (they always underestimated).[96] They also measured the time taken to achieve climax – 7.8 minutes – though it has to be said that 12 of the original 40 subjects (28 eventually participated) withdrew because of their inability to reach orgasm under laboratory conditions.[97]

Several generations of German university students were questioned about their masturbatory habits by a Hamburg research team to chart changing attitudes and practices from 1966 to 1996, with the findings published in 2003. Did they reach orgasm? Were they sexually satisfied?

Was it fun?[98] Kentucky male prison inmates were asked about their habits in 2000, and although less than 20 per cent responded to the questionnaire (perhaps the others were too busy practising), almost all (apart from one inmate) admitted to masturbating – 30 per cent several times a week, 20 per cent once a day, and over 20 per cent more than once a day.[99] Do the asexual self-pleasure? A 2016 study concluded that 'those who do not experience any sexual attraction' certainly did: 70 per cent of asexual woman and 90 per cent of asexual men masturbated 'at least monthly'.[100] Regardless of the reliability of these masturbation surveys, their significance is that they were carried out at all. In another study, published in 2014, US women were contacted on Craigslist and asked about their masturbatory experiences, including clitoral stimulation and vaginal penetration.[101]

Autoeroticism is pervasive on film and television; Lauren Rosewarne's *Masturbation in Pop Culture* (2014) was able to draw on over 600 such scenes.[102] My favourites are the *Seinfeld* episode 'The Contest' (1992), in which the 'm' word is never uttered, and where George's mother tells her adult son that he is 'treating his body like it was an amusement park'; the film *Spanking the Monkey* (1994), in which the main character is trying to masturbate in the bathroom, while the family dog, seemingly alert to such behaviour, pants and whines at the door; and the scene in the television comedy *Fleabag* (2016), with the brilliant Phoebe Waller-Bridge masturbating to a political speech by Barack Obama!

Self-pleasure has featured in literature, most famously of course in Philip Roth's *Portnoy's Complaint* (1969), a veritable 'poetics of masturbation'.[103] The activity intrudes early on in the novel, with adolescence, and in capitals, in the section 'WHACKING OFF'.[104] There are so many memorable moments in Alex Portnoy's frenetic quest for solitary pleasure, including sex (can we call it that?) with a cored apple at a friend's picnic, rushing off in the midst of a family dinner to jerk off in the bathroom and then fretting over 'the sticky evidence' upon his return to the table (is it on his shoe? 'in my *hair?* my *ear?*'), and even (though the word 'even' seems inappropriate in the context of Roth's inventiveness) ravaging offal: '"Come, Big Boy, come", screamed the maddened piece of liver that, in my own insanity, I bought one afternoon in a butcher shop and, believe it or not, violated behind a billboard on the way to a bar mitzvah lesson.'[105] Portnoy ejaculates on to an overhead light bulb (Kinsey would have pointed out the possibility, if unlikelihood, of that), thinks about self-pleasuring to reach a climax while being masturbated by an unappealing woman ('instead of making believe that I am getting laid, as I ordinarily do while jerking off, I make believe that I am jerking off'), and engages in one-handed reading of Freud – with little Alex in the other hand.[106] Lawrence Scher has argued that in *Portnoy's Complaint*, masturbation becomes a metaphor not just for sex but for life itself.[107]

But autoeroticism is there in more recent writing too, including Chuck Palahniuk's disturbing short story 'Guts' (2004) and Charlotte Roche's controversial *Wetlands* (2010).[108] Jonathan Safran Foer's *Here I Am* (2016) has both female masturbation involving a door knob, and much male self-pleasuring, including a passage nominated (unjustly) for the 2016 Bad Sex in Fiction Award: 'He jerked off with the determination of someone within sight of Everest's summit, having lost all his friends and Sherpas, having run out of supplemental oxygen, but preferring death to failure.'[109]

Solitary sex (and its traces) have showcased in artistic expression: in Jordan McKenzie's sperm and charcoal canvases (2007), for example, or with Marina Abramović's reprising of Vito Acconci's *Seedbed* at the Guggenheim in 2005, and her video *Balkan Erotic Epic* of the same year.[110]

Philosophers philosophise about solitary sex, much as Jacques Derrida had with Jean-Jacques Rousseau's autoeroticism, 'that dangerous supplement'.[111] What are the 'necessary and sufficient conditions for sexual activity to be masturbatory'? Is it in fact sexual activity? Alan Soble has had productive fun with such thinking.[112] Damon Young, prompted by Karl Marx's sneer about philosophers as 'wankers' (Young's word, not Marx's), has penned a defence of both autoeroticism and philosophy.[113] Social scientists have questioned masturbation's actual definition. Does it have to involve orgasm? Must it be solitary? Does it have to consist of particular acts? Does stimulating the anus for pleasure, without climax, comprise masturbation? (70 per cent of men and 80 per cent of women in one study thought that it did.) Can having a sexual fantasy to orgasm, without any touch, be considered as masturbation? (42 per cent of men and 35 per cent of women thought it could.)[114]

Masturbation's recent history, however, is actually far more complex than this characterisation, and deserves more attention. One might say that the dangerous supplement has a dangerous supplement. The effects of the campaign against the solitary vice lingered long into the twentieth century. A counsellor at Duke University in the 1930s surveyed 75 of his male freshmen and found that over 80 per cent of them believed that masturbating caused serious physical or mental damage, including a significant minority (16 per cent) who thought that it resulted in insanity. Significantly, as the author of the report pointed out, the beliefs of these boys ran counter to 'the best medical and psychological opinion'.[115]

It would be a mistake, then, to present a rigid contrast between past condemnation and present acceptance. After all, it was in the early 1960s, on the eve of the sexual revolution, that the writer Norman Mailer proclaimed that masturbation 'cripples people', wastes life, and makes man a machine (he seemed to think that only men masturbated). 'I think masturbation is bad . . . The ultimate direction of masturbation always has to be insanity.'[116] When his interviewer supported solitary sex, the best that he could do was to justify it as a substitute, as a temporary practice for adolescents, and as recognisably absurd.[117] Roth recalled that when *Portnoy's Complaint* was published, there were rumours that its author 'had had to be carted off to that mythical lunatic asylum to which folklorists have been consigning unregenerate onanists since self-abuse began'.[118] Shortly afterwards, in the 1970s, a survey of US medical students found that nearly 30 per cent of graduates in residencies believed that masturbation caused emotional and mental instability, so consulting a physician then would not always have been helpful.[119]

So this modern history is complicated. It was not long ago (1994) that the US Surgeon General, Joycelyn Elders, the operational head of public health in that country, lost her job for saying that masturbation should be part of the health curricula in schools. She had to explain later that she was not advocating that 'schoolchildren should be taught how to masturbate' but merely that the topic should be discussed as part of sex education.[120]

A recent article explaining Western Islam's view of masturbation advanced an argument not far removed from the attitudes encountered in past times. Masturbation led to 'poor physical health', depression, high blood pressure, 'prostatic and penile pathology', and was generally counter to the benefits of 'penile–vaginal intercourse'; 'masturbation is unlawful in Islam'.[121] For its part, the Catholic Church still holds masturbation as sinful, 'objectively disordered or intrinsically evil', in the precise words of the *New Catholic Encyclopedia*. It encourages selfishness and immaturity. It represents adultery in the heart. It stands outside the justified conjugal relations between husband and wife – though self- and mutual stimulation in preparation for married, potentially procreative, sexual intercourse seems to leave open a rather large stable door through which to drive the metaphorical masturbatory horse.[122]

In Judaism (Portnoy excepted) there is an eerie silence. The word never appears in *Marriage, Sex, and the Family in Judaism* (2005) and *The Cambridge Companion to American Judaism* (2005), despite mention of Roth's self-pleasurer in the latter.[123] A young graduate student from New York, prompted to email me after I wrote a short essay on the history of masturbation, said that growing up in a modern Orthodox household in New Jersey in the late 1990s and early 2000s he was 'told often in Jewish school that spilling seed meant that the would-be-babies your sperm could've created would haunt you in the afterlife'.[124] (Foer's *Here I Am* refers to a 'mass grave being dug and filled with sperm'.)[125] The *Historical Dictionary of Judaism* (2015) tells us that male masturbation is strongly condemned in the Talmud, that rabbis censure its practice because of its waste of potential life and its simulation of sexual desire, but that female masturbation 'is not clearly covered in the traditional codes'.[126] In short, to quote Rebecca Alpert, 'according to Jewish tradition, solitary sex is unthinkable for men and rarely considered for women' – though it must be said that her essay (she had read Laqueur) was a progressive Jewish justification for self-loving.[127] Roth himself reflected more pithily (and with regard to men) that a Jew 'is not expected to make a spectacle of himself, either by shooting off his mouth or by shooting off his semen, and certainly not by shooting off his mouth about shooting off his semen'.[128]

Soble once observed that people brag about casual sex and infidelities but remain silent about solitary sex.[129] For Philippe Brenot, who penned a short defence of masturbation, that was its 'great drama', the fact that it was universally practised but never talked about.[130] Martha Cornog, author of *The Big Book of Masturbation*, whose friends must have been more liberal than most on sexual matters, encountered awkwardness or silence when she told them about her masturbation research.[131] Kristen Blinne, the owner of the experimental, masturbatory auto-ethnography discussed at the start of this chapter, acknowledged that admitting to masturbation 'places me in troublesome territory: I run the risk of judgment, harassment, embarrassment, or stigmatization . . . Perhaps my research will be declared as "not research", "illegitimate", "self-indulgent", or maybe even masturbatory.'[132] Anne-Francis Watson and Alan McKee's 2013 focus group of 14–16-year-old Australians revealed that their young informants knew that masturbation was normal yet still made 'negative or ambivalent statements' about it.[133]

Watson and McKee's study found that not only their participants but also their families and teachers were more comfortable talking about almost any other sexual matter than they were about self-pleasuring.[134] The National Health and Social Life Survey (1992), the Sex in America report, found that masturbation was 'generally felt to be the most sensitive topic of any we discussed, making both respondents and interviewers the most uncomfortable' – a far cry from Kinsey.[135] 'Masturbation remains in the shadows', the surveyors wrote in their popular version of their findings, 'a practice that few discuss.'[136] Presumably this accounts for the large numbers of those surveyed who reported that they never masturbated – over 40 per cent of men aged 18–24 and nearly 65 per cent of women in the same age range – and the substantial percentages of those who did engage in autoeroticism who said that they felt guilty afterwards – nearly 60 per cent of 18–24-year-old males and females.[137] Masturbation 'remains an activity that is viewed as shameful and problematic' warns the *Encyclopedia of Adolescence* (2011).[138] In a study of the sexuality of students in a western US university, where they were asked about sexual orientation, anal and vaginal sex, condom use, and masturbation, it was the last topic that occasioned reservation; 28 per cent of the participants 'declined to answer the masturbation questions'.[139] Women experiment with masturbation more than men and have more multiple orgasms; masturbation is important to their erotic lives.[140] Yet the researchers Breanne Fahs and Elena Frank have found that while women derive immense satisfaction from self-pleasuring, and demonstrate no shame about practising it, they can still be reluctant to talk to others about the details.[141] It is surely significant that the topic rarely surfaces in two highly publicised books about young American women, Peggy Orenstein's *Girls & Sex* (2016) and Nancy Jo Sales's *American Girls* (2016). Masturbation remains, to some extent, taboo.

Belief in the evils of masturbation has resurfaced in the figure of the sex addict and in the obsession with the impact of Internet pornography. Throughout their relatively short histories, sexual addiction and hypersexual disorder have included masturbation as one of the main symptoms of their purported maladies. What would be considered normal sexual behaviour in a sex-positive environment has been pathologised in another. Of the 152 patients in treatment for hypersexual disorder in clinics in California, New Mexico, Pennsylvania, Texas, and Utah, in a study published in 2012, most characterised their sexual disorder in terms of pornography consumption (81 per cent) and masturbation (78 per cent).[142] The *New Catholic Encyclopedia*'s supplement on masturbation (2012–13), too, slips into a lengthy disquisition on sex addiction and the evils of Internet pornography: 'The availability of internet pornography has markedly increased the practice of masturbation to the degree that it can be appropriately referred to as an epidemic.'[143]

The masturbator is now the pornography consumer and sex addict 'enslaved by masturbation'. In Google's Ngram, usage of the words pornography and porn rise as masturbation dips (see Figure 54). The sociologist Steve Garlick has suggested that negative attitudes to masturbation (of the type discussed in this chapter) have been reconstituted to 'surreptitiously infect ideas about pornography'.[144] Pornography has become

54 Usage of words 'masturbation', 'pornography', and 'porn' in the printed book from Google Ngram. Google and the Google logo are registered trademarks of Google Inc., used with permission.

masturbation's metonym. Significantly, when the New Zealand politician Shane Jones was exposed in 2010 for using his taxpayer-funded credit card to view pornographic movies, the unnamed shame was that his self-pleasuring activities were proclaimed on the front pages of the nation's newspapers – thus the jokes about 'the matter in hand' and not shaking hands with him at early morning meetings. It might have been less humiliating, one assumes, if he had used the public purse to finance the services of sex workers.[145]

Boundaries are drawn, even in the climate of general clinical acceptance. There is good and bad masturbation. Certain forms of male self-pleasuring are pathologised as 'idiosyncratic masturbatory style', masturbation that is too frequent, or . . . awkward, as a 2014 study expressed it: 'For the purpose of this study we have defined awkward or unusual masturbation as masturbatory techniques that do not resemble intercourse and are not easily duplicated by their partner's hand, mouth, or vagina.'[146] Ever-increasing syndromes require the appropriate masturbatory modification. Diminished ejaculatory disorders (DED) include 'retarded ejaculation' (RE), with symptoms that can involve 'greater arousal and enjoyment from masturbation than from intercourse', perhaps accompanied by 'an idiosyncratic and vigorous masturbation style'.[147] Predictably, treatment includes 'masturbation retraining'.[148] Michael Perelman, a New York psychiatrist, and David Rowland, an Indiana psychologist, recommended for men a version of the 1970s treatments of preorgasmic women (discussed above) but without the vibrators, which seems something of a failure of imagination on their part.[149]

There is a new male disorder, 'traumatic masturbatory syndrome' (TMS). One sufferer, a patient in a religious order who had been told by a priest that touching his penis for pleasure 'was the equivalent of "recrucifying Christ"', would masturbate, hands-free, against his bedding to the point of exhaustion, always losing his erection.[150] 'You may wonder why your position during masturbation would have any effect on you at all', writes an online sex therapist, with a pictured sufferer, face down, hands by side, to demonstrate the incorrect posture:

> Ordinarily it doesn't. If you lie on your side, or on your back, or even sit while jerking off, your face and body are exposed to your surroundings. Your hands are likely encircling your penis and stroking your thighs, chest and testicles.
>
> In TMS, none of this is true. Boys who learn this masturbatory technique tend to become isolated with their fantasies during arousal and ejaculation. They close their eyes and go inside – these are not porn watchers. Since they are not touching themselves, they do not learn to associate touch with the

> pleasure of sex. Also, their rigid body form certainly does not mimic the fluid lovemaking they will be enjoying in later years.
>
> It is the transference of erotic patterning from solo to partnered sex that prompted sexologists to dub this 'traumatic' masturbatory syndrome, for these fellows experience great difficulty relating erotically to another person. Everything about partnered sex feels wrong to them. The touch of another's skin, so much a turn-on for a man who has learned to associate stroking with pleasure, is a distraction and/or an annoyance for one who lies silently, internally focused, clenching and releasing his muscles, hands balled into fists. Eye contact is difficult, as are relaxing and changing positions during lovemaking. Murmuring sweet nothings? Not likely. In fact, sharing the journey from erotic stirrings to orgasm is next to impossible for a man who has learned to masturbate on his stomach without touching his genitals. He becomes sexually crippled in terms of partnered sex.[151]

It is not a warning about masturbation per se – self-pleasuring is advocated for future self-development – but rather a condemnation of a form of masturbating.

Nor is there consensus on the health benefits of solitary sex. Despite masturbation's continued use in therapy, some therapists question its usefulness and propriety. 'It is a mystery to me how conversational psychotherapy has made the sudden transition to massage parlor technology involving vibrators, mirrors, surrogates, and now even carrots and cucumbers!' was the reaction of a psychologist in the late 1970s to the *Journal of Consulting and Clinical Psychology* study referred to earlier. He was concerned about issues of client–patient power and a blinkered pursuit of the sexual climax 'ignoring . . . the more profound psychological implications of the procedure'.[152] This critic was not, it should be noted, worried about the privileging of vaginal over clitoral stimulation. The irascible Thomas Szasz reflected that in the nineteenth century 'masturbating was an illness and not masturbating was a treatment; today, not masturbating is a disease and masturbating is a treatment'. He singled out the work of the University of Oregon Psychology Clinic (cited earlier), quipping that such therapists treated the clitoris as 'a kind of household appliance whose owner has not understood the instruction manual'.[153]

In fact there has long been an implicit favouring of intercourse over masturbation, captured perfectly in Donald Mosher's criticism of therapists' focus on masturbatory technique: 'If masturbation is not associated with erotic *and* loving, specifically partner-oriented fantasies, then what is being scripted is not in the service of bonding the marital unit.'[154] As Joseph LoPiccolo and Wendy Stock summarised the situation in the mid

1980s, some therapists treated as problematic women who were achieving orgasm in perfectly normal ways, including masturbation, and even multiple orgasms through partner stimulation, but just not orgasm through penis in vagina, no hands sex.[155] And this was despite the numerous studies showing the statistical improbability of attaining 'coital orgasm', and the fact that, as these critically aware and practically experienced therapists claimed, 'orgasm achieved during intercourse may be an unrealistic goal of treatment'.[156] We see a partnered bias too in current treatment of inhibited ejaculation (IE), with the man encouraged to masturbate to match 'vaginal stimulation'; 'masturbatory retraining, integrated into sex therapy as a form of "dress rehearsal" for sex with a partner'.[157]

In terms of effectiveness, critics think that therapeutic masturbation might reinforce individual pleasure and sexual selfishness rather than creating sexual empathy and sharing. Leslie Farber was censorious about the Masters and Johnson experiment for precisely those reasons; but he used a critique of laboratory autoeroticism, 'the Lady of the Laboratory', as an indictment of masturbation more generally and the role of sex in society (he was writing in 1967). 'Clearly', he observed sardonically, 'the perfect orgasm is the orgasm achieved on one's own. No other consummation offers such certainty and moreover avoids the messiness that attends most human affairs.'[158] 'The onanist', he continued,

> may choose the partner of his dreams . . . or he may have his orgasm without any imagined partner . . . True, this solitary experience may leave him empty and ashamed. But as a citizen of his times he will try to counter this discomfort by reminding himself that sexology and psychoanalysis have assured him that masturbation is a morally indifferent matter . . . Nor should we be too surprised if such solitary pleasure becomes the ideal by which all mutual sex is measured – and found wanting.[159]

As another critic of therapeutic masturbation observed in the pages of the *Journal of Sex & Marital Therapy* in 1995, 'Ironically, the argument against masturbation in American society was originally religiously founded, but may re-emerge as a humanist argument.'[160] The critic oversimplified the origins of the argument against American masturbation, but was perceptive about its more modern connotations. The trauma of traumatic masturbatory syndrome, we should recall, resides in its anti-social nature. The aforementioned Jewish graduate student captured such reservations beautifully:

> over time I came to associate masturbation not with self-exploration or pleasure, but with loneliness and self-indulgence. I came to feel, as I do now, that

> the only meaningful acts of sex occur with another, when one reaches out beyond one's self . . . When I read your article, I felt you'd touched on exactly the sort of fears masturbation stirs in me – of the horrifying impulse to be with oneself over others, to be self-sufficient rather than self-giving.[161]

People remain disturbed by the solitariness of solitary sex. Perhaps this is why the entry on masturbation in James McConnachie's sex-positive *Rough Guide to Sex* (2010) is mostly about masturbating others.[162]

So it is a complicated and conflicted history. Why has what the Japanese rather charmingly call 'self-play' become such a forcing ground for sexual attitudes?[163] Have we moved in modern history from a time when masturbation was much written about, nearly always to condemn, to an era where the discourse of self-pleasure has proliferated but where this mainstreaming is far from unconditional and stalked by new proscriptions? Is the taboo of one era even remotely comparable to the unacceptability of another? Alternatively, is the assumed and accepted vulgarity of the practice in ancient times at all analogous to modern mockery and embarrassment?

Is masturbation's uncontrollability a factor? It is perhaps the queerest sex of all: non-procreative, incestuous, adulterous, always homosexual, 'often pederastic', and (in imagination at least) sex with 'every man, woman, or beast to whom I take a fancy', to quote Soble (inspired no doubt by Rousseau).[164] We may recall Samuel Steward's endorsement of its superiority: 'you can have the world's pick if you just use your head'.[165] Self-pleasure is a lingering perversity in a heteronormative world. For the ever-astute Laqueur, masturbation is 'that part of human sexual life where potentially unlimited pleasure meets social restraint'.[166] Its secrecy, potential excess, and boundless imaginativeness worried countless generations. In the eighteenth and nineteenth centuries, the focus was on social restraint; in more pleasure-conscious modern times, the balance has tipped towards personal gratification. But fears of unrestrained fantasy and indulging of the self, as we have seen, still permeate the present. We discussed how the old fear of masturbation has been replaced by a new fear of sex addiction and pornography, masturbation's proxies. Laqueur has noted that Tissot's complaints about the lack of restraint of solitary sex are not light years away from those of modern addictionology.[167]

We have traced the 'what', but what about the 'why'? Why did masturbation become the modern problem that it was and, for some, still is? For Laqueur it began with developments in eighteenth-century Europe, with the cultural rise of the imagination in the arts, the seemingly unbounded future of commerce, the role of print culture, the rise of private, silent reading, especially novels, and the democratic ingredients of this transformation. Masturbation's condemned tendencies – solitariness, excessive desire, limitless imagination, and equal-opportunity pleasure – were an outer limit or testing of these valued attributes, 'a kind of Satan to the glories of bourgeois civilization'.[168]

In more pleasure-conscious times, the balance has tipped towards personal gratification. The acceptance of personal autonomy, sexual liberation, and sexual consumerism, together with a widespread focus on addiction and the ubiquity of the Internet, now seem to demand their own demon. Fears remain of unrestrained fantasy and endless indulging of the individual. *Onania*'s eighteenth-century complaints about the lack of restraint of solitary sex are not, ultimately, all that far from today's fear of boundless, ungovernable, unquenchable pleasure in the self.

Notes

1 K. C. Blinne, 'Auto(erotic)ethnography', *Sexualities*, 15:8 (2012), 953–77.
2 Ibid., 954–5.
3 Ibid., 955, emphases in original.
4 Ibid., 959.
5 A. Hunt, 'The great masturbation panic and the discourses of moral regulation in nineteenth- and early twentieth-century Britain', *Journal of the History of Sexuality*, 8:4 (1998), 575–615, quote at 576; T. W. Laqueur, *Solitary Sex: A Cultural History of Masturbation* (New York, 2003), p. 23.
6 A. Giddens, *The Transformation of Intimacy* (Cambridge, 2008 [1992]), p. 15.
7 Ibid., p. 16.
8 Quoted in L. Hilderbrand, 'The uncut version: the Mattachine Society's pornographic epilogue', *Sexualities*, 19:4 (2016), 449–64, quote at 451.
9 B. Dodson, *Sex for One: The Joy of Selfloving* (New York, 1996), pp. 5, 74–82. First published in 1974 as *Liberating Masturbation*.
10 B. Dodson, 'Getting to know me: a primer on masturbation', *Ms.*, August 1974, reprinted in *Ms.*, Spring 2002.
11 Boston Women's Health Collective, *Our Bodies Ourselves* (Boston, MA, 1973).
12 E. Johnson, 'Loving yourself: the specular scene in sexual self-help advice for women', in J. M. Gaines and M. Renov (eds), *Collecting Visible Evidence* (Minneapolis, MN, 1999), ch. 11.
13 G. Tuck, 'The mainstreaming of masturbation', in F. Attwood (ed.), *Mainstreaming Sex: The Sexualization of Western Culture* (New York, 2010), ch. 5, quote at p. 78.
14 Accessed 18 July 2017.

15 http://www.goodvibes.com/s/content/c/masturbation-hall-of-fame (last accessed 26 April 2018).
16 For the former, see http://www.cfnmvillage.com/forum/viewtopic.php?f=38&t=1231 (last accessed 26 April 2018); and for the latter, see M. Way, 'Rain City Jacks is Seattle's premier masturbation club', *Vice*, 11 September 2011: https://www.vice.com/en_us/article/rain-city-jacks-is-seattles-premier-masturbation-club (last accessed 26 April 2018).
17 See A. Sprinkle, 'Masturbating onstage': http://anniesprinkle.org/masturbating-onstage/ (last accessed 26 April 2018).
18 A. Sprinkle, *Hardcore from the Heart: The Pleasures and Profits of Sex in Performance*, ed. G. Cody (New York, 2001), pp. 52–3.
19 L. Williams, 'A provoking agent: the pornography and performance art of Annie Sprinkle', *Social Text*, 37 (1993), 117–33; M. Carlson, 'Performative pornography: Annie Sprinkle reads her movies', *Text and Performance Quarterly*, 19:3 (1999), 236–47; C. Straayer, 'The seduction of boundaries: feminist fluidity in Annie Sprinkle's art/education/sex', in P. C. Gibson (ed.), *More Dirty Looks: Gender, Pornography and Power* (London, 2004), ch. 19.
20 Sprinkle, 'Masturbating onstage'.
21 A. Czekay, 'Distance and empathy: constructing the spectator of Annie Sprinkle's Post-POST PORN MODERNIST – Still in Search of the Ultimate Sexual Experience', *Journal of Dramatic Theory and Criticism*, 7:2 (1993), 177–92, at 181.
22 See A. Sprinkle, *Post-Porn Modernist: My 25 years as a Multimedia Whore* (San Francisco, 1998); Sprinkle, *Hardcore from the Heart*; A. Sprinkle, 'The sex addiction myth': http://anniesprinkle.org/the-sex-addiction-myth/ (last accessed 26 April 2018); http://sexecology.org/ (last accessed 26 April 2018).
23 Williams, 'Provoking agent', 126–7.
24 S. Aydt, 'Annie Sprinkle: the lost interview', *These New Old Traditions*, 10 February 2011: https://newoldtraditions.wordpress.com/2011/02/10/annie-sprinkle-the-lost-interview/ (last accessed 26 April 2018).
25 M. Gillies, D. Pear, and M. Carroll (eds), *Self-Portrait of Percy Grainger* (Melbourne, 2006), p. 97.
26 K. Dreyfus (ed.), *The Farthest North of Humanness: Letters of Percy Grainger, 1901–14* (London, 1985), p. 188.
27 San Francisco History Center, San Francisco Public Library, Louis Graydon Sullivan Papers, Box 4, Folder 168: Material relating to Jack and Jill Clubs.
28 The New York Public Library, Humanities and Social Sciences Library, Manuscripts and Archives Division, MSS Col 353, David Louie Bowie Diaries 1978–93. In chronological order, see Bowie Diaries, 6 and 7 September 1978; 10 September 1978; 17 February 1980; 2 September 1981; 30 August 1982; 18 October 1985; 29 November 1985; 27 June 1987; 30 January 1988; 8 April 1988; 9 June 1988.

29 L. Eighner, *Elements of Arousal: How to Write and Sell Gay Men's Erotica* (New York, 1994), p. 130.
30 G. Talese, *The Voyeur's Motel* (New York, 2016).
31 Ibid., p. 191.
32 Quoted by Laqueur, *Solitary Sex*, p. 109.
33 J. Stengers and A. Van Neck, *Masturbation*, trans. K. A. Hoffman (New York, 2001), p. 36.
34 Ibid., p. 38.
35 P. Singy, 'Friction of the genitals and secularization of morality', *Journal of the History of Sexuality*, 12:3 (2003), 354–64.
36 M. Stolberg, 'The crime of Onan and the laws of nature: religious and medical discourses on masturbation in the late seventeenth and early eighteenth centuries', *Paedagogica Historica*, 39:6 (2003), 701–17.
37 M. Tissot, *Onanism: Or, a Treatise Upon the Disorders Produced by Masturbation*, trans. A. Hume (London, 1766), p. 2.
38 *Onania: Or the Heinous Sin of Self-Pollution* (London, 1776), Sig. A2.
39 M. Foucault, *Abnormal: Lectures at the Collège de France, 1974–1975*, trans. G. Burchell (New York, 2003), p. 237.
40 *Onania*, pp. 12, 15.
41 Ibid.
42 Tissot, *Onanism*, p. 21.
43 Ibid., pp. 23, 25, 27.
44 *Onania*, Sig. A2.
45 Tissot, *Onanism*, p. 41.
46 *Le Livre Sans Titre* (Paris, 1830).
47 A. R. Haynes, *Riotous Flesh: Women, Physiology, and the Solitary Vice in Nineteenth-Century America* (Chicago, 2015), p. 94.
48 N. F. Cooke, *Satan in Society* (Chicago, 1871), p. 100.
49 N. F. Barker, *A Secret Book for Men* (Brighton, 1888), pp. 7, 9.
50 E. Lyttelton, *The Causes and Prevention of Immorality in Schools* (London, 1883), pp. 7, 8.
51 Ibid., p. 7; Hunt, 'Great masturbation panic', 587.
52 J. H. Kellogg, *Plain Facts for Old and Young* (Burlington, IA, 1891 [1877]), p. 233.
53 Ibid.
54 J. Money, *Lovemaps* (New York, 1988), p. 165.
55 R. Darby, 'The masturbation taboo and the rise of routine male circumcision: a review of the historiography', *Journal of Social History*, 36:3 (2003), 737–57.
56 J. Juffer, *At Home with Pornography: Women, Sex, and Everyday Life* (New York, 1998), ch. 2. Note that Juffer's chapter has a question mark: 'The mainstreaming of masturbation?' See also N. Richardson, C. Smith, and A. Werndly, 'Sexualization, commodifying sex and the mainstreaming of masturbation', in

their *Studying Sexualities: Theories, Representations, Cultures* (New York, 2013), ch. 9.

57 P. Robinson, 'Alfred Kinsey', in his *The Modernization of Sex* (New York, 1976), ch. 2, quote at p. 64.

58 A. C. Kinsey, W. B. Pomeroy, and C. E. Martin, *Sexual Behavior in the Human Male* (Philadelphia, PA, 1949), p. 339; A. C. Kinsey, W. B. Pomeroy, C. E. Martin, and P. H. Gebhard, *Sexual Behavior in the Human Female* (Philadelphia, PA, 1953), p. 142.

59 Kinsey et al., *Sexual Behavior in the Human Female*, p. 132.

60 Ibid.

61 Ibid., p. 401.

62 Ibid., p. 139.

63 Kinsey, Pomeroy, and Martin, *Sexual Behavior in the Human Male*, pp. 339, 490–1.

64 Kinsey et al., *Sexual Behavior in the Human Female*, pp. 166–8.

65 P. Robinson, 'William Masters and Virginia Johnson', in his *Modernization of Sex*, ch. 3, quote at p. 142.

66 Ibid., pp. 142–5.

67 W. H. Masters and V. E. Johnson, *Human Sexual Response* (Boston, MA, 1966), pp. 63, 65.

68 Ibid., p. 313. My percentage calculations from the figures provided.

69 Ibid., p. 133.

70 A point made by J. M. Irvine, *Disorders of Desire: Sexuality and Gender in Modern American Sexology* (Philadelphia, 2005 [1990]), p. 65.

71 See Chapter 3 above.

72 Masters and Johnson, *Human Sexual Response*, p. 15; R. Morrow, *Sex Research and Sex Therapy: A Sociological Analysis of Masters and Johnson* (New York, 2008); T. Maier, *Masters of Sex* (New York, 2009); D. J. Drucker, *The Machines of Sex Research: Technology and the Politics of Identity, 1945–1985* (New York, 2014), ch. 3.

73 Masters and Johnson, *Human Sexual Response*, p. 305.

74 L. H. Farber, 'I'm sorry, dear', in R. Brecher and E. Brecher (eds), *An Analysis of Human Sexual Response* (London, 1967), pp. 291–318, quote at p. 297.

75 S. Hite, *The Shere Hite Reader* (New York, 2006), p. 60.

76 D. Herbenick et al., 'Sexual behavior in the United States', *Journal of Sexual Medicine*, 7:Suppl. 5 (2010), 2655–65.

77 B. Dodge et al., 'Sexual behaviors of US men by self-identified sexual orientation: results from the 2012 National Survey of Sexual Health and Behavior', *Journal of Sexual Medicine*, 13:4 (2016), 637–49.

78 K. L. Goldey, A. R. Posh, S. N. Bell, and S. M. van Anders, 'Defining pleasure: a focus group study of solitary and partnered sexual pleasure in queer and heterosexual women', *Archives of Sexual Behavior*, 45:8 (2016), 2137–54.

79 A. Jagose, *Orgasmology* (Durham, NC, 2013), ch. 3; B. Reay, 'Transgender orgasms', *Feminist Formations*, 28:2 (2016), 152–61.
80 Jagose, *Orgasmology*, p. 109.
81 Reay, 'Transgender orgasms'.
82 Ibid.
83 E. Coleman, 'Masturbation as a means of achieving sexual health', *Journal of Psychology & Human Sexuality*, 14:2–3 (2003), 5–16.
84 W. C. Lobitz and J. LoPiccolo, 'New methods in the behavioral treatment of sexual dysfunction', *Journal of Behavior Therapy and Experimental Psychiatry*, 3:4 (1972), 265–71, quote at 267.
85 Ibid., 269.
86 L. G. Barbach, 'Group treatment of preorgasmic women', *Journal of Sex & Marital Therapy*, 1:2 (1974), 139–45, quotes at 140, 141.
87 Ibid., 142.
88 A. Zeiss et al., 'Orgasm during intercourse: a treatment for women', *Journal of Consulting and Clinical Psychology*, 45:5 (1977), 891–5.
89 See, for example, J. LoPiccolo and W. E. Stock, 'Treatment of sexual dysfunction', *Journal of Consulting and Clinical Psychology*, 54:2 (1986), 158–67.
90 J. van Lankveld, 'Self-help therapies for sexual dysfunction', *Journal of Sex Research*, 46:2–3 (2009), 143–55.
91 D. Servan-Schreiber and Y. M. Binik, 'Extending the intelligent tutoring system paradigm: sex therapy as intelligent tutoring', *Computers in Human Behavior*, 5:4 (1989), 241–59, quote at 252.
92 This is not the place to discuss the rise of the drug companies. However, it is possible to detect this shift in guides to therapy, where use of masturbational therapy seems marginal but androgen and pharmaceutical use is prevalent: see S. R. Leiblum (ed.), *Treating Sexual Desires: A Clinical Casebook* (New York, 2010).
93 See Z. D. Peterson (ed.), *The Wiley Handbook of Sex Therapy* (Malden, MA, 2017), pp. 19, 20, 21, 60, 62, 79, 85, 86, 272, 273, 276, 277, 295–6, 299.
94 M. Bacci and M. Porena, 'Masturbation injury resulting from intraurethral introduction of spaghetti', *American Journal of Forensic Medicine and Pathology*, 7:3 (1986), 254–5; J. F. Flores-Martin et al., 'Penile incarceration secondary to masturbation with a steel pipe', *Archives of Sexual Behavior*, 42:3 (2013), 337–9.
95 D. L. Mosher and P. R. Abramson, 'Subjective sexual arousal to films of masturbation', *Journal of Consulting and Clinical Psychology*, 45:5 (1977), 796–807.
96 R. J. Levin and G. Wagner, 'Orgasm in women in the laboratory – quantitative studies on duration, intensity, latency, and vaginal blood flow', *Archives of Sexual Behavior*, 14:5 (1985), 439–49.
97 Ibid.
98 A. Dekker and G. Schmidt, 'Patterns of masturbatory behaviour', *Journal of Psychology & Human Sexuality*, 14:2–3 (2003), 35–48.

99 C. Hensley, R. Tewksbury, and J. Wright, 'Exploring the dynamics of masturbation and consensual same-sex activity within a male maximum security prison', *The Journal of Men's Studies*, 10:1 (2001), 59–71, figures at 66.

100 M. A. Yule, L. A. Brotto, and B. B. Gorzalka, 'Sexual fantasy and masturbation among asexual individuals: an in-depth exploration', *Archives of Sexual Behavior*, 46:1 (2017), 311–28, quote at 315.

101 B. Fahs and E. Frank, 'Notes from the back room', *The Journal of Sex Research*, 51:3 (2014), 421–52.

102 L. Rosewarne, *Masturbation in Pop Culture* (Lanham, MD, 2014).

103 L. R. Scher, 'Fragments of a poetics: Bonnetain and Roth', in P. Bennett and V. A. Rosario (eds), *Solitary Pleasures: The Historical, Literary, and Artistic Discourses of Autoeroticism* (New York, 1995), ch. 9, quote at p. 225.

104 P. Roth, *Portnoy's Complaint* (New York, 1969), p. 11.

105 Ibid., pp. 12–13. Emphasis in original. The come on the ear is reprised in the famous Ben Stiller masturbation scene in the movie *There's Something About Mary* (1998).

106 Roth, *Portnoy's Complaint*, pp. 13, 127, 131.

107 Scher, 'Fragments of a poetics', p. 228.

108 http://chuckpalahniuk.net/features/shorts/guts (last accessed 26 April 2018); C. Cox, 'Masturbation: literature's last taboo', *The Guardian*, Fiction Books Blog, 21 April 2010: https://www.theguardian.com/books/booksblog/2010/apr/20/masturbation-literature-last-taboo (last accessed 26 April 2018).

109 J. S. Foer, *Here I Am* (New York, 2016), pp. 76, 331. For the *Literary Review*'s award, see https://literaryreview.co.uk/bad-sex-in-fiction-award (last accessed 26 April 2018).

110 M. van Driel, *With the Hand: A Cultural History of Masturbation* (London, 2012), pp. 230–1; S. Watanabe, 'Marina Abramović "Seven Easy Pieces" at the Guggenheim Museum: looking for others whom you've never seen' (2011): http://www.shinyawatanabe.net/en/writings/content57.html (last accessed 26 April 2018). Abramović's *Balkan Erotic Epic* (2005) has enjoyed a somewhat ephemeral presence on YouTube.

111 J. Derrida, *Of Grammatology*, trans. G. C. Spivak (Baltimore, MD, 1976), pp. 141–64.

112 A. Soble, *Sexual Investigations* (New York, 1996), ch. 2.

113 D. A. Young, 'Knowing thyself . . . in private: masturbation and philosophy', *Sexuality & Culture*, 9:4 (2005), 58–79.

114 A. Kirschbaum and Z. D. Peterson, 'Would you say you "had masturbated" if . . .?: the influence of situational and individual factors on labeling a behavior as masturbation', *The Journal of Sex Research*, online 2017: http://dx.doi.org/10.1080/00224499.2016.1269307 (last accessed 26 April 2018).

115 E. V. Pullias, 'Masturbation as a mental hygiene problem – a study of the beliefs of seventy-five young men', *The Journal of Abnormal and Social Psychology*, 32:2 (1937), 216–22, quote at 221.

116 N. Mailer, *The Presidential Papers* (New York, 1968 [1963]), pp. 151–5.
117 Ibid., pp. 152–3.
118 P. Roth, *Reading Myself and Others* (New York, 2001), p. 256.
119 W. R. Miller and H. I. Lief, 'Masturbatory attitudes, knowledge, and experience: data from the Sex Knowledge and Attitude Test (SKAT)', *Archives of Sexual Behavior*, 5:5 (1976), 447–67, figures at 457.
120 'The politics of masturbation', *The Lancet*, 24 December 1994.
121 S. S. Hoseini, 'Masturbation: scientific evidence and Islam's view', *Journal of Religion and Health*, 56:6 (2017), 2076–81.
122 *New Catholic Encyclopedia Supplement 2012–13*, online: http://www.catholiceducation.org/en/marriage-and-family/sexuality/masturbation.html (last accessed 26 April 2018).
123 M. J. Broyde and M. Ausubel, *Marriage, Sex, and Family in Judaism* (Lanham, MD, 2005); D. Biale, 'The body and sexuality in American Jewish sexual culture', in *The Cambridge Companion to American Judaism* (New York, 2005), ch. 14.
124 The essay is B. Reay, 'The body as amusement park: a history of masturbation', *Aeon*, 2016: https://aeon.co/essays/the-body-as-amusement-park-a-history-of-masturbation (last accessed 26 April 2018).
125 Foer, *Here I Am*, p. 330.
126 N. Solomon, *Historical Dictionary of Judaism* (Lanham, MD, 2015), 'Masturbation'.
127 R. T. Alpert, 'Reconsidering solitary sex from a Jewish perspective', in D. Ruttenberg (ed.), *The Passionate Torah* (New York, 2009), ch. 12.
128 Roth, *Reading Myself*, p. 258.
129 Soble, *Sexual Investigations*, p. 60.
130 P. Brenot, *In Praise of Masturbation*, trans. P. Buck and C. Petit (London, 2005), pp. 73–4.
131 M. Cornog, *The Big Book of Masturbation: From Angst to Zeal* (San Francisco, 2003), p. 301.
132 Blinne, 'Auto(erotic)ethnography', 955.
133 A-F. Watson and A. McKee, 'Masturbation and the media', *Sexuality & Culture*, 17:3 (2013), 449–75.
134 Ibid.
135 E. O. Laumann, J. H. Gagnon, R. T. Michael, and S. Michaels, *The Social Organization of Sexuality: Sexual Practices in the United States* (Chicago, 1994), p. 69.
136 R. T. Michael, J. H. Gagnon, E. O. Laumann, and G. Kolata, *Sex in America: A Definitive Survey* (New York, 1994), p. 158.
137 Laumann et al., *Social Organization of Sexuality*, p. 82.
138 R. J. R. Levesque, 'Masturbation', in R. J. R. Levesque (ed.), *Encyclopedia of Adolescence* (New York, 2011), pp. 1654–5.
139 S. Pinkerton et al., 'Factors associated with masturbation in a collegiate sample', *Psychology & Human Sexuality*, 14:2–3 (2003), 103–21.

140 B. Fahs, *Performing Sex: The Making and Unmaking of Women's Erotic Lives* (Albany, NY, 2011), p. 156.

141 Because of this 'relative invisibility' women can be influenced by negative stereotypes while simultaneously flaunting them through their actual practice – using clitoral stimulation, for example, while still privileging (though not employing) vaginal penetration: Fahs and Frank, 'Notes from the back room', 241.

142 B. Reay, N. Attwood, and C. Gooder, *Sex Addiction: A Critical History* (Cambridge, 2015), p. 144.

143 J. J. Farraher, T. Friedrichsen, and R. P. Fitzgibbons, 'Masturbation', *New Catholic Encylopedia Supplement 2012–13: Ethics and Philosophy*: http://www.catholiceducation.org/en/marriage-and-family/sexuality/masturbation.html (last accessed 26 April 2018).

144 N. Garlick, 'Masculinity, pornography, and the history of masturbation', *Sexuality & Culture*, 16:3 (2012), 306–20, quote at 318.

145 This is now the stuff of folk memory, and Jones has staged a political resurrection.

146 G. Bronner and I. Z. Ben-Zion, 'Unusual masturbatory practice as an etiological factor in the diagnosis and treatment of sexual dysfunction in young men', *The Journal of Sexual Medicine*, 11:7 (2014), 1798–1806, quotes at 1799–1800.

147 M. A. Perelman and D. L. Rowland, 'Retarded ejaculation', *World Journal of Urology*, 24:6 (2006), 645–52, quotes at 645, 647. For a more recent restatement of the ailment and its therapy, see M. A. Perelman, 'Psychosexual therapy for delayed ejaculation based on the Sexual Tipping Point model', *Translational Andrology and Urology*, 5:4 (2016), 563–75.

148 Perelman and Rowland, 'Retarded ejaculation', 649.

149 Ibid.

150 L. S. Sank, 'Traumatic masturbatory syndrome', *Journal of Sex & Marital Therapy*, 24:1 (1998), 37–42, quote at 38.

151 P. Ren, 'Traumatic masturbatory syndrome', *Smartsextalk*, 16 December 2016: http://www.smartsextalk.com/traumatic-masturbatory-syndrome/ (last accessed 26 April 2018).

152 K. G. Bailey, 'Psychotherapy or massage parlor technology', *Journal of Consulting and Clinical Psychology*, 46:6 (1978), 1502–6, quote at 1503.

153 T. Szasz, *Sex by Prescription: The Startling Truth about Today's Sex Therapy* (Syracuse, NY, 1990), pp. 64, 66.

154 D. L. Mosher, 'Negative attitudes toward masturbation in sex therapy', *Journal of Sex & Marital Therapy*, 5:4 (1979), 315–33, quote at 332. Emphasis in original.

155 LoPiccolo and Stock, 'Treatment of sexual dysfunction', 158–9.

156 Ibid., 160–1. The current consensus (in 2017) seems to be for variety in women's experiences of orgasm, including 'both genital and non-genital stimulation'. An online survey of over 1,000 women in 2015 found that a significant

number of women can experience orgasm from 'penetration alone', though clitoral stimulation was still an important factor. (The researchers do not seem to have allowed for clitoral stimulation via the positioning of the penis during intercourse.) See D. Herbenick et al., 'Women's experiences with genital touching, sexual pleasure, and orgasm: results from a U.S. probability sample of women ages 18 to 94', *Journal of Sex & Marital Therapy*, online 2017: http://dx.doi.org/10.1080/0092623X.2017.1346530 (last accessed 26 April 2018).

157 D. L. Rowland and S. E. Cooper, 'Treating men's orgasmic difficulties', in Peterson (ed.), *Wiley Handbook of Sex Therapy*, ch. 6, quotes at pp. 83, 85.

158 Farber, 'I'm sorry, dear', p. 306.

159 Ibid., pp. 306–7.

160 C. Christensen, 'Prescribed masturbation in sex therapy: a critique', *Journal of Sex & Marital Therapy*, 21:2 (1995), 87–99, quote at 98.

161 Email to author, 29 July 2016.

162 J. McConnachie, *The Rough Guide to Sex* (London, 2010), pp. 91–102.

163 Cornog, *Big Book of Masturbation*, p. 21.

164 Soble, *Sexual Investigations*, p. 60. For Rousseau, see V. A. Rosario, 'Phantastical pollutions: the public threat of private vice in France', in P. Bennett and V. A. Rosario (eds), *Solitary Pleasures: The Historical, Literary, and Artistic Discourses of Autoeroticism* (New York, 1995), ch. 4, esp. quote at p. 101.

165 Kinsey Institute, University of Indiana, Bloomington, Samuel Steward Collection, Series 2, F, S.S. 1955 Diary, 25 April 1955.

166 Laqueur, *Solitary Sex*, p. 13.

167 Ibid., pp. 238–9.

168 Ibid., p. 278.

9

Queer Baltimore: the photography of Amos Badertscher

with Branka Bogdan

The central male figure in Amos Badertscher's *Club Kids*, flanked by his topless female friends, is young, slim, and relatively clean-cut (see Figure 55). He appears detached, the object of desire: the other figures in this image (including Badertscher with his Nikon) are attentive, surrounding him, the women with their arms draped around his waist and neck and the blond with her hand resting on his crotch, the centre point of the photograph. 'Photographs flirt', writes Julia Adney Thomas; their relationship with those who represent the past is both 'voluptuous and analytical'.[1] Who is the young man? Is this group portrait a fashion shoot, or something else? The female subjects, whose bodies are either turned inward towards the male or hidden behind him, although their breasts are visible, are secondary figures. It is the male's open, forward-facing stance that invites admiration, which holds the photographer's attention (eye contact is implied through the mirror used to photograph the group). The posing of the females suggests the male's heterosexuality; he has his arm around one woman and the other is touching his hand. But the presence of the photographer hints at (perhaps one-sided) same-sex desirability. The man's youthful masculinity is pivotal. However, so too is the three's engineered androgyny, the most obvious representation of which comes from their shared wardrobe, as all three are wearing baggy jeans with boxer shorts visible over the top (a classic 1990s American masculine fashion-statement), and the fact that all three are topless. Or does the portrait hint at something more? Bisexuality? Queer sex? Are the two female clubbers lesbians? Are they posing before, or after, group sex? We can probably agree that the image is palpably sexual; when Jane Gallop distinguished between 'sexuality *in* photography' and 'the sexuality *of* photography', she might almost have been referring to *Club Kids*.[2] While the nature of that sexuality is unresolved, it is unlikely that Badertscher is endorsing

55 Amos Badertscher, *Club Kids* (1), 1999, Badertscher Collection.

heteronormativity. It is a queer historical image within a larger archive of queer history in Baltimore.

When we first came across this photograph in Amos Badertscher's Baltimore basement studio/office, he explained that it captured a chance encounter with young aficionados of the late 1990s club scene. He met them at a gay pride block party near the city's famous gay club The Hippo during the summer of 1999, where they happened to be at the time; they 'basically pursued raves in and out of state'.[3] The brief narrative written in hand around the photograph, Badertscher's trademark, corroborates his astonishing memory about thousands of such interactions. What we also learned was that the photographer was mainly interested in the young man but that he could only persuade him to pose if the young women appeared alongside him. The photograph is part of a series; other images have the man naked in high-heels, stockings and a boa, with a small American flag subversively draped across his genitals, the women still trousered, or him wearing boots and a modesty pouch, with one of the women clutching his thigh (see Figures 56–7).[4] Badertscher is extremely attracted to female as well as male androgyny, but in this instance his focus is more on the male. The photographer's presence within the frame in the first image from *Club Kids* may perhaps seem unusual to those who first encounter his work but is typical of many of the images he took. The photograph is representative not only of this artist's extensive oeuvre and of his take on urban Baltimore's street culture, but also of that culture's constructions of gender and sex.

Club Kids is merely one in Badertscher's vast collection of photographs of Baltimore's street youth, drag queens, performance artists, sex workers, and drug addicts, hundreds of which have neither been exhibited nor published. Although he could never have comprehended it when he began his venture, indeed was not even aware that there was such a project, his total output is a forty-year exploration of Baltimore's sexual cultures from the 1960s to 2005 (when the photographer stopped photographing), including the city's much-publicised, inner-urban disintegration. It is surely the most extensive known photographic collection of imagery of hustlers (male sex workers). But it is much more than that. Badertscher was active in the hustling street scene before deciding to turn to photography to capture that arena. He began in the 1960s with Polaroids and other photographs of his hustler sexual contacts. He moved on to more formal portraits of male prostitutes and their girlfriends, transgender, the 1990s Baltimore and Washington club culture, and then to charting the drug-addled sex work of the post-industrial city. The result is what Michael Mezzatesta describes as 'an archival record of a city and its illicit fringe culture'.[5]

Counter-archival might, however, be a better term to describe work that is so intensely personal. This is no detached, dispassionate chronicle of the sexual life and culture of a major US city – one, incidentally, with no

56 Amos Badertscher, *Club Kids* (2), 1999, Badertscher Collection.

57 Amos Badertscher, *Club Kids* (3), 1999, Badertscher Collection.

such study, though there are compelling sexual histories of other American urban centres. Tim Dean has referred to the 'archives of affect', the counter-archives, where intimacy enters the record, the personal is central, the 'passions of the collector' are valued, 'nonnormative pleasures' are tracked, and categories of sexual identity challenged.[6] Jennifer Evans has analysed what she terms an 'archive of experience' in the photography of Herbert Tobias in West Berlin in the 1950s, with his images of rent boys (fitting, given the subject matter of Badertscher's pictures) capturing 'queer desire' in an 'iconography of emotions'.[7] We might recall discussion of the photography of Nan Goldin (Chapter 1), who charted her world and history much in the way that Badertscher did his, with the same blending of subject and artist, admittedly with different aesthetics but with themes that were not vastly different (club kids, drug addicts, drag queens, the impact of AIDS) – what Sarah Ruddy has defined as 'affective documentary'.[8] The aim of this chapter is to introduce another such significant archive of affect.

Although Badertscher continued on for years, unconcerned with recognition until it came by chance in the 1990s, it should be conceded that this photographer is not exactly obscure.[9] He has had major solo exhibitions at the Duke University Museum of Art (1995) and the Leslie–Lohman Museum of Gay and Lesbian Art in New York (2005), and his work recently featured in the latter's 'The 1970s: The Blossoming of a Queer Enlightenment' (2016), in the gallery where much of his collection now resides. His photographs have been catalogued in the Stonewall Inn series publication *Badertscher* (1998) and, most notably, in Duke University Press's *Baltimore Portraits* (1999).[10] His images have appeared – rather incongruously – in the fashion magazine *Dust* (2015).[11] However, Badertscher is not famous. His work was not in the Smithsonian Institution's (controversial) 2010–11 exhibition on same-sex desire in American portraiture.[12] Nor is he included in Catherine Lord and Richard Meyer's *Art & Queer Culture* (2013), although it features the work of many photographers.[13] He is not even in *Aperture* magazine's 2015 *Queer* issue, despite new queer photography's rediscovery of its own past.[14] He deserves to be better known.

Badertscher's techniques and processes changed over the course of the years that he was photographing his subjects. From the 1970s to the 1990s he lived in a top-floor apartment on Madison Street in Mount Vernon, only a short walk from The Hippo and the Mount Vernon meat rack, where young men waited for a trick. Before noon the sun would stream in through one set of windows and drench the room in vivid natural light (these images are easily identifiable, with the subjects standing by the window, awash with rich sunlight). After nights out with hustlers, he would invite them to stay overnight to photograph them in the morning. When he moved to his current townhouse, Badertscher established a photography studio and darkroom in his basement (he had the windows blocked out) where he began using artificial light, white backdrops, and mirrors to capture self- and group portraits and expand the size of the space (many of the images disguise the narrow span of the room). We have visited his studio, and the effect of experiencing an archive of personal photography while being in the space that was used as a backdrop for much of that photography is surreal, adding to its counter-archival quality. It was not until the late 1990s and early 2000s that Badertscher turned his attention to the disused and decaying areas of post-industrial Baltimore, places where, according to the photographer, many of the street kids whom he wanted to photograph existed rather than lived.

Badertscher challenges ideas about the relationship between subject and artist and subject and spectator. He uses taboo ideas to express precisely what many youths could be exposed to and what they willingly or unwillingly confronted. Many of his images are of siblings and close friends, who have been photographed in subversively intimate positions. He was both the client, who was paying these subjects for their time and their bodies, as well as the artist in charge of the final product. We should not see him as an impartial observer, whether or not his motivations were simply to expose the lives of Baltimore's abandoned generations, to chronicle a sexual milieu or the impact of a drug culture, or, more grandly, to condemn the state of modern America. His work would not be as striking if his subjects were not presented to the viewer at their most vulnerable and exposed. Badertscher's vantage point as a customer of young male prostitutes allowed him to document this world. He said that the hustlers called him 'the early morning john' and would visit him in the morning to get enough money to get a hit to take them to their major appointments later in the day and then the big score . . . and so it went on. It was a paper-thin line between hustling and modelling. He has written about one of these morning guests:

> It was 1981 and Kerry was serious. It was too early in the morning and I was just as serious about sleeping and fighting the excessive dimensions of a hangover – the price you just have to pay for Paradise. He was banging the door and viciously ringing the bell because I had promised him a photo session and he was a glutton for attention and he always needed cash. My god! Artaud had come back to haunt me because I was refusing to read his stuff and this was not the first time. With a sinking and ailing heart I was suddenly remembering the existences of some of the other tenants in the building. I was already on their xxxx list, and so, as usual, Kerry prevailed. The sun was not yet in the correct position and I really needed to use the bathroom. But now, at any rate, I didn't have to promise Antonin anything.[15]

Unlike the transience that we often associate with his subjects, Badertscher remains deeply attached to Baltimore, the backdrop to his images. He is very attuned to Baltimore's changing past – as in this textual commentary on a grainy picture from the early 2000s of a grave on a median strip on Wilkins Avenue:

> Along Wilkins avenue: It goes through the heart of the Westside of Baltimore. In the 50's and 60's this was a large working class community and included many smaller successful diverse neighborhoods. Most of the residents worked in the shipyards or for Bethlehem Steel. As these industries left town, the neighborhood started [to] decline. During the 80's and 90's drugs and prostitution were what it was mostly about here. It was ground zero for the setting of the book 'The Corner' . . . as well as the setting for the television drama 'The Wire'. Today, despite valiant efforts by city government, it is considerably worse. This is where a large portion of the boys and girls whom I photographed, lived.[16]

It is a potted history of the area and its place in the lives of his photographic subjects. Or consider this longer prose poem, 'Billy on Baltimore Street – Faster Than a Heartbeat' (2015):

> For generations in this city the areas around and within Patterson Park on the east side of Baltimore were significant magnets for hustlers and their clients. And this was just one of the main meat racks in a city seemingly composed of meat racks and almost all of them within and around working class neighborhoods. There were the obvious reasons for this. The average age of the boys was about 17 but this could run anywhere from 12 to 19 or 20. On Eastern Avenue, 'The Avenue', running along the south side of the Park, boys would be sitting on the white marble steps of so many row houses, hitch-hiking in either direction as long as it took, or cryptically signaling with their eyes and a slight movement of the head, their availability. Many men traveled to Baltimore from other cities and other districts, like the District of Columbia, to bear witness. They weren't casual observers preparing to write tour guides.
>
> On the opposite side of the Park, the north side, along Baltimore Street, there were about 15 street corners for casual loitering: Montford, Luzerne, Glover, Lakewood, Belnord, Kenwood and Streeper. The long steps in front of Saint Elizabeth of Hungary made an excellent launching pad as well, but some of the boys living close by would not want to be seen in such an obvious location. The non-local boys didn't care.
>
> Some evenings Billy could be found at the corners of Belnord or Kenwood, maybe Streeper. Street lights made shadows form at each house corner and he would be there, in the late nights, for one, maybe two summers, mid-70's. Always he was casual and friendly with a large black comb at the ready in his left front pocket.

> Oh! (as Rimbaud could so often begin a line of poetry) Those hot, heavy and so humid Baltimore evenings, each night having its own particular smell, its own particular fantasy, its own particular ecstasy or danger. In those times the city seemed so labyrinthine, so compelling, so endless and resistant to change. And I, for one, really believed that it would continue forever. It was so sanctioned by the ages. I was much younger, so clueless and obsessed and I knew no tomorrow. Yet all of this did change. Within a heartbeat.[17]

There is much to discuss in this evocation of hustling. It is anchored in place, the row houses and parks, localities within localities, for the sexual economy of hustling drew both clients and providers into the ambit of Baltimore, and, within that city, into the zones of paid sex. It is a knowing sexual geography by someone who had driven and walked, literally cruised, those streets – and for decades rather than months. But it is also a social geography. The zones were proximate to the working-class sectors of the city; 'There were the obvious reasons for this', Badertscher writes. And it is history, a sexual history of a city by someone who knew that the steps of a church could be religious threshold by day and then, as night fell, a meat rack with a parade of male flesh, filled with promises of an entirely different kind. It is a history by someone who was there to observe over time, amid all the coming and going, the transience, the young men 'for one, maybe two summers', and their johns (their customers) who came from DC and elsewhere.

Or take this tetraptych of two young men, boys really, shooting up on a bench in Baltimore's Patterson Park (see Figures 58–61). The multiple images, *Dennis and Marty in Patterson Park*, provide the sense of an action shot, the grainy appearance adding to a documentary feel, creating a sense of intimacy as the photographer and viewer become almost complicit in preparing and delivering the hit, the high. In the photographer-artist's trademark style, image is combined with text. The writing on the first image explains that the setting was near a key historic site of the Battle of Baltimore in 1812, when American forces engaged with the British, and in a park donated by a wealthy nineteenth-century merchant and then added to by the city, segregated until 1956 (Baltimore, as everyone knows, has a large African American population), a major hustling ground from the 1950s, and drug-ravaged in the 1990s. Although Badertscher wrote that the park had been gentrified and order restored, the content of his photographs (from 2002–03) contradicts the extent of the clean-up. It is a weird juxtaposition of heritage and contemporary culture, a battle site that later became, as he put it, a place of 'exercise, festivals, fun, hustling, drugs and sexual encounters' – of shootings up with entirely different meanings.

58 Amos Badertscher, *Dennis and Marty in Patterson Park* (1), 2002–2003, Badertscher Collection.

59 Amos Badertscher, *Dennis and Marty in Patterson Park* (2), 2002–2003, Badertscher Collection.

60 Amos Badertscher, *Dennis and Marty in Patterson Park* (3), 2002–2003, Badertscher Collection.

61 Amos Badertscher, *Dennis and Marty in Patterson Park* (4), 2002–2003, Badertscher Collection.

The earlier references to *The Corner* and HBO's *The Wire* are significant. Perhaps Badertscher's photography could be considered a form of visual ethnography. It is not the photo-ethnography employed by Philippe Bourgois and Jeff Schonberg in their immersed study of homeless, middle-aged, San Francisco addicts, harrowing in its detailed anthropology of their physical and psychological disintegration.[18] The motivations were different. Badertscher's were aesthetic and sexual: Bourgois and Schonberg wrote of 'the politics within aesthetics' and urged public policy application – there was no sexual attraction involved and any payments made were for cooperation, not sex.[19] What we have in mind is more the 'ethnographic imaginary' that Linda Williams found so compelling in *The Wire* – that the critically acclaimed television series is so emblematically Baltimore (for better or worse, it has come to represent the city) is a curious coincidence.[20] But if the TV series is multi-sited (police, drug gangs, unions, city government, schools, press), the photographer's focus is firmly on the streets of what Marc Levine has termed 'The Underclass City'.[21] Whereas *The Wire*'s Baltimore is resolutely black (apart from Season Two's dockworkers), Badertscher's is whiter. The poor white population, relatively absent from both *The Corner* and *The Wire*, is certainly represented in the photographer's pictures.[22] And Badertscher deals with sex; apart from the queerness of the characters Omar and Kima, and Bubbles's mentoring of young men, sexual matters, including the link between drugs and male prostitution, rarely appear in the television series.

Trade (the sexual appeal of ostensibly straight and proudly masculine men who might engage in same-sex sex) was pivotal to Badertscher's photography. He observed in one interview that his earliest photographs were of hustlers whom he encountered on the street – 'The predominant drive was sexual contact' – and that he never formed relationships with them.[23] (The situation was more complex: there were several whom he saw regularly and photographed over long periods of time – such as Dennis, whose framed images are prominent on the walls of Badertscher's home.) These were men with girlfriends, who hustled to survive, and their girlfriends frequently did the same. One young hustler, John, and his girlfriend, photographed together in 2001 under the interstate in various states of undress, worked the streets together (see Figure 62). Billy and Shannon, and Steve and Malisa, pictured later, 'hustled men' and 'frequently worked the west side along Wilkins Avenue'.[24] Heterosexual–homosexuality or homosexual–heterosexuality was taken for granted in the world that Badertscher chronicled.[25]

The imagery of same-sex contact – sometimes explicit, sometimes implied by context or text – certainly conveyed homoeroticism and suggested

62 Amos Badertscher, *John and girlfriend*, 2001, Badertscher Collection.

homosexuality. These were young men whom Badertscher paid for sex and/or posing. However, there are pictures too of heterosexual sex; and of female subjects – of which Badertscher's beautiful photograph of Michelle in 2002 is among the more unforgettable (see Figure 63). His friend Jackie provided him with an entry to the clubs in Baltimore in the 1970s

63 Amos Badertscher, *Michelle*, 2002, Badertscher Collection.

'when the gay bars . . . were still a visual sexual paradise attracting so many straights and bisexuals'.[26] 'When you walked into a bar of a certain type with Jackie, everyone noticed – young males and women.'[27] Badertscher and Jackie went cruising together, though her particular obsession was with rockers. Her 1976 portrait is still on his wall (see Figure 64). Then there are

64 Amos Badertscher, *Jackie*, 1976, Badertscher Collection.

the photographs of Billy and Shannon tongue kissing, his hand cupping her breast, of Steven and Malisa and Badertscher (see Figures 65–6). The assumed heterosexuality of off-scene sex with girlfriends was rendered visible in these rarer, on-scene moments. Yet queer is probably the best description of what is portrayed. Dennis was photographed, aroused, with both male and female companions. Steve 'liked men or women'.[28] Danny's sexuality was 'totally fluid'.[29] As for Charles, 'Sexual preference is not an issue.'[30]

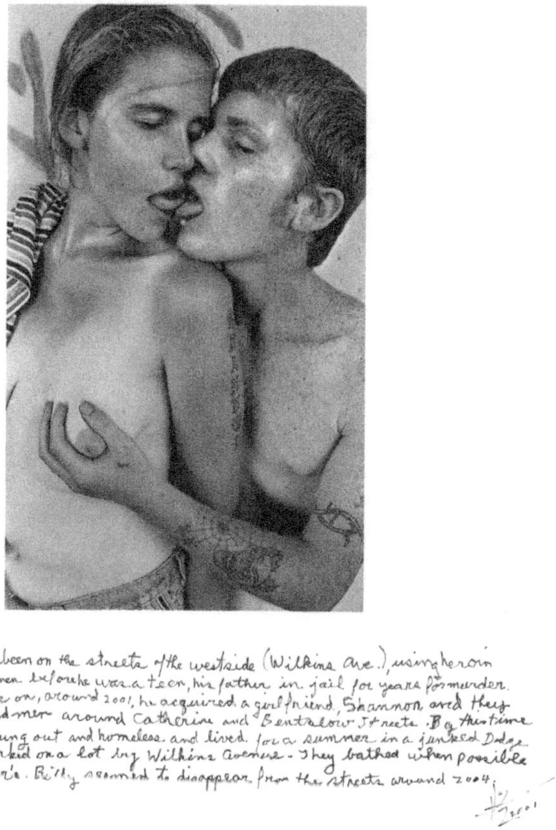

65 Amos Badertscher, *Billy and Shannon*, 2001, Badertscher Collection.

The employment of a female presence in some of Badertscher's prints is reminiscent of Larry Clark's photographs of rough white teens in Tulsa and Oklahoma City, and the 42nd Street hustlers, portraits that (whatever Clark's intent) depend upon a sexualised female presence and heterosexual sex as well as a more obvious appeal to male same-sex tastes. The very young hustlers in *Teenage Lust* (1983), who posed for Clark quite blatantly ('they were looking at me with those come-on looks'), picked up a drugged teen and had group sex with her, which Clark also photographed.[31] Yet the heterosexuality in Clark's work is fragile. José Esteban Muñoz is perceptive in his claims for the way in which 'queerness continues to hum in the background' of such photographs, and how the female is used to anchor

66 Amos Badertscher, *Steven and Malisa*, 1997, Badertscher Collection.

them in heterosexuality. He argued that Clark's heterosexuality became particularly stretched in the last section of *Teenage Lust*, with the pictures of young Puerto Rican hustlers.[32] The mix of hetero and homo, intimated already in Badertscher's *Club Kids*, is present in Clark's teens, where naked male flesh and homoerotic interaction combines with heterosexual sex with women, or where the focus of that heterosexual sex is the male – as in the plate from the Oklahoma section of Clark's book, 'prostitute gives teenager his first blowjob'.[33]

There are other archives of hustler images. One is David Hurles's mail-order, black-and-white and colour photography of amphetamine-addicted, hustler drifters and ex-cons in 1960s to 1990s San Francisco and Los Angeles, with their dangerous, oiled, muscular, fist-clenched, tumescent hypermasculinity – what John Waters referred to as sexual taste 'for the outer limits of straight men'.[34] These were men whom the photographer himself said 'like women as fuck of first choice but men for convenience'.[35] The artist Rex claimed that Hurles encouraged his subjects to abuse him verbally in order to capture the required rage, his low-angled, crotch-focused shots exaggerating their menacing allure.[36] He also thought that Hurles's earlier use of the backdrop of the hustler's 'natural habitat – cheap motel rooms' heightened the pictures' erotic appeal, whereas in his later photographs, shot in the affluence of the photographer's Hollywood home, the *mise-en-scène* was merely distracting.[37]

Or there is the archive of the early 1990s photography of Philip-Lorca diCorcia, who deliberately played with the 'fantasy of trade'.[38] He set up his photographic equipment and assistant in locations near Hollywood's Santa Monica Boulevard – motel rooms, building entries, streets, parking lots – and then drove to the noted hustling strip, and, when approached by a hustler, asked them to pose for him for the same money that they would for sex. If they agreed ('they normally said yes'), they were photographed in frames reminiscent of trade imagery and captioned with name, age, home town, and a dollar amount, $50, $30, $25, indicating the fee paid for their posing, in effect their sexual price.[39] When the images initially appeared as 'Hollywood 1990–1992', lush in their lighting and Californian colour, the hustler status of his subjects was more opaque. It was claimed that he had approached men on the street to be photographed (a little different to them approaching him), that they were not necessarily hustlers but may well have been, and that their dollar captions indicated sexual promise.[40] But his republication of these photographs in their entirety, with his notes on the context of individual shots and explanation of the project, makes it clear that these men were selling sex. Entries on his subjects seem pretty clear: 'was going to get some ribs and some crack. Went with women'; 'said he was hustling because he & his friend ran out of money soon after arriving'; 'Porn movie actor . . . Said he could fuck himself'. 'The original title for the project was Trade', writes diCorcia, 'as in the street word for prostitutes, as the exchange of services for money, as the role reversal which voyeurs indulge and photography provides, as the desire to be anybody but you.'[41] This time the photographic archive was called *Hustlers* (2013).

Eve Fowler's portraits of 1990s New York and Los Angeles hustlers, many photographed on the street, are very similar in terms of composition and colour to those of diCorcia (Internet commentary on *Dazed* magazine continually referenced him as an influence).[42] However, Fowler's portraits are intentionally captionless: 'The lack of verbal prompts . . . jars at first', Fowler explained, 'you feel cheated out of their stories somehow, but by the end it's that same lack of backstory that frees these hustlers from categorisation.'[43]

In contrast to other portraits of hustlers, many of Badertscher's images are of the generations post AIDS and post crack cocaine. Many are dirty, shaven-headed, lean, and marred: 'His face at 20 has severe markings, his arms and legs viciously scarred with the signs of heroin use.'[44] Badertscher's collection reflects the change from the long-haired, fresh-faced portraits from the 1970s (the early plates in *Badertscher* are from that period) when young men hustled for the money to finance weekends with their girlfriends. The photographer noted a shift in the 1980s in Baltimore, when what he called the 'old style street hustling' – 'almost too common to register on the cultural Richter scale' – was replaced by something 'more desperate & emotionally dysfunctional . . . more dangerous'.[45]

In the sadly confronting photograph of Marty, taken in 2002, the naked 20-year-old looks at the photographer – us – as he displays his needle-ravaged arms (see Figure 67). Badertscher, who updated his marginal notations long after the photograph was taken, explained that his young subject had already spent a lifetime selling his body to survive and feed his habit, had robbed his clients, served time in jail, and had lost his younger brother at the age of 14 when he was hit by a speeding car at a notorious Baltimore drug corner. If there is a punctum in this affecting image, Roland Barthes's photographic element that wounds or pierces, it is Marty's eyes.[46] The writing around the image tells us that Marty died in a crack house in 2010.

The potential danger, traditionally part of the sexual allure of trade, is clearly chronicled in Badertscher's work: 'a knife appears so fast at my throat it takes a few seconds to realize it's really a knife and he's holding it at my throat and it's really happening'.[47] *Exit 52: Boy with a Knife* pictures a young man, naked, brandishing a pointed knife by a track running under a freeway, his weapon undercutting (so to speak) the vulnerability of his nakedness: 'I met him hustling on Patterson Park Avenue in 2001. He never had the slightest chance for a stable life' (see Figure 68).[48] Badertscher recorded that the illiterate Branch, photographed in homeboy style with the naked photographer, had 'owned 26 or 27 guns & been arrested at least 135 times'.[49] Michael strangled a john in 2004, after an argument about

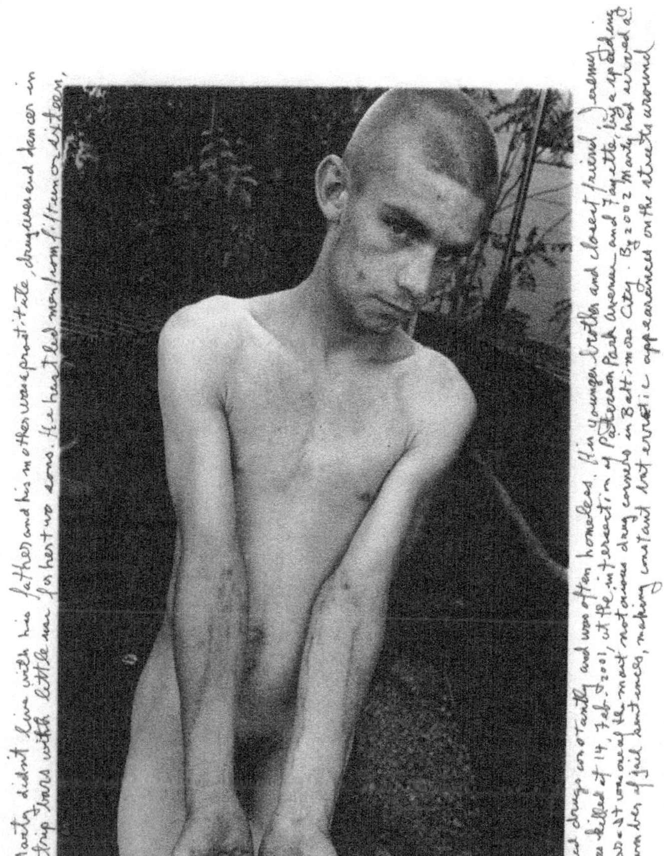

67 Amos Badertscher, *Marty*, 2002, Badertscher Collection.

money, and then attempted to disguise the murder by burning the man's house down.[50] Badertscher once observed of the area under the interstate highway, where he took many of his 2000s photographs, that it was 'a hot location for bringing city prostitutes, checked almost never by the police', and 'a nice place to be mugged or shot'.[51] So the hazards were real. However,

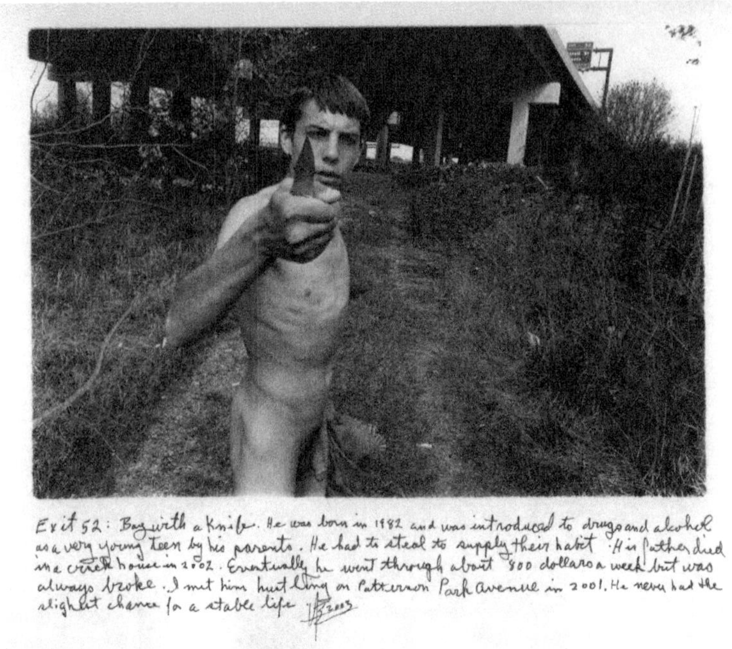

68 Amos Badertscher, *Exit 52: Boy with a Knife*, 2003, Badertscher Collection.

he insists that he saw them as calculated risks rather than opportunities for heightened sexual interaction.

Badertscher commonly employed a documentary style in his photography, what has been termed (without reference to our artist) 'insider documentary' or 'subcultural photography'.[52] He prefers the description 'subversive'; we would favour Ruddy's 'affective documentary'.[53] Such artists depict scenes of people in the streets, framed by buildings and the city itself as a spatial reference. They often use manipulation to make their images seem even more biting, or they leave their photography untouched in order to give it a more authentic feel. They show familiarity by using the language of the streets, by depicting the codes and understandings of that milieu – Michael Moon argues that during the 1960s and 1970s an unprecedented level of attention was given to urban sexual subcultures.[54] Though it is tempting to merge such artists and their subjects into a homogeneous group, their motivations, backgrounds, and approaches are anything but uniform, even when they employ similar narratives and techniques and their work seems to reflect some broader artistic and literary trends.

The photograph uses a mechanical instrument to offer a fleeting snap of a particular scene or event, and generally captures (or at least claims to capture) a candid or impromptu moment. Liz Kotz characterises such work as 'gritty, quasi-documentary . . . presented in an apparently intimate, unposed manner, shot in an off-kilter, snapshot style, often a bit grainy, unfocused', what she calls the 'aesthetics of "intimacy"'.[55] But of course photographs are constructed pieces of work. The developmental stages of photography can be heavily invasive, cropping and manipulating the image with chemicals or various tools that add texture; and the places that a photograph is displayed, in what surroundings, context, and with what purpose, are also highly contrived. They provide glimpses of an instant, claiming that it reflects some wider social phenomenon or commonality, or that it is an 'honest' or 'truthful' depiction of the people and spaces involved. They inevitably tell us as much about the artist as they do about the subjects captured or depicted. Elsa Dorfman says of portrait photographs that they 'aren't the whole person, the real person. They are one mini-second, only as representative as any other mini-second would be . . . They seem so real and yet they're no more real than blatant fantasy.'[56]

While Badertscher's studio portraits do seem more deliberately arranged because of the sterile white background and the use of props and sexual accessories, the street imagery is just as constructed and composed. When discussing the authentic feel of his street image *JESUS CHRIST WILL SAVE YOU FROM HELL*, Badertscher said that it and every such scene, including other blowjobs, were choreographed and posed (see Figure 69).

In terms of Badertscher's outdoor photographic images, the *mise-en-scène* is crucial to our sense of this being an untouched documentation of reality: random objects, such as industrial equipment, homeware, bedding, and debris, are strewn about, giving the illusion that they serve no premeditated purpose in the shot. Badertscher's subjects seem to naturally *fit* into the marginal areas of the city. The way that they are pictured within the dilapidated city implies that the people themselves are considered part of this debris, discarded by society. The diptych *Dennis* is a perfect example of these photographs, but there are many others (see Figures 70–1). Again we have a brief history to go with the imagery:

> Dennis hustled on the west end of Patterson Park in Baltimore City or close by on Eastern Ave. He is unusually thin and looks much younger than his age. His home life was perpetually chaotic as both his parents were drug addicts and he himself is a chronic heroin user. His father died in an abandoned house

69 Amos Badertscher, *Jesus Christ*, 1999, Badertscher Collection.

70 Amos Badertscher, *Dennis* (1), 2001, Badertscher Collection.

71 Amos Badertscher, *Dennis* (2), 2001, Badertscher Collection.

> in 2002 from a drug overdose, his mother still on the streets. Dennis went through about $800 a week, was always broke and never sure where he would spend the night. It was not unusual to see him nodding out on a transit bench along Eastern Avenue.

The decaying city unmistakably frames their figures within the photographic view, as does the presence of graffiti, a form of public art that, like them and their activities, is decreed as illicit and troublesome. Standing surrounded by rubble and graffiti, amid industrial ruins, might also emphasise the subjects' ability to survive in desolate conditions and to prevail despite their youth and tragic upbringing (see Figure 72).

Even though there is an undeniable feeling of discomfort when viewing Badertscher's work, he also attempts to create a sense of trust in his audience. Badertscher uses mirrors to create space, depth, and texture. In an earlier cited image, *Steven and Malisa*, he is candid about his position as an artist, photographing the mirror image of himself with his camera between the two posing subjects. Malisa sits between the photographer's legs, and Steven holds his shoulder. Badertscher presents himself as the clear artistic personality in the shot – he has the camera, they are in his studio, the constructed nature of a studio photoshoot is consciously exposed for the viewer.

So he is often there, naked apart from his camera and footwear, entwined with his subjects and reflected back to the viewer. Occasionally, he is the only

72 Amos Badertscher, *Untitled*, 2003, Badertscher Collection.

subject (see Figure 73). In his homage to Arthur Rimbaud's 'Season in Hell', he photographs himself photographing, and the viewer looks at him as he fictively photographs them: 'Finally I came to regard as sacred the disorder of my mind.' And there is a Rimbaudian disclaimer in the same marginalia: 'This gentleman knows not what he does: he is an angel.'[57] His is no invisible presence. The critic Arthur C. Danto once observed of Robert Mapplethorpe that what distinguished his work from the detached observations of Diane Arbus and Henri Cartier-Bresson was that he was part of the (S/M) milieu that he photographed; whatever the inevitable artifice in any image or composition, 'Mapplethorpe was never outside the human reality of the photographic reality'.[58] The same is true of Badertscher. The hustler world was his world.

Whatever way Badertscher photographed Baltimore, the subjects of most of the images were actively connecting with the camera, and, inherently, with the artist and viewer. They were often confronting the lens, engaging directly with it. They do not seem like vulnerable victims. They are apparently willing to show themselves in compromising positions. They are shooting up heroin, or clearly portraying themselves as hustlers, their stance, one leg bent, leaning against the wall, emphasising or showing their wares, or posing languidly as if they have just had sex.[59] Or they display alternative sexual interests and embrace multiple personalities/identities through performance. Dennis is injecting.[60] He poses with Luna Aviance, a gay performer.[61] He wears lipstick in a double-portrait with Michelle (see Figure 74). He has Michelle on a leash and is visibly erect.[62] He is naked on a couch with Gary.[63] He is engaged in oral sex with David.[64] Dennis was one of Badertscher's favourite models, described by the photographer as his 'constant subject' for five years: 'A fluid and mobile personal identity allowed him, like a brilliant actor, to instantly and innocently assume any role.'[65]

These are images with what Tyler Curtain has termed 'a damaged, intense affect'.[66] But the text is part of the visual presentation, the stories that tell the pictures: 'Just as his subjects' lives bleed into and out of the defining white spaces of the photograph, his subjects' lives bleed into the underwritten text.'[67] It is important to grasp the centrality of Badertscher's retrospective biographies to his photographic project; he rarely relies merely on the impact of the visual image – or rather the visual image frequently includes the written word, always handwritten rather than typed. The text for the 1993 portrait of Charles or 'Chubbs', naked apart from sneakers, against a graffiti-covered wall, is arguably more important than his picture, arresting though it is (see Figure 75).

73 Amos Badertscher, undated self-portrait, Badertscher Collection.

74 Amos Badertscher, *Michelle and Dennis*, 2002, Badertscher Collection.

> Born on the 4th of July 1972, a masterpiece of neglect and abuse. Charles was introduced to drugs early by his parents, frequently ran away from home and school and said he hustled men by 13 or 14. He developed a heroin habit, was in and out of emergency rooms, alcohol and drug re-hab and jail. If 'Chubbs' ever did a day's work it was by mistake. I ran into him in the neighborhood about 2005 on crutches, his right leg missing up to the knee cap. He died of an overdose in 2009.

And the brevity of these sexual histories can be devastating – as in the 1979 picture, *Sandy the mild prostitute – at eighteen*:

> Her haunt was Eastern Avenue supplying services all her life to men who needed people like Sandy. Initially, a sexually abused child from Armistead Gardens in Baltimore City, uneducated, her only indulgences were a few beers, fun with her friends and later on in life, a little witchcraft. For this she earned a few years in prison for prostitution. Her last years were lived with drag queen Mary on Monument St. and she died in September of 1993 of AIDS at age 32. Her real name: Steve . . .[68]

This was a life in eighty-eight words and a haunting photograph.

Badertscher's combination of text and image is not unique. Duane Michals employed the technique in the 1970s, including handwriting on photographic

75 Amos Badertscher, *Born on the 4th of July* [Charles], 1993, Badertscher Collection.

paper in the absence of any other image – 'I am making black marks on white paper. These marks are my thoughts. You are reading my thoughts' – though his text was philosophical rather than socio-historical.[69] Elsa Dorfman used handwritten words in 1974 and Jim Goldberg incorporated observations by the photographic subjects themselves in work published in 1984.[70] Goldberg's *Raised by Wolves* combined both textual commentary and short, written observations – 'Sleezy old men Jack'n off in front of me you have to get high to do it' – next to his harrowing photographs of Californian runaways.[71] Danny Lyon experimented with textual explanations around a few of his images in the 1970s and 1980s.[72] But the idea of little personal histories, used consistently with the photographic print, seems exclusive to Badertscher.

Badertscher's histories, presumably based on street gossip as well as direct personal testimony, are remarkably similar in tone and narrative. They were written in pen after the photograph had been developed, sometimes supplemented years later, modified and repeated for different pictures of the same subject; but, when viewed together, image and text impart a sense of common experience much like the tropes in Charles's story: a tragic and neglected childhood (a familiar narrative), teenage hustling, drugs, a marginal existence.

Badertscher's storytelling technique has grown in confidence as the years have progressed, changing from short, pithy observations or quotes to more sustained narratives. The effect of drug abuse is a constant refrain, unsurprising given the state of Baltimore in the 1990s and 2000s and the link between hustling and narcotic use. Badertscher was aware that the drug-addicted hustlers he was photographing in the 2000s were the children of 'seriously addicted young parents' of the early 1980s, 'many of them no longer around'.[73] He is dealing with generations of dependency.

Many of these marginal biographies are posthumous, alluding to the sum of an embattled life, and invariably ending in death from AIDS, an overdose, or violence. Mike overdosed and drowned in a tub of water.[74] Eddie was beaten to death in the Westside, 'a drug war zone'.[75] Apart from his idiosyncratic charms, Todd's life was representative of so many of Badertscher's models:

> Todd had too many personalities and the lightest fingers in Charm City. He lifted a window curtain right next to me and I never knew it until the owner of the apartment pointed it out. He always carried a big bag over his shoulder and holy crosses and the sacred implements of the Mass were never safe. Thank God 'Miss Toddles' didn't make it to Rome. But Todd was an early genius of thrift store chic and the Roman churches had too much stuff in them anyway. I took him to dinner and at some point all the glasses on the table began disappearing until only this large glass pitcher of water was left. And I said 'What

> about that one Todd?' Ha! I was dining with a master. But for a restaurant that kept its cash in a cigar box I guess paying attention to the glassware was not a priority. Abandoned by his mother at 10 years old and the lonely product of a children's home, his was an outrageous fantasy world, manipulative, cold, and inventive. Todd was on the streets of Baltimore like the Mt. Vernon meat rack, pocket book and makeup, hustling for drugs, cash and sex before he was 14. Here he is in 1975, at 21, as a young Katherine Hepburn. Todd's life became increasingly violent and erratic (and what part of his life wasn't erratic) through drug and alcohol use and he died of A.I.D.S. about 1986 and not too many people, including Todd, gave a shit.[76]

Even when the biographies are not posthumous, they imply the inevitability of a tragic and lonely death, both social and physical. In a post-AIDS era, these are familiar descriptors and narratives, serving as what one commentator terms memento mori.[77] Indeed it could be said that photographs of hustlers are always inhabited by a sense of doom, the subject matter compounding what Barthes described as 'that rather terrible thing which there is in every photograph: the return of the dead'.[78] 'Wondering what became of these sixty-nine guys who appear in this book is futile', diCorcia writes of his own *Hustlers* portraits; 'Twenty years later they probably have come to a bad end, or they wouldn't have been there to begin with.'[79]

If death was not personal it was cultural, sometimes nostalgic as in the prose poem cited earlier: 'And I, for one, really believed that it would continue forever. It was so sanctioned by the ages. I was much younger, so clueless and obsessed and I knew no tomorrow. Yet all of this did change. Within a heartbeat.'[80] Geoff Tuck observes of Eve Fowler's 1990s portraits of young male sex workers that they are 'like relics or icons from a time that's gone away [he was writing in 2010] . . . it was disappearing even as she took the photos . . . that scene is gone culturally . . . It's bittersweet, this new morality. As is the attendant assimilation of otherwise queer culture.'[81]

It is impossible in such limited space to do justice to the range of Badertscher's work. It also includes visual imagery from the early history of transgender, since Baltimore's Johns Hopkins Hospital was a centre for what was then termed transsexual surgery and attracted a large trans population to the city. These were mainly what would come to be termed trans women who were hoping to gain support for their transitions and who, in the interim, did what they could to survive and raise the cash needed for costly treatment. Tony was someone the artist had trouble recalling, other than the fact that she was a 'sex worker' (see Figure 76). 'Who her clients were and how she found them, I don't know.'[82] He knew

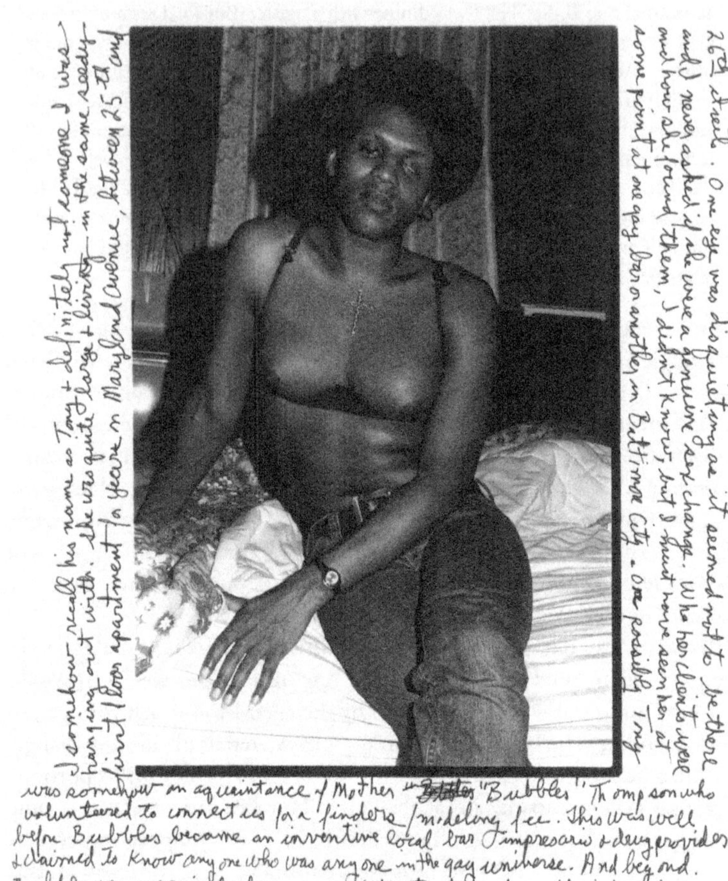

76 Amos Badertscher, *Tony*, 1976, Badertscher Collection.

more about Steven, one of a series of androgynous portraits of a waif-like individual, from that transsexual moment of the 1970s (see Figure 77). Steven, a working-class teenage hustler and transitioning trans woman, told Badertscher that she considered herself a woman, acquired breasts, and transformed herself into the far from fragile Marilyn Mansfield, performing first in topless bars and then in trans pornography.[83] Badertscher photographed Marilyn Mansfield in 1994 (see Figure 78). Or there was

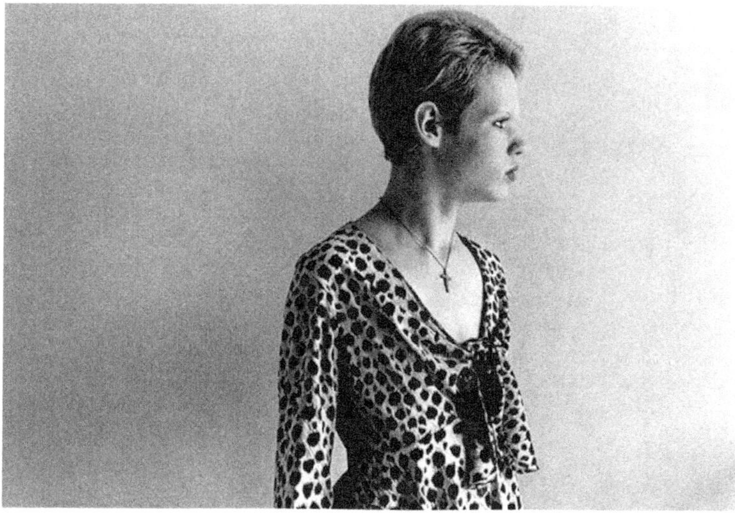

77 Amos Badertscher, *Steven*, 1977, Badertscher Collection.

Todd, subject of one of the posthumous biographies quoted above, whose make-up and cross-dressing was part of his teen hustling.[84] There are pictures of him in 1975, at the age of 21, a 'young Katherine Hepburn' (see Figure 79). Androgyny and gender ambiguity, understated female masculinity, slender youthful male bodies, and fusions of maleness and femaleness fascinated Badertscher.

His imagery, as already intimated, is especially strong on the culturally innovative club life of the 1990s. The photograph *Vita Opulence* is of just one of the performers at a variety of Washington DC and Baltimore venues, an assertive, arresting proclaiming of male femininity or female masculinity, it is difficult to decide which. The appeal of the image lies both in the gender hybridity of its subject and the power of the captured performance (see Figure 80). Badertscher has written an accompanying history, not all of which is conveyed in the writing around the picture:

> Vita Opulence (Shawn . . .) started out in full drag in Pittsburgh about 1992, just out of his teens. He performed at Metropol and Pegasus in that city and came to Washington in 1994 where he performed, organized and hosted drag performances (Zeigfeld's, Remington's, Velvet Nation). Shawn had long been intrigued by all those men who pursued him as a woman but pointedly ignored him as a man. He called these transi-chasers. But he dressed only to be a performance artist, not to be a woman. Sometime following this session

78 Amos Badertscher, *Marilyn Mansfield*, 1998, Badertscher Collection.

> in 1999 he went through a very difficult period and left Washington, a lot of the depression due to his positive HIV status. He returned briefly to the drag scene, his health deteriorated and he died of AIDS in 2002.[85]

But the hustler images dominate Badertscher's oeuvre. We keep returning to what Scott Herring refers to as the gay photographer/poor straight

79 Amos Badertscher, *Todd*, 1975, Badertscher Collection.

guy dynamic.[86] The success of Badertscher's Baltimore hustler images in inducing discomfort in the viewer relies on the fact that an uncomfortable relationship is playing out between the artist and his subjects – Badertscher is certainly aware of this tension. '[T]here has to be this absolute aura of straightness about the boys', he told Craig Seymour in 2011, 'I really do have to identify with the straight image.' There was a psychosexual element to the exchange. Badertscher saw them as everything that he was not when he was their age: 'I wanted to be these boys.'[87] The photographer Larry Clark had wanted to recapture his teenage years by befriending teenagers and then photographing them having sex and doing drugs. The difference was that Clark had been the subject of his photographing – 'fucking in the backseat, gangbangs with the pretty girl all the other girls in the neighborhood hated' – and Badertscher never had.[88]

Herring's article on Michael Meads's images of young men in the American South discusses how the photographer used intelligible signifiers to complicate ideas of sexual identity. The positioning and posing of Meads's Southern boys creates an uncomfortable and irritatingly ambiguous image: they are posed in same-sex intimate moments, lying in bed naked together, or standing together with their penises showing. But the viewer also knows that they may not be interested in same-sex sex, that the photographer has posed them this way, and that the only reason that they are so placed might

80 Amos Badertscher, *Vita Opulence*, 1999, Badertscher Collection.

be because he is paying them for their presence. With Badertscher's Dennis especially – but also the other young men in the photographer's countless images – it is largely impossible to produce a stable heterosexual reading, given the same-sex intimacy that he is pictured engaging in. Yet it is also impossible to read Dennis as gay because the idea of exchange obscures our ability to read his performance as anything other than posing. Any stable or easy reading of Badertscher's images is negated by the contradictory coupling of the homoerotically charged image and the heterosexually themed textual narrative that surrounds it. As discussed earlier, images of men hugging naked or actually engaging in oral sex with each other are displayed with writing that relays the subjects' heterosexual relationships.

If there is a common thread in Badertscher's project, it is what Herring has said of the work of Meads: 'a disidentification that pitches his photographs out of a discernible imaginary of gay (or straight) male types' and that threatens 'urban sexual legibility'.[89] Badertscher's hustlers have girlfriends but seek out men for survival and the supply of drugs: 'Like all boys of his class he is "straight" but has been hustling men since 14.'[90] As Curtain observes, in the Baltimore working-class world charted by Badertscher, 'sexual identity doesn't operate in the same way that it does among the WASPy middle classes . . . Having sex with men is about a lot of things – authority, abuse, thrills, aspirations, boredom, survival – but it isn't necessarily about identity.'[91]

We have invoked the work of other photographers and artists and even the visual ethnographic imaginary of *The Wire*, but perhaps the best comparison for Badertscher is with the work of a writer who has been characterised as producing a 'style of writing that merges heights of creative imagination with fictive "anthropological" journeys into outsider spaces'.[92] Like our photographer, Bruce Benderson focuses on what he calls 'congress with the dislocated'; 'white nights in the company of Midtown Manhattan hustlers, ex-cons and junkies, sponging up their speech and vampirising their emotions to write about'.[93] Like Badertscher, he participates in the culture that he represents without really being of it, 'a very shaky balance between the stances of voyeur and participant', separated exponentially by education and social background.[94] The two men inhabit sexual milieus that demonstrate sexual flexibility, 'a polymorphous sexuality that mocks our reductive categories of sexual identity', where there are 'sexual impulses that are too fragmented to base an entire sociological identity upon'.[95] Benderson is very consciously writing about a lost world, that of Times Square before its gentrification and Disneyfication in the 1990s, and felt that he had to move to Eastern Europe to recapture that sexual culture. Meanwhile, in post-industrial Baltimore, Badertscher managed to maintain access to its inhabitants' fragmented sexual impulses and the feminine sides of masculine personalities – into the 2000s.

Amos Badertscher is a unique photographer. Others have chronicled similar lives and immersed themselves in their assignments – and then left. However, Badertscher lived his project for the whole of his working life; it was his life. He has said that while he felt out of place in 'normal' society, he was completely at home with those on that society's borders. He felt comfortable on the street. The result is one man's extraordinary visual record of Baltimore's sexual history, truly an archive of affect

Notes

1 J. A. Thomas, 'The evidence of sight', *History and Theory*, 48:4 (2009), 151–68, quotes at 151.
2 J. Gallop, 'The pleasure of the phototext', in G. Batchen (ed.), *Photography Degree Zero: Reflections on Roland Barthes's Camera Lucida* (Cambridge, MA, 2011), p. 53.
3 Here and elsewhere, these direct observations come from conversations between the authors and Amos Badertscher in Baltimore in late June and early July 2015 and again in June 2016.
4 *Club Kids* series, 1999. The Badertscher archive is divided between his residence in Baltimore (hereafter BB) and the Leslie–Lohman Museum of Gay and Lesbian Art in New York (hereafter L–L), where the whole collection will eventually reside. Our figures are all high-quality digital images of the original photographs (usually 8" x 10") from Badertscher's personal archives.
5 M. P. Mezzatesta, 'Foreword', in A. Badertscher, *Baltimore Portraits* (Durham, NC, 1999), p. xi.
6 T. Dean, 'Introduction: pornography, technology, archive', in T. Dean, S. Ruszczycky, and D. Squires (eds), *Porn Archives* (Durham, NC, 2014), pp. 1–26. For affect in photography, see E. H. Brown and T. Phu (eds), *Feeling Photography* (Durham, NC, 2014).
7 J. V. Evans, 'Seeing subjectivity: erotic photography and the optics of desire', *American Historical Review*, 118:2 (2013), 430–62, quotes at 432, 462. She tends to over-justify the use of photography in history as representing subjectivity, perhaps for the perceived readership of the journal, which, in itself, is a rather dispiriting admission.
8 S. Ruddy, '"A radiant eye yearns from me": figuring documentary in the photography of Nan Goldin', *Feminist Studies*, 35:2 (2009), 347–80, quote at 350.
9 'For the better part of . . . twenty years his work was ignored', wrote the director of the Degen Scharfman Gallery in New York in 1998: G. Scharfman, 'Introduction', in A. Badertscher, *Badertscher* (New York, 1998), p. vii.
10 Badertscher, *Badertscher*; Badertscher, *Baltimore Portraits.*
11 A. Badertscher, 'The souls around us', *Dust*, 7 (2015), no pagination.
12 J. D. Katz and D. C. Ward, *Hide/Seek: Difference and Desire in American Portraiture* (Washington DC, 2010). This book is the companion volume to the exhibition that ran from 30 October 2010 to 13 February 2011.
13 C. Lord and R. Meyer, *Art & Queer Culture* (New York, 2013).
14 See R. Meyer's observations in 'Queer photography?', *Aperture*, 218 (2015),

28–9, and the contributions by S. M. Cane and D. Sameshima in that same issue.

15 A. Badertscher, 'Kerry and the French Connection, 1981', unpublished writing for a photograph, 2017, BB.

16 *Along Wilkins Avenue*, no date, L–L.

17 A. Badertscher, 'Billy on Baltimore Street – faster than a heartbeat', unpublished writing for a photograph, 2015, BB.

18 P. Bourgois and J. Schonberg, *Righteous Dopefiend* (Berkeley and Los Angeles, 2009).

19 Ibid., p. 11.

20 L. Williams, 'Ethnographic imaginary: the genesis and genius of *The Wire*', *Critical Inquiry*, 38:1 (2011), 208–26; L. Williams, *On The Wire* (Durham, NC, 2014). See also T. Porter and C. W. Marshall (eds), *The Wire: Urban Decay and American Television* (New York, 2009); and A. Chaddha and W. J. Wilson, '"Way down in the hole": systematic urban inequality and *The Wire*', *Critical Inquiry*, 38:1 (2011), 164–88.

21 M. V. Levine, '"A third-world city in the first world": social exclusion, racial inequality, and sustainable development in Baltimore', in M. Polèse and R. Stren (eds), *The Social Sustainability of Cities: Diversity and the Management of Change* (Toronto, 2000), ch. 5.

22 This criticism of *The Corner* is made too by K. Alexander, D. Entwistle, and L. Olson, *The Long Shadow: Family Background, Disadvantaged Urban Youth, and the Transition to Adulthood* (New York, 2014), pp. 3–12, which looks at a cohort of Baltimore school children from the same area of West Baltimore and during the same period (1982–2005) as that covered by Badertscher and in *The Corner* and *The Wire*. *The Long Shadow* does not neglect the urban white poor.

23 C. Seymour, 'A conversation with Amos Badertscher', *The Archive: The Journal of the Leslie/Lohman Gay Art Foundation*, 38 (2011), 4–7, quote at 5.

24 *Billy and Shannon*, 2001, and *Steven and Malisa*, 1997, L–L.

25 For studies of a mix of the hetero and homo, see B. Reay, *New York Hustlers: Masculinity and Sex in Modern America* (Manchester, 2010); C. R. Johnson, *Just Queer Folks: Gender and Sexuality in Rural America* (Philadelphia, PA, 2013); J. Ward, *Not Gay: Sex Between Straight White Men* (New York, 2015).

26 *Jackie*, 1976, L–L.

27 A. Badertscher, 'Biographies of models', BB.

28 *Steve and His Older Brother Fire Up*, 1997, L–L.

29 *Danny*, 2001, L–L.

30 *Charles*, 1993, L–L.

31 L. Clark, *Teenage Lust* (New York, 1983), no pagination. The section on the 42nd Street hustlers begins with such a plate.

32 J. E. Muñoz, 'Rough boy trade: queer desire/straight identity in the photography of Larry Clark', in D. Bright (ed.), *The Passionate Camera: Photography and Bodies of Desire* (New York, 1998), pp. 167–77, quote at p. 173.

33 Clark, *Teenage Lust*, no pagination.
34 D. Hurles and Rex (text and design), *Speeding: The Old Reliable Photos of David Hurles* (San Francisco, 2005); D. Hurles, *Outcast: David Hurles' Old Reliable in Living Color* (San Francisco, 2010); J. Waters, 'Outsider porn', in his *Role Models* (New York, 2010), p. 217.
35 Old Reliable/David Hurles, from the interview by J. Fritscher, 'Old Reliable: a legend in his own time', September 1982, as published at www.JackFritscher.com (last accessed 26 April 2018).
36 Hurles and Rex, *Speeding*, p. 114.
37 Ibid., p. 124.
38 R. Montez, '"Trade" marks: LA2, Keith Haring, and a queer economy of collaboration', *GLQ*, 12:3 (2006), 425–40, quote at 428.
39 P. L. diCorcia, *Hustlers* (Göttingen, 2013), no pagination.
40 See P. Galassi and P. L. diCorcia, *Philip-Lorca diCorcia* (New York, 2000), pp. 12–13, 50–73.
41 diCorcia, *Hustlers*, no pagination.
42 S. Dolding, 'Hustling on the streets of New York and LA', *Dazed Digital*, May 2014: www.dazeddigital.com/photography/article/20021/1/hustling-on-the-streets-of-new-york-and-la (last accessed 26 April 2018). For Fowler, see E. Fowler, *Hustlers* (New York, 2014); G. Blank, 'Interview with Eve Fowler', *Influence*, 2 (2004): www.gilblank.com/texts/intvws/fowlerintvw.html (last accessed 26 April 2018).
43 Eve Fowler quoted in Dolding, 'Hustling on the streets of New York and LA'.
44 *Marty*, 2002, L–L.
45 Badertscher, 'Biographies of models', and *Wade*, 1980, L–L.
46 R. Barthes, *Camera Lucida: Reflections on Photography*, trans. R. Howard (London, 1993), pp. 26–7.
47 A. Badertscher, 'David: the boy in collage with flowers', unpublished writing for a photograph, 2015, BB.
48 *Exit 52*, 2003, L–L.
49 *Branch*, 2000, L–L.
50 Badertscher, 'Biographies of models'.
51 Ibid.
52 L. Kotz, 'Aesthetics of "intimacy"', in Bright (ed.), *The Passionate Camera*, pp. 204–15, quotes at p. 204.
53 Ruddy, 'A radiant eye', 350.
54 M. Moon, 'Outlaw sex and the "search for America": representing male prostitution and perverse desire in sixties film (*My Hustler* and *Midnight Cowboy*)', *Quarterly Review of Film and Video*, 15:1 (1993), 27–40.
55 Kotz, 'Aesthetics', p. 204.
56 E. Dorfman, *Elsa's Housebook: A Woman's Photojournal* (Boston, MA, 1974), p. 52.
57 *This Gentleman Knows Not What He Does*, no date, L–L.

58 A. C. Danto, *Playing With the Edge: The Photographic Achievement of Robert Mapplethorpe* (Berkeley and Los Angeles, 1998), quote at p. 45.
59 *Big Daddy: Sunday: Under an Interstate*, in Badertscher, *Baltimore Portraits*, unpaginated plates.
60 *Dennis and Marty in Patterson Park*, 2003, L–L.
61 *Dennis* series, 2002, L–L.
62 *Michelle and Dennis*, 2002, L–L.
63 *Two Boys*, 2003, L–L.
64 The three-part series, *Under the Interstate*, 2004, L–L.
65 A. Badertscher, 'Dennis and the latter', unpublished writing for a photograph, 2015, BB.
66 T. Curtain, 'A Baltimore essay: photography, sexuality, community', in Badertscher, *Baltimore Portraits*, p. 3.
67 Ibid., p. 4.
68 *Sandy*, 1979, in Badertscher, *Baltimore Portraits*, unpaginated plates.
69 D. Michals, *Photographs With Written Text* (Amsterdam, 1981), no pagination.
70 Dorfman, *Elsa's Housebook*; J. Goldberg, *Rich and Poor* (Göttingen, 2013); L. Benedict-Jones, 'Duane Michals: storyteller', in L. Benedict-Jones (ed.), *Storyteller: The Photographs of Duane Michals* (Pittsburgh, PA, 2014), pp. 54–5.
71 J. Goldberg and P. Brookman, *Raised by Wolves* (New York, 1995), p. 230.
72 J. Cox et al., *Danny Lyon: Message to the Future* (New Haven, CT, 2016), pp. 162–3, 183, 186, 194,
73 Badertscher, 'Biographies of models'.
74 *Mike*, 2001, L–L.
75 Badertscher, 'Biographies of models'.
76 Badertscher, 'Todd, 1975', unpublished writing for a photograph, 2017, BB.
77 Mezzatesta, 'Foreword', p. xi.
78 Barthes, *Camera Lucida*, p. 9.
79 diCorcia, *Hustlers*, no pagination.
80 Badertscher, 'Billy on Baltimore Street – faster than a heartbeat', unpublished writing for a photograph, 2015, BB.
81 G. Tuck, 'Notes on looking: contemporary art in Los Angeles', 15 July 2010. From Tuck's blog, 'Notes on looking', no longer available on the Internet.
82 See *Tony*, 1976, and *Black Transvestite Sex Worker*, 1977, L–L.
83 See http://shemale-vod.co.uk/marilyn-mansfield-movies.html (last accessed 26 April 2018).
84 Badertscher, 'Todd, 1975', unpublished writing for a photograph, 2017, BB.
85 Badertscher, 'Biographies of models'.
86 S. Herring, 'Caravaggio's rednecks', *GLQ*, 12:2 (2006), 217–36, quotes at 222, 224.
87 Seymour, 'A conversation with Amos Badertscher', 5.
88 The quote comes from Clark, *Teenage Lust*, unpaginated.
89 Herring, 'Caravaggio's rednecks', 221, 232.

90 *Portrait of Walt MacNew*, in Badertscher, *Baltimore Portraits*, unpaginated plates.
91 Curtain, 'A Baltimore essay', p. 2.
92 D. Johnson, 'Carrying her liver in a shopping cart (and other bohemian notions): an interview with Bruce Benderson', *Social Text*, 114 (2013), 109–25, quote at 110.
93 B. Benderson, *Sex and Isolation and Other Essays* (Madison, WI, 2007), p. 63; B. Benderson, *The Romanian: Story of an Obsession* (New York, 2006), p. 20.
94 Benderson, *Sex and Isolation*, pp. 173–4.
95 Ibid., pp. 178, 179.

Index